my revision notes

AQA GCSE (9–1)

RELIGIOUS STUDIES

SPECIFICATION A

HODDER
EDUCATION
AN HACHETTE UK COMPANY

Hachette UK's policy is to use papers that are natural, renewable and recyclable products and made from wood grown in sustainable forests. The logging and manufacturing processes are expected to conform to the environmental regulations of the country of origin.

Orders: please contact Bookpoint Ltd, 130 Park Drive, Milton Park, Abingdon, Oxon OX14 4SE. Tel: 01235 827827. Fax: 01235 400454. Lines are open 9.00 a.m.–5.00 p.m., Monday to Saturday, with a 24-hour message answering service. You can also order through our website: www.hoddereducation.co.uk

ISBN 9781510404793

© Lesley Parry and Jan Hayes 2017
First published in 2017
Hodder Education,
An Hachette Company
Carmelite House
50 Victoria Embankment
London EC4Y 0DZ

www.hoddereducation.co.uk

Impression number   7

Year   2021 2020

Cover photo © SamalMike - Shutterstock

Illustrations by Integra Software Serv. Ltd

Typeset in India by Integra Software Serv. Ltd

Printed in Spain

A catalogue record for this title is available from the British Library.

My revision planner

REVISED   TESTED   EXAM READY

Answers at **www.hoddereducation.co.uk/myrevisionnotesdownloads**

	REVISED	TESTED	EXAM READY

Introduction

It is very common practice for schools to recommend to students that they get a revision guide to support their final revision for GCSE (and in fact any formal exams). The point being that you, the student, can do some reading and studying at home with a set of reliable notes. This is crucial to GCSE success – just working in school is not enough. This book is to help you revise, covering the whole Specification.

Of course, revision guides are just shortened forms of the textbook (which is a shortened form of what you should be covering in class). They don't give you every detail and do expect you to have some knowledge to start with. This guide is no different, though it should give you enough detail and clues to be able to revise effectively. It is meant to support your revision, not teach you anew.

Doing well in exams is about knowing and understanding the subject content in a course. It is also very much about being able to understand the questions you are faced with and what they want of you. This usually means you have to apply your knowledge, and demonstrate clear understanding and insight. This guide gives you lots of exam advice, practice questions and practice answers to think about.

Hopefully your teachers have taught you a few revision techniques. Make sure you try them out, bearing in mind that some people use the same method effectively for every subject, while others use a variety of methods depending on the subject they are revising. Your revision programme will be unique to you – just make sure you have one! This guide suggests a small number of revision strategies which have been effective for GCSE students in the past – feel free to try them, use them as described or tailor them to your style.

How does it work?

- Each topic lists the **key terms** you need to know so that you can answer questions. Knowing key terms is the bedrock of your success.
- A **glossary of terms** gives you the words used in the Specification itself – you can be asked questions using any of these terms, so they are the most important.
- Each topic is written in bitesize chunks – read and learn them all. There are four religions in this book – study only the two you studied in school. All six Themes are here, but in the exam you answer four.
- Key teachings are found throughout the book. Those prescribed by the Specification are there, but we have added quite a few extras. It always impresses examiners if you use teachings that are specific to a question.

- As well as activities throughout, there are also extra activities on the Hodder Education My Revision Note website.
- At the end of each section there is a page of exam-style questions – great practice for you. And as a bonus, you will gain increased familiarity with exam question wording, which reduces anxiety and confusion in the exam.
- There is a section on revision techniques. Try them all – you never know what might work for you. Try them in other subjects, too.
- Throughout the book we have scattered quick tips and hints – tips for revision, for the exam, and common mistakes.
- We also give you a checkpoint page which doubles as the contents page. You can track your revision progress and feel your confidence grow as you tick the boxes.

Good luck!

Features to help you succeed

These revision notes will help you to revise for AQA's GCSE (1–9) Religious Studies Specification A. It is essential to review your work, learn it and test your understanding. Tick each box when you have:

- revised and understood a topic
- checked your understanding and practised the exam questions.

You can also keep track of your revision by ticking off each topic heading in the book. You may find it helpful to add your own notes as you work through each topic.

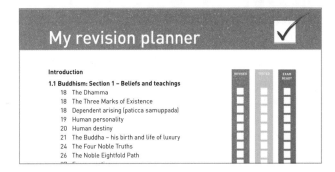

Exam question practice

Practice exam questions are provided for each topic. Use them to consolidate your revision and practise your exam skills.

Religious teachings

It is crucial that you can write about religious teachings in your exam. Almost all the questions demand this. This book includes many teachings to use, but you should look to add your own.

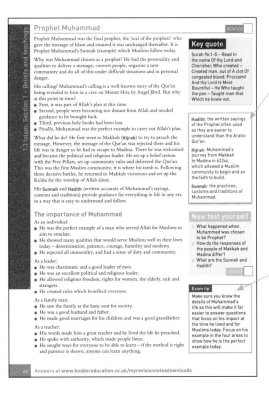

Key terms

Key terms are highlighted and defined throughout the book. There are lists of specification-specific terms at the back, but you should familiarise yourself with all the highlighted terms.

Exam tip

Throughout the book there are tips to help you boost your grade.

Revision tip

Throughout the book there are tips to help you improve your revision.

Full Course and Short Course outlines

If you have this book and you are revising for the Full Course RS GCSE check the following:

- You have studied **two** world religions. This book covers Buddhism, Christianity, Judaism and Islam. Do not use the material from the religions you didn't study in class.
- You know both the **beliefs** and the **practices** for the two religions you have studied.
- You have studied **four Themes** – there are six covered in the book so make sure you are revising the ones your teacher has taught you. The attitudes of all six world faiths are referred to in each Theme.

You will have one exam paper for the religions: Paper 1.
- Religion 1 – Beliefs = 24 marks (+ 3 SPaG)
- Practices = 24 marks Total 48 marks
- Religion 2 – Beliefs = 24 marks (+ 3 SPaG)
- Practices = 24 marks Total 48 marks
- Total marks for Paper 1 = 96 (+ 6 SPaG) = 102 marks and you will have 1 hour 45 minutes.

You will have one exam paper for the Themes: Paper 2.
- You will answer four full questions, each worth 24 marks.
- Total marks for Paper 2 = 96 (+ 3 SPaG) = 99 marks and you will have 1 hour 45 minutes.

The questions within each religion (both beliefs and practices) and Themes have a common structure made up of five part-questions of 1, 2, 4, 5 and 12 marks.

If you have this book and you are revising for the Short Course RS GCSE, check the following:

- You have studied **two** world religions (two from Buddhism, Christianity, Islam and Judaism). **Do not** use the material from the religions you haven't studied in class.
- You know the **Beliefs** for the two religions you have studied. **Do not** revise the Practices sections for religions.
- You also need to have studied **two Themes** – there are six covered in the book so make sure you are revising Theme A Relationships and families and Theme B Religion, peace and conflict. Note: Theme B for the Short Course is actually Theme D in this book.
- You will have one exam paper: Paper 1.
  - Religion 1 – Beliefs = 24 marks
  - Religion 2 – Beliefs = 24 marks
  - Theme A – Relationships and families = 24 marks
  - Theme B – Religion, peace and conflict = 24 marks
  - Total = 96 (+ 6 SPaG)

Total marks for Paper 1 = 96 (+ 6 SPaG) = 102 marks and you will have 1 hour 45 minutes.

The questions within each religion (beliefs) and Themes have a common structure made up of five-part questions of 1, 2, 4, 5 and 12 marks.

The exam

All of your work for Religious Studies is summed up in your performance in two exam papers, each lasting 1 hour and 45 minutes. You can look at each paper as being four sets of 24 marks; the mark breakdown in each 24 set is rigid, that is always the same.

	Four sets	Questions	Total marks
Paper 1	Religion 1 – Beliefs and teachings	Questions worth 1/2/4/5/12 marks	24 × 4
	Religion 1 – Practices	Questions worth 1/2/4/5/12 marks	plus 6 marks for SPaG
	Religion 2 – Beliefs and teachings	Questions worth 1/2/4/5/12 marks	
	Religion 2 – Practices	Questions worth 1/2/4/5/12 marks	
Paper 2	Theme choice 1	Questions worth 1/2/4/5/12 marks	24 × 4
	Theme choice 2	Questions worth 1/2/4/5/12 marks	plus 3 marks for SPaG
	Theme choice 3	Questions worth 1/2/4/5/12 marks	
	Theme choice 4	Questions worth 1/2/4/5/12 marks	

You need to aim to score at least 14 marks per set if you want to reach the higher grades. You will most likely achieve this if you score evenly across all your sets. If you know you have a weaker set – you don't like your second religion Practices set, or you hate the fourth of your four Themes – then you need to do extra revision work to bring that weak set up to the level of your stronger ones. Eradicate the weakness!

Command phrases in the exam – what they are and what they mean

The wording of the exam questions is fixed and examiners have to write questions which fit into the prescribed wording. The wording is specific for Religion Beliefs (RB), Religion Practices (RP) and the Themes (T). So what are they seeking?

Which section?	Wording	Explanation	Marks
All	Give two …	For 2-mark questions you just list two things – could be words or phrases.	2
RB	Explain two ways in which … influences _____ today	You must give and explain two ways, but you must show the impact on behaviour/thinking of people in that religion today.	4
RP/T	Explain two contrasting _____ in contemporary British society	You must give and explain two beliefs/teachings/practices, but they must be contrasting or different.\n\nIn the Themes, there are only three 'contrasting' topics to know about and you must answer from a Christian perspective for one view.	4
T	Explain two similar …	You must give and explain two beliefs/teachings/practices. Can be from any aspect of the topic.	4
T	Explain two contrasting …	You must give and explain two teachings/practices. Can be from any aspect of the topic and any religion.	4
RB	Explain two (religion) teachings about …	You must give and explain two teachings. Using the quote or a version of it will gain the fifth mark. It is easier to get the marks by using clear, specific teachings.	5
RP	Explain two contrasting ways in which …	You must give and explain two ways in which something is done. Use of a quotation/teaching will earn the fifth mark.	5
T	Explain two religious beliefs about …	You must give and explain two beliefs (attitudes really). Use of a quotation/teaching will earn the fifth mark.	5
RB/RP	Refer to (religion) teaching	Your answer must include clear and repeated reference to the teachings of the specified religion in order to reach higher levels.	12
All	Give reasoned arguments in support of this statement.	You must support the statement and explain the reasons you give.	12
All	Give reasoned arguments to support a different point of view.	You must provide a different point of view and explain the reasons you give for it.	12
T	Should refer to religious arguments	You must use religious arguments in your answer – it can't be entirely non-religious (that will limit you to fewer than half the available marks).	12
T	May refer to non-religious arguments	You could – but don't have to – use non-religious arguments.	12
All	Should reach a justified conclusion.	You should provide a concluding paragraph which comes from what you have said but is not just a repeat of it – keep some reasons back to explain in your conclusion as your own view.	12

Question mark	Wording examiners follow	What that means to you
1	Award a mark for a correct answer	Right answer gets the mark.
2	Award a mark for each correct answer up to 2 marks	Two correct points made get the 2 marks.
4	**First belief/way/etc.** Simple explanation of relevant and accurate point – 1 mark Detailed explanation of relevant and accurate point – 2 marks	First set of 2 marks comes from first making the point or giving the relevant teaching, second explaining that point/teaching and showing how it is relevant to the question.
	Second belief/way/etc. Simple explanation of relevant and accurate point – 1 mark Detailed explanation of relevant and accurate point – 2 marks	Second set of 2 marks is given for doing the same thing for a new point.
5	**First teaching/belief/way/etc.** Simple explanation of relevant and accurate point – 1 mark Detailed explanation of relevant and accurate point – 2 marks	First set of 2 marks comes from first making the point or giving the relevant teaching, second explaining that point/teaching and showing how it is relevant to the question.
	Second teaching/belief/way/etc. Simple explanation of relevant and accurate point – 1 mark Detailed explanation of relevant and accurate point – 2 marks	Second set of 2 marks is given for doing the same thing for a new point.
	Relevant and accurate reference to scripture and/or sacred writing	You get a mark for a relevant teaching – make sure it is clearly relevant.
12 (in four levels)	Level 4: 10–12 marks A well-argued response, reasoned consideration of different points of view. Logical chains of reasoning leading to judgement(s) supported by knowledge and understanding of relevant evidence and information	You give several arguments from at least two points of view. These are mostly/all explained and expanded in a clear and effective way. Your points are all clearly relevant to the statement. There is a strong element of religious argument in your answer. The examiner won't have to think about what you are trying to say because you have argued logically and coherently.
	Level 3: 7–9 marks Reasoned consideration of different points of view. Logical chains of reasoning that draw on knowledge and understanding of relevant evidence and information.	You give several arguments from at least two points of view. You explain/expand some of these. Most of them will be obviously relevant to the statement, so that your points are clear. You will have put more than just a hint of religious argument in your answer. You will be evaluating the statement, not just writing attitudes about the topic of the statement.

→

Question mark	Wording examiners follow	What that means to you
	Level 2: 4–6 marks	If you write about only one point of view, you cannot achieve a higher level than this one.
	Reasoned consideration of a point of view. A logical chain of reasoning drawing on knowledge and understanding of relevant evidence and information	It might be one-sided. If it is, it will have several arguments which are explained and expanded well, and which clearly weigh up the statement.
	Or	Or
	Recognition of different points of view, each supported by relevant reasons/ evidence.	You give a series of arguments for more than one point of view with limited explanation of any argument.
	Level 1: 1–3 marks	You are unlikely to have explained very much at all; rather to have listed a few reasons to support what you think.
	Point of view with reason(s) stated in support.	

NB: while the wording of the 4- and 5-mark questions may vary, essentially the awarding of marks is as above (idea – explanation – idea 2 – explanation = 4 marks; idea – explanation – idea 2 – explanation – teaching = 5 marks), whether it be asking for a teaching or belief, whether similar or contrasting or open. We have used 'point' in place of belief/teaching/way, etc.

Your written English (SPaG)

REVISED ☐

You will be judged on your written English in certain 12-mark questions you answer. This is worth up to 3 marks and is based around the quality of your spelling, punctuation and grammar. You get up to 3 marks per 12-mark Beliefs question. While awarded to each answer in the Themes Paper, the best of these is what you actually get – you don't get any extra up to 3 four times, you just get one award of up to 3 marks.

So how are the marks awarded? Here is a simple guide.

0	You haven't written anything, e.g. not answered any of the 12-mark questions.
	You have written answers which have nothing to do with the question, so don't answer it.
	It is almost impossible to work out the points you are trying to make (there are so many errors, what you have written doesn't make sense).
1	Called 'threshold performance'.
	You will have used only a limited range of specialist words.
	While probably making a lot of errors in grammar, what you write is still understandable.
	Your punctuation and spelling are reasonably accurate.
2	Called 'intermediate performance'.
	You will have used a good range of specialist terms and used them in the right context.
	You are generally accurate with grammar.
	Your spelling and punctuation are good, with few mistakes.
3	Called 'high performance'.
	You use lots of specialist language, in the right context and showing clear understanding of how to use it very appropriately.
	Your grammar is almost always correct and you use complex grammar (extended sentences and paragraphs, high-level grammatical constructions, etc.).
	Your spelling and punctuation are almost flawless, again beyond simple constructions.

You can improve your SPaG by paying attention to your English over the whole time you are studying – it isn't something you can fix overnight as it is about your habitual way of writing. Learning and using key language helps. Using connectives to make more complex sentences also helps. Ask your teacher what you need to do to hit a better performance descriptor and so get better marks.

Answers at www.hoddereducation.co.uk/myrevisionnotesdownloads

Using specific religious teachings

How well you are able to learn and to use religious teachings in your exams will determine the grade you achieve. The wider the range of teachings you can refer to, the better your answers will be.

The exam Specification refers to the following teachings in the four religions covered in this book.

The exam questions can refer specifically to the content of these quotes, so be aware of their content. They are all explained in the relevant section of this guide.

You can use them in your answers, which will show your direct understanding of the religion.

Buddhism:	Christianity:	Islam:	Judaism:
Dhammapada 190–191	Genesis 1:1–3	Surah 112	Genesis 12:1–3
Jataka 075	John 1:1–3	Surah 96:1–5	Exodus 20:1–17

Will it really make a difference to an exam grade to learn teachings?

REVISED

Look at the following. On the **Religions** paper the 5- and 12-mark questions specifically instruct you to 'refer to religious teachings in your answer'. This means that 17/24 marks are reliant on you using teachings to explain your answers. Over the whole paper: 68/102 marks! Probably the 4-mark questions will be easier to answer if you have teachings you can refer to as well. You need the teachings to use as the core of your answers for the 4- and 5-mark questions or to support ideas in your 12-mark evaluations.

On the **Themes** paper the 5- and 12-mark questions specifically instruct you to 'refer to religious teachings in your answer'. Again 17/24 marks are reliant on you using teachings to explain your answers. Over the whole paper: 68/99! Also, in the 4-mark questions where you are asked to comment on 'contrasting, similarities or differences' in beliefs, quotes will really help you, so add another 16 marks to your 68 – total 84/99 marks!

By knowing the teachings, explaining them in relation to the topic of the 4- and 5-mark questions, and using these to build arguments in your 12-mark evaluations, your answers will be able to access higher marks.

It is well worth the effort in your revision to learn teachings.

There are two ways to do this

REVISED

On page 113 you will find 'general teachings' that can be used again and again across the Religions paper and the Themes paper. They are called general because they can be applied to many topics, but as they aren't specifically linked it will take more work, exam time and writing for you to make them relevant to the question. For example:

'Explain two religious beliefs about why fighting a war may be wrong.'

Two teachings – 'Love your neighbour'; 'Those who live by the sword, die by the sword.'

Using the first teaching you would need to explain that loving your neighbour means not to harm others and that as most wars include killing others (clearly harming and not loving others) then wars

must be wrong to fight. Most wars are also fought against neighbouring countries, so this would not follow the teaching, etc.

The answer would be rather rambling, a little contrived – you would have to make the link more obvious. If you wrote it any more briefly, the examiner might not get the point you are making (they can only mark what you write, after all, not what you were thinking when you wrote it).

Using the second teaching you can simply say that 'war is wrong because those who take up arms will end up dying by them too so war is futile to fight'. The second is far more concise and direct, making clear sense for the examiner.

Good advice from an examiner would be to learn three teachings from two religions for each theme.

So four themes = 12 quotes each from the two religions studied. The revision guide provides those teachings for you. They are simple to learn and they do not have to be absolutely exact – as long as your examiner can tell which quote/teaching you are referring to, that will be enough. Hopefully you have been using these throughout your course so you should be familiar with many of them. If not, it's not too late – learn six per week for the month leading up to your exam … job done! It's never too late.

Remember that teachings/quotes you revise for the Themes might also be useful to you on the Religions paper. For example, teachings about helping the poor could be used as reasons why street pastors in Christianity carry out their work.

Once you begin to see how the teachings can be used across Themes and Religions, then your revision is going well and you are getting nearer to being prepared to take the exam.

From the start of revision to the exam itself

Doing GCSEs is like running a race. You do the preparation and training (your study and revision), then you turn up to the race putting yourself in the right frame of mind (that is, your last-minute revision, and calming yourself to hit the ground running in the exam itself), and finally you run the race (the exam itself). You don't see the outcome when you finish the exam, as you would with a race – that comes later. However, better than a race where only one person gets to win, in GCSEs everybody who meets the grade (and has given the right answers) gets to be a winner.

On your marks ...

REVISED

Make sure you have good notes covering all the topics – you can't have anything missing. You can revise only what you have studied already (otherwise it is study, not revision). Use your class and other notes to make a set of revision notes, in a style that suits you (check out the revision strategies in the back of this guide if you don't know any). This book could be the start of your notes – if it belongs to you, write on it. Then use your notes along with revision techniques to fix the information in your head/memory.

Where there are questions in the book, do them all – it is good practice. Also check out the AQA website for further assessment materials you could use for practice. Always do timed practices – that helps you in the exam where time is precious. Work to a minute a mark, perhaps allowing a couple extra for the 5- and 12-mark questions.

Get set ...

REVISED

- Prepare yourself for the specific exam.
- Get a good night's sleep beforehand.
- Have breakfast (your brain needs fuel). If it is an afternoon exam, avoid a stodgy lunch (it will put you to sleep when you need to be alert).
- Any revision now should be light, as it really should only be a case of refreshing your memory.
- Be in good time for the exam – rushing and arriving at the last minute encourages panic.

Go ...

REVISED

- Sitting in the exam room, breathe slowly and relax yourself (carefully reading every word of the exam paper cover is a good way to do this). Focus on your space, not the big room. Make sure you can see a clock so you can keep track of time.
- Read the exam paper and decide which questions are best for you. Answer your strongest first to give yourself confidence – if you started with your weakest, you could undermine your confidence and thus not perform so well.
- Within the exam, take mini-breaks. After completing a question take a moment to clear your head so you can get your focus clearly for the next. If you feel yourself panicking, just give yourself a breathing break to calm yourself down.
- If your mind goes blank on a question, just leave it, move on and come back to it later. Mark the question paper to remind yourself that you need to do that.
- Finished? Check your answers. Do this by reading the question, thinking of an answer, then reading your answer – you stand more chance of spotting any gaps. Also remind yourself of technique. What does the 4-marker require? Check you have done it.

On the podium ...

REVISED

It is a big podium for GCSE. With the right revision, you will be on it and receiving a good grade in the summer.

Let's get going then.

1.1 Buddhism: Section 1 – Beliefs and teachings

The Buddhist religion originated in India in the 5th century BCE, begun by a man named Siddhartha Gotama (the Buddha). It is called the Middle Way. It is very influential in Asia and the Far East, but is found in most Western countries as well. Buddhism is a way of living, not just a religion.

The Dhamma

This is the teaching of the Buddha. The Dhamma is the way the universe operates, like 'cosmic law'. It existed before the Buddha. The Buddha put it into words and explained it for others to understand. So what the Buddha taught is, to Buddhists, a form of law. The Buddha's teachings include the Three Marks of Existence, the Four Noble Truths and the Noble Eightfold Path (aka the Three Fold Way).

The nature of reality

There are two basic beliefs in Buddhism about the nature of reality: first, the Three Marks of Existence and second, 'dependent arising'.

> **Key quote**
>
> Dhammapada 183: to avoid all evil, to cultivate good, and to cleanse one's mind – this is the teaching of the Buddhas.

The Three Marks of Existence

These are also known as the Three Universal Truths. The Buddha taught that:
- everything is impermanent and illusory. Everything changes and is constantly in flux – this is **anicca**
- since everything is constantly changing, there can be no permanent self or soul, as the elements which might make this are in constant flux – this is **anatta**
- everything is constantly changing, which causes unsatisfactoriness, which leads to suffering – this is **dukkha**.

> **Anatta**: there is no permanent soul.
>
> **Anicca**: impermanence is the reality.
>
> **Dukkha**: everything is unsatisfactory.

Dependent arising (paticca samuppada)

'If this exists, that comes to exist': Buddhists believe that we have many thousands of rebirths – we are each a changing bundle of elements (skandhas) born into many lifetimes, each time trying to attain enlightenment. Together these elements are enough to keep the illusion going, but the chain of existence comes from **paticca samuppada**, or *dependent arising* (that there are interdependent events which cause the existence or occurrence of other events).

This is usually described as 12 links:
- Links 1–2: relate to past existence and are what makes the present.
- Links 3–10: relate to this existence and are shaping the future.
- Links 11–12: relate to the future, based on links 1–10.

> **Paticca samuppada**: dependent arising, meaning there are interdependent events which cause the existence or occurrence of other events.

> **Now test yourself**
>
> 1 What are the Three Marks of Existence? What does each mean?
> 2 What is 'dependent arising'?
>
> TESTED

Answers at **www.hoddereducation.co.uk/myrevisionnotesdownloads**

Human personality

The skandhas

According to Buddhism, a person is made up of five elements (aggregates), known as **skandhas**. These are constantly changing even from second to second – hence anatta. All skandhas are impermanent, so lead to dukkha.

- Physical form (rupa) – made up of the elements of air, earth, fire and water.
- Sensations/feelings (vedana) – caused when the eye sees, ear hears, mouth tastes, nose smells, body touches, or mind thinks. For example, we taste something (feeling) which we decide is not pleasant (sensation).
- Perception (samjna) – perceptions of sense.
- Mental formations (samskara) – the decision-making bit of our brain, which makes us say/think/do something.
- Awareness/consciousness (vijnana).

Consider this: are you exactly the same person as the person that woke up this morning? Or have you learned something new? Since then, you have certainly shed skin cells. So you are not the same – hence anatta.

> **Skandhas**: five aggregates which make up each person.
>
> **Sunyata**: emptiness, void.

Sunyata

Sunyata means 'emptiness'. It is the skilful (upasala) means by which a person disentangles themselves from the impurity of existence and from unsatisfactoriness. To realise sunyata is to cease attachment and craving. It leads to enlightenment. Meditation is a means to that understanding, hence meditation is being able to deliver enlightenment (as for the Buddha).

Buddha described sunyata as 'void', 'no rising and falling', 'calmness' and 'extinction'. Without having this, he would not have been able to attain enlightenment.

> With any concept, it isn't enough to 'understand' something; 'realising' it means you have both understood and experienced it – it is full understanding based on knowledge, a form of wisdom.

Attaining Buddhahood and the Buddha-nature

There are two schools of Buddhism – Theravada and Mahayana. In Theravada Buddhism, enlightenment is a personal goal, sought by monks who become **arhats** (perfected beings); in Mahayana, individuals can support others to achieve enlightenment. So, while both forms show everyone can become a Buddha (eventually), the journey may be very different.

The ultimate goal and ambition is to become Buddha. This can be done in many ways, particularly by following the Buddhist Path, namely living according to the teaching of the Buddha, the path of Dhamma. This means having faith in the Buddha, showing determination to achieve enlightenment and not give up, cultivating wisdom in oneself, and perfecting compassion and loving kindness towards others.

Mahayana Buddhism believes that everyone has **Buddha-nature** – that is, the potential to become Buddha, to become enlightened. It is the practice of Buddhism which helps us to realise our Buddha-nature for ourselves.

> **Arhat**: in Theravada Buddhism, a perfected being (the stage before enlightenment).
>
> **Buddha-nature**: the belief that everyone possesses the capacity to become Buddha.

Now test yourself

1 What are the five skandhas?
2 How can it be said that the skandhas explain anatta?
3 Explain sunyata.
4 How does sunyata explain anatta?
5 Why do Buddhists believe it is possible for everyone to become Buddha?

Human destiny

Buddhahood

Buddhists believe that every person has within them the potential to become Buddha. This means there are an infinite number of Buddhas now and to come. The different groups within Buddhism see our capacity for this slightly differently.

Arhat

Found in Theravada Buddhism, arhat means 'perfected being', one who has gained insight into the true nature of existence and has achieved nibbana. Being an arhat is the goal of Theravadins.

Realistically, one is unlikely to become an arhat unless a monk in a monastery. This means a female cannot become an arhat. Monks follow the **sila** (Ten Precepts), developing their morality, discipline and insight to become arhats. Most importantly, they develop wisdom (prajna).

Bodhisattva

Found in Mahayana Buddhism, this means 'one whose essence is bodhi (enlightened)'. Siddhartha Gotama (the Buddha) was a **bodhisattva** in life prior to his enlightenment.

Mahayanans believe the bodhisattva has made a vow to postpone their full enlightenment in order to help other beings. They see this as a higher being than the Theravadin arhat (who is focused on their own enlightenment). Compassion (karuna) than wisdom (prajna), because this is what drives them to put off full enlightenment.

The bodhisattva can transfer their own merit to their followers, thus helping them.

Stages of being a bodhisattva are:
● first, declaring the intention to put off **Buddhahood** to help others
● second, taking vows to show determination – a vow to become a buddha, and one to help others achieve enlightenment
● third, living as a bodhisattva, so working hard to develop and perfect the Six Perfections (charity, morality, patience, energy, meditation and wisdom)
● fourth, becoming enlightened and attaining Buddhahood. This is really the realisation that the person has been buddha all along because everything they have done has been selfless.

Bodhisattvas include Avalokiteshvara, Maitreya and Manjushri.

Pure Land Buddhism

Amitabha Buddha was a monk who vowed that after he achieved his own enlightenment, anyone male or female who called his name could live in his heaven (Sukhavati, or Western paradise) until they attained enlightenment for themselves. Sukhavati heaven is a beautiful place free from pain and need/want.

The **Pure Land** school of Buddhism, formed in Japan in the 12th–13th century CE, emphasises faith in Amitabha. However, a version existed in China from the 4th century CE. In Japan this form of Buddhism is known as Jodo.

Influences

If I believe that everyone can become Buddha, I know that following the Buddha's teachings will help me achieve that, so I follow them. Also that wisdom and compassion are important, so I try to show these qualities in my daily life when dealing with others.

Sila: Ten Precepts kept by monks.

Bodhisattva: a being who has postponed enlightenment after taking a vow to help others.

Buddhahood: the realisation of perfect enlightenment.

Amitabha: the Buddha of infinite light; the most important form of Buddha for Japanese Buddhists, who resides in the Pure Land heaven (Sukhavati).

Pure Land: Sukhavati heaven, the residence of Amitabha.

Answers at **www.hoddereducation.co.uk/myrevisionnotesdownloads**

The Buddha – his birth and life of luxury

Siddhartha Gotama was the man born to be the Buddha in 563 BCE. Stories of his life were written after his death, some many centuries later.

Special birth

Queen Maya, his mother, dreamed that an elephant with six tusks and a head coloured like rubies came down from heaven, entering her womb from the right side. The King sought advice from Brahmin priests about this dream – it meant Maya would have a holy child who would achieve perfect wisdom.

Siddhartha was born in the gardens of Lumbini, as his mother walked. A sala tree bent its branch for her to hold and from her side came Siddhartha. He immediately walked seven paces and from each footprint grew a lotus flower. He said this would be his last rebirth and that he would end the sorrow of birth and death.

Shortly after his birth, a holy man, Asita, told the King that Siddhartha would become either a great king or a great holy man. His father wanted him to rule, so he shaped Siddhartha's life and experiences around that aim. He was given a life of luxury, but he was kept ignorant of death, illness and other suffering in order to prevent him from becoming concerned about the meaning of life.

Points of importance

- Even before conception, Siddhartha Gotama was special.
- Prophecies were made saying Gotama would become a holy man and renounce his life of extreme wealth, and these prophecies later came true.
- His statements at birth show that we are driven by past lives.

The Four Sights – illness, old age, death, holy man

Asita had said that Siddhartha would become a great religious leader if he saw the Four Sights. Siddhartha grew curious about the world outside the palace. Jataka 075 tells the story. Aged 29, during four visits outside the palace Siddhartha encountered an old man (realising that aging happened to all regardless of wealth), then a sick person (realising that illness is an unavoidable part of life) and then a dead body (realising that we all crumble to dust eventually). These sights troubled and saddened him greatly and made him totally dissatisfied with his extreme wealth, but he had no solution – until he saw a holy man. This man had renounced the material life to find the truth, and seemed happy. It inspired Siddhartha to try for himself, vowing to find a solution to suffering.

Points of importance

- The encounter with death shows the impermanence of the material world – no amount of money can stop this.
- Seeing the Four Sights with no comprehension of them beforehand was mind-blowing – it resulted in Siddhartha renouncing his life of extreme wealth, rejecting it as not being satisfactory. This was the trigger for his spiritual journey to enlightenment.
- The last of the Four Sights (the holy man) gave him a potential solution to the dissatisfaction caused by the other three – a religious path.

Now test yourself

TESTED ☐

1 What was the human name of the Buddha?
2 What dreams and prophecies suggested Siddhartha was special?
3 What were the Four Sights?
4 Why did Siddhartha's father not want him to see the Four Sights?

Ascetic life

Having seen the Four Sights, which made him realise that suffering was unavoidable, Siddhartha left the palace and his luxurious life. He rejected them as unsatisfactory. He spent the next few years learning meditation techniques from different Hindu masters. He wanted to gain insight into the problem of suffering. He also lived a very austere life, denying himself the things he craved, especially food. This period of his life lasted six years, during which he almost starved to death – but he did not find the solution to suffering.

One day, while meditating, he heard a man telling his son about stringing an instrument – fasten the strings too tightly they snap, too loosely they will not play. Either way, no music is made. Siddhartha saw this as a metaphor for what he was doing – his life of luxury had not worked, and neither did the extreme austerity he now practised. He washed and ate proper food for the first time. His companions deserted him, seeing him as a failure.

Points of importance

- This was the opposite extreme to Siddhartha's life of luxury – he had now experienced both extremes, neither of which worked. To him, this meant the solution had to be between these – hence Buddhism is a Middle Way.
- Siddhartha reflected on the Four Sights as he saw them, then learned to meditate from masters. He later reflected that as a child he had meditated, though he had not known that was what he was doing. Meditation became a central theme in his life and in his teachings.

Enlightenment

Siddhartha sat beneath a bodhi tree and vowed to meditate without stopping until he achieved enlightenment. At first, the demon Mara tried to stop him – he tried to frighten him with fierce armies, then sent his daughters to tempt Siddhartha and so distract him from his purpose. Finally, Mara challenged his very right to achieve enlightenment. Siddhartha called on the earth goddess Vasundhara to act as witness that he was fit to achieve enlightenment. Mara left. Four periods were then marked out in the actual enlightenment:

1 Siddhartha recalled all his past lives, thus being able to see that he was ready to become enlightened.
2 He understood how all living things come to exist – paticca samuppada. He understood that everything is impermanent.
3 He realised that suffering comes from a desire or craving for things to stay as they are, or for the better. Overcoming those cravings was the key.
4 With these realisations, he attained nibbana – the three poisons (greed, hatred and ignorance) stopped within him, so no longer controlling him, and he was left with a sense of calm and happiness.

Answers at **www.hoddereducation.co.uk/myrevisionnotesdownloads**

Points of importance

- We are reminded that it takes many lifetimes to attain enlightenment – and we learn in each one.
- Even with great determination, a person can be distracted and have doubts, which must be ignored or pushed away to be successful.
- Enlightenment comes from the power of the human mind, not a divine intervention.
- Siddhartha's realisations form the basis of Buddhist teaching (paticca samuppada, Three Marks of Existence, Noble Eightfold Path). These teachings have the status of 'law' to Buddhists.

After enlightenment

The Buddha was not sure that he could teach others, so he did not turn to teaching immediately. However, the god Brahma spoke to him. He likened people to the lotus flower, a plant that grows in water – while some see only their mundane lives (like the roots of the plant in mud), others are ready to be taught (like the flower bud breaking the surface of the water) and others are ready to attain enlightenment (like the flower bursting open in the sun). The Buddha sought out the ascetics who had left him as a failure. He taught them first and then anyone who came to listen.

Points of importance

- The lotus is one of the symbols of Buddhism – for example, a statue of a seated Buddha will be sitting on an opened lotus flower, while a standing Buddha may be holding out a closed flower to the worshipper. In many Buddhist countries it is the norm for worshippers to give lotus flowers as offerings at the temple.
- Having taught the ascetics – who were close to enlightenment – Siddhartha taught anyone. This shows Buddhism is for anyone, regardless of gender, age or creed, which reflects the Buddha's compassion and concern for all.

> **Revision tip**
>
> Know the story of the Buddha's life so that you can refer to it in your answers. It is perhaps more important to know why each aspect was important in itself and any symbolic features, as these are more likely to be the basis of questions.

> **Activity**
>
> Which bit of the Buddha's life was the most important? Evaluative questions could easily focus on this, for example 'Seeing the Four Sights was the most important part of the Buddha's life'. Complete this chart to prepare yourself for any question like that.
>
> | Reasons why it is... | Birth | Four Sights | Ascetic life | Enlightenment |
> | --- | --- | --- | --- | --- |
> | **Most important** | | | | |
> | **Not most important** | | | | |

> **Revision tip**
>
> Watch the film 'Little Buddha', starring Keanu Reeves as the Buddha. It has really good depictions of the key elements of the Buddha's life. Seeing this visually will help you learn the story to use in answers.

> **Influences**
>
> As a Buddhist, the Buddha is my role model. That he became enlightened by his own efforts tells me that I can as well. From him I learn compassion for others – because he became a teacher of the Middle Way. So I work hard in my religion and try to be kind to others always.

The Four Noble Truths

This teaching flows from the Three Marks of Existence, as it explores suffering and impermanence. During his enlightenment, the Buddha realised these Truths. The Four Noble Truths are the essence of the Dhamma.

The Buddha was known as the 'great physician' and the Four Noble Truths can be seen as following a medical model of diagnosis (First Truth), cause (Second Truth), cure (Third Truth) and prescription (Fourth Truth).

Dhammapada 190–191: He who has gone for refuge to the Buddha, the teaching and his Order, penetrates with transcendental wisdom the Four Noble Truths – suffering, the cessation of suffering, and the Noble Eightfold Path leading to the cessation of suffering.

First Noble Truth

Since all existence is impermanent, all existence must involve suffering (**dukkha**). Three forms of dukkha are everyday pain and unpleasantness, that caused by the experience and realisation of impermanence (anicca/anatta), and that caused by what has gone before (our karmic programming).

Dukkha is caused by desire/craving, our attitude, and **attachment**. It is also caused by the Three Poisons (or 'fires') – greed, ignorance and hatred.

In Buddhism, there is no value to suffering, though suffering is endless until a person can cease attachment (and hence achieve enlightenment).

> **Attachment:** upadana/clinging/not wanting to be separated from someone or something.
>
> **Dukkha:** suffering.
>
> **Tanha:** craving.

Second Noble Truth

Dukkha is caused by craving (**tanha**). We suffer because we continue to crave – we want bad things to stop, we want good things to never end, we want more of what makes us feel good. This may all sound fine, but it perpetuates the craving, which is itself suffering.

Paticca samuppada (dependent arising) explains how tanha comes about because it explains how all things come to exist. 'He who perceives paticca samuppada perceives the Dhamma,' said the Buddha. Essentially, our past lives shape our present and future, but in the present life desire and attachment build to keep us bound to the cycle of rebirth (samsara).

This is considered to be the lynchpin of the Buddha's teaching and its realisation was the trigger for his enlightenment.

> **Useful quote**
>
> This being, that comes to be;
>
> from the arising of this, that arises;
>
> this not being, that ceases;
>
> from the ceasing of this, that ceases.

Third Noble Truth

End tanha by achieving non-attachment (**nirodha**) – stop wanting = stop suffering. This is also nibbana (cessation of suffering) – when a person stops being attached to the material world and what is in it, they have the calm of enlightenment and are not affected by the Three Poisons because of non-attachment.

Nirodha is described in many ways in Buddhist scripture – the destruction of the skandhas, supreme happiness, the stopping of becoming, the ending of craving, final destruction of the intentions, the end of suffering. It can be seen as a state of being (peace, blessing, purity), or a place (the unborn, the unbecome, the eternal).

> **Nirodha:** cessation of suffering.

Fourth Noble Truth

The way to nirodha is by the path (**magga**). This is Buddhist practice, known as the Noble Eightfold Path. It is the Middle Way.

Magga has eight elements, all of which are important – a Buddhist cannot focus on just one or two. Think of the Buddhist wheel (Figure 1). The eight spokes (Noble Eightfold Path elements) lead to the hub (enlightenment) and those not following the spokes are on the outer rim (wheel of rebirth, samsara). This is one reason the wheel (Dharmachakra) is such an important symbol for Buddhism.

Magga: the path, the Fourth Noble Truth.

Wheel of rebirth – samsara

Enlight-enment

Figure 1 The Buddhist wheel

The eight elements are Right View, Right Thought/Intention, Right Speech, Right Action, Right Livelihood, Right Effort, Right Mindfulness, Right Concentration.

Magga can also be understood as the Threefold Way – this still uses the elements of the Eightfold Path but grouped into three aspects of wisdom (Right Thought/View), morality (Right Action/Speech/Livelihood) and meditation (Right Effort/Meditation/Concentration).

Now test yourself
TESTED

1 Which of these is not one of the Four Noble Truths?
(a) Nirodha   (b) Tanha   (c) Samsara   (d) Dukkha
2 Which of these is the First Noble Truth?
(a) Magga   (b) Nirodha   (c) Tanha   (d) Dukkha
3 How many parts are there to the path of Buddhism (Magga)?
(a) 3   (b) 4   (c) 8   (d) 5
4 Explain the Four Noble Truths.
5 Explain how belief in the Four Noble Truths might influence a Buddhist in their daily lives.

Influences

These teachings affect my life every day. I try to always see things – good and bad – as transient, they will pass. This helps me get through difficulties, but also means I try not to hold on to good happenings. The important thing is not to hold on, because that attitude causes me angst on top of the hurt already felt – if I get ill, for example, the illness makes me suffer, so I accept it; moaning on about it only makes it worse (for everyone!). So I suppose a side effect of believing these Truths is to be determined to be detached.

The Noble Eightfold Path

Magga – the Fourth Noble Truth – is the Noble Eightfold Path. It is the eight-part system for living for a Buddhist. The Dharmachakra ('wheel symbol' for Buddhism) reflects the idea that we are on the rim of life, but by following the Eightfold Path (spokes) we reach enlightenment (hub).

Each part of the Eightfold Path must be followed as the eight elements are linked. A Buddhist would not try to perfect just one element at a time, they would be working on all of them.

It can also be split three ways: wisdom (**panna**) – Right Thought, Right View; morality/ethics (**sila**) – Right Speech, Right Action, Right Livelihood; and meditation (**samadhi**) – Right Effort, Right Mindfulness and Right Concentration (Figure 2). This is called the **Threefold Way** and is seen in Dhammapada 183 – to avoid all evil, to cultivate good, and to cleanse one's mind – this is the teaching of the Buddhas.

> **Panna**: wisdom.
>
> **Samadhi**: meditation.
>
> **Sila**: morality.

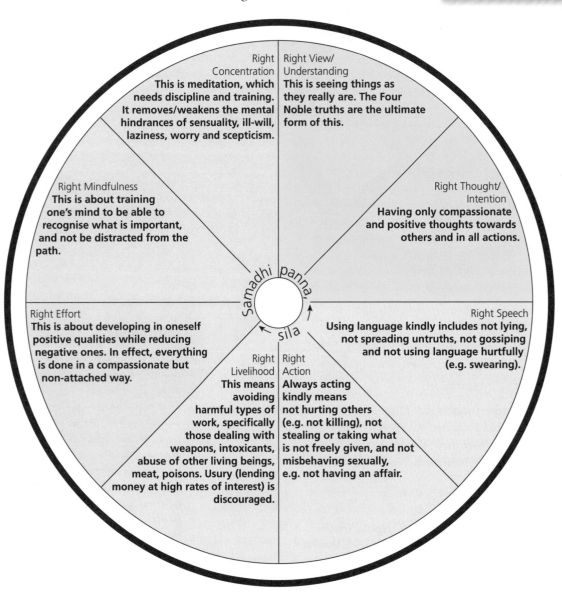

Figure 2 The Noble Eightfold Path

Exam practice

What questions on this section look like:

Buddhism: Beliefs and teachings

This page contains a range of questions that could be on an exam paper. Practise them all to strengthen your knowledge and technique while revising. Check back to pages 13–14 to see the marking grids that examiners use: this will help you to mark your answers.

1 What is meant by dukkha?
   (a) Suffering   (b) Charity   (c) Loving kindness   (d) Craving   [1]

2 Which of the following is not a place associated with the Buddha's life?
   (a) Lumbini   (b) Sarnath   (c) Bodh Gaya   (d) Calcutta   [1]

3 Give two of the Four Noble Truths.   [2]

4 Give two of the Four Sights.   [2]

5 Give two of the five skandhas.   [2]

6 Explain two ways in which belief in the Pure Land influences Buddhists today.   [4]

7 Explain two ways in which belief in the Three Marks of Existence influences Buddhists today.   [4]

8 Explain two ways in which belief in magga (the Path) influences Buddhists today.   [4]

9 Explain two ways in which a belief in dependent arising influences Buddhists today.   [4]

10 Explain two Buddhist teachings about the human personality. Refer to sacred writings or another source of Buddhist belief and teaching in your answer.   [5]

11 Explain two Buddhist teachings about enlightenment. Refer to sacred writings or another source of Buddhist belief and teaching in your answer.   [5]

12 Explain two Buddhist teachings about the importance of the Buddha. Refer to sacred writings or another source of Buddhist belief and teaching in your answer.   [5]

13 'The enlightenment of the Buddha was the most important event in his life.' Evaluate this statement.
In your answer you should:
- refer to Buddhist teaching
- give reasoned arguments to support this statement
- give reasoned arguments to support a different point of view
- reach a justified conclusion.   [12]

14 'Buddhists cannot expect to become enlightened if they are not a monk.' Evaluate this statement.
In your answer you should:
- refer to Buddhist teaching
- give reasoned arguments to support this statement
- give reasoned arguments to support a different point of view
- reach a justified conclusion.   [12]

15 'Dependent arising is the most important part of the Buddha's teachings.' Evaluate this statement.
In your answer you should:
- refer to Buddhist teaching
- give reasoned arguments to support this statement
- give reasoned arguments to support a different point of view
- reach a justified conclusion.   [12]

ONLINE ☐

Commentary

Grade 2 students have limited knowledge of the content of the course. They write very short answers, sometimes giving no answer at all. If this is you, get notes that you can revise from and learn methods of revision so that you can tackle the exam more effectively.

Grade 5 students have general knowledge of the topics, but they don't go into detail often enough. Their answers can be vague or woolly, or they can be great on one question and poor on another, showing patchy knowledge and understanding. If this is you, make sure you have notes that make sense to you, that cover every bit of the Specification, and practise by making yourself explain everything – which comes from understanding the content better.

Grade 8 students have a strong understanding of the content – their answers are detailed and clear, reflecting that good understanding. Their writing demonstrates that they understand the connections between the different elements they have studied.

1.1 Buddhism: Section 2 – Practices

Buddhist ethics

Buddhists follow the Noble Eightfold Path to attain enlightenment. The Path is also known as the Threefold Way. One of these is sila or morality/ethics, covering Right Speech, Action and Livelihood. Let's face it – if everyone behaved compassionately in all these three 'Rights', the world would be much nicer, since they provoke most problems.

Karma and rebirth

Karma/kamma means 'action'. Buddhists believe that all intentional actions/thoughts/words have consequences. Actions can be skilful (upaya kusala) or unskilful (akusala) – skilful actions bringing positive future consequences, unskilful actions bringing negative ones. The consequence can come in this lifetime, the next one or many lifetimes away, but Buddhists believe it will happen as an automatic outcome, without someone giving a judgement or sentence. A current lifetime is a result of karma from previous one(s). Since the key is 'intention', having generally good morality can outweigh unskilful action to some extent (i.e. one unskilful action does not necessarily define a future lifetime, and may even have no consequence). Many Buddhists believe in merit-making – building good karma by good deeds – which offsets previous bad karma. Essentially, our rebirth (**samsara**) – positive or negative – is defined by our karma.

Karuna

This is mercy or compassion. It is one of the four sublime states (**Brahma-viharas**) which Buddhists are constantly urged to develop in themselves. It is a virtue or state of mind which leads to a sense of selflessness. The bodhisattva exemplifies this virtue, as a bodhisattva has vowed to help others. Amitabha welcomes Buddhists into his heaven as an act of karuna. The Buddha is the model of compassion and wisdom – compassion without wisdom can lead to harmful actions. The whole point of the Noble Eightfold Path is to develop wisdom and compassion.

Metta

Metta is loving kindness. It is selfless – kindness not done for personal gain. It is another of the Brahma-viharas. It is a concern for the well-being of others – actions flow from that concern. The act of kindness can be small or large, done for those near or for those far away.

The Metta Sutta says, 'Whatever beings there may be … may all beings, without exception, be happy-minded.' Mettabhavana meditation makes the meditator think loving thoughts to push out to the world in stages from those closest to us those we dislike to those we do not even know. The Dalai Lama once said, 'My religion is simple, my religion is kindness.'

Brahma-viharas: four sublime states – living kindness, compassion, sympathetic joy and equanimity.

Karma/Kamma: the ethical quality or value of all intentional actions/words/thoughts.

Metta: loving kindness.

Samsara: cycle of birth, death and rebirth.

Now test yourself

1 What is karma? How does it bind us?
2 What is rebirth? How does it link to karma?
3 What are karuna and metta?

TESTED

Activity

Develop the notes

A student ran out of time in their exam and had to write their answer in notes. Use them to write a well-argued, detailed answer. Remember it needs a conclusion.

Metta and karuna are the most important Buddhist virtues. [12 marks]

Agree – Buddha's example – did not keep what he learned to himself; helped many to achieve enlightenment; selfless = non-attachment; Dalai Lama – 'compassion is my religion'.

Disagree – wisdom more important; misguided compassion causes more trouble; being faithful to Dharma more important; metta/karuna not always possible in a situation.

The Six Perfections (paramitas)

In Mahayana Buddhism the **Six Perfections** (prajna–paramita) are the virtues perfected by a bodhisattva in the course of their spiritual development and journey towards enlightenment. For a bodhisattva, they are often seen to replace the Noble Eightfold Path. They are considered to be perfected when even the most difficult actions can be carried out with a mind free of discriminatory ideas, without reference to self, without ulterior motives and with no thought of reward. As with the Noble Eightfold Path, practice is the key to perfecting these. However, any person can try to be better at any of them – they neither have to be Buddhist nor bodhisattva.

> **Five Precepts** – panca sila: five guidelines which all Buddhists must follow in order to live compassionately.
>
> **Six Perfections** – prajna-paramita: six virtues which bodhisattvas work to perfect in themselves.

Perfection (paramita)	How to cultivate this in oneself
Giving/generosity (dana)	Someone who practises perfect giving sees no difference between the giver and the receiver. This includes giving guidance on the Dhamma, material items, accumulated merit and his/her own life, if necessary (the Buddha in one lifetime gave his life to a she-tiger who had no food for her cubs).
Morality (sila)	Keeping all the Ten Precepts. It is also the understanding of how one can break a Precept yet still be acting in a skilful (kusala) way, e.g. killing someone to prevent them murdering another person.
Patience (ksanti)	Non-anger/non-agitation. This is going beyond enduring suffering, but rather accepting any difficulties one has. Accepting sunyata means that the bodhisattva sees no difference between themselves as sufferer and the cause of the suffering.
Effort/energy (virya)	This means never getting bored/tired of working for one's vows. It is unrelenting energy in overcoming one's faults and cultivating the virtues of the bodhisattva.
Meditation (bhavana)	Following all forms of meditation. This is about becoming able to always see things as they are so as to help others more effectively.
Wisdom (prajna)	Realisation of sunyata. This is perfect wisdom.

The Five Precepts (panca sila)

The **Five Precepts** are five guidelines for living which all Buddhist laity (ordinary people) must keep to. They are not laws. They are followed in skilful (upaya kausala) or unskilful (akusala) ways. To follow them in skilful ways results in good karma, while following them in unskilful ways results in bad karma being generated. Keeping them in a skilful way is also a good counter to the Three Poisons (greed, hatred, ignorance). Unskillful means ignoring Precepts, as well as deliberately breaking them. Buddhism emphasises intention, so thoughts and words matter just as actions do. A Precept can be kept or broken in mind as well as in practice.

Skilful example	Precept	Unskilful example
Helping a homeless person by feeding them	First Precept Abstain from harming sentient beings (any form of feeling life)	Murdering another person
Being kind with one's possessions so as to share them with others	Second Precept Abstain from taking that which is not freely given (including not forcing others to give)	Persuading someone to give you something when you know they don't want to really
Being faithful in marriage	Third Precept Abstain from sexual misconduct (physical or emotional)	Making unwanted sexual comments to someone
Being honest but kind in speech	Fourth Precept Abstain from using false speech (including being untruthful or unkind with language)	Telling lies about someone
Not drinking alcohol so as not to be unaware of actions	Fifth Precept Abstain from using intoxicating drinks and drugs causing heedlessness (not being concerned about consequences)	Taking drugs not prescribed as medicines

Monks keeping the Precepts

Monks are required to follow ten Precepts (dasa sila), as are any non-monks who are focused on their religious path. As well as the Five Precepts, these are abstaining from taking untimely meals, abstaining from dancing/music/singing, abstaining from the use of garlands/perfumes/jewellery, abstaining from use of high seats/luxurious beds and abstaining from accepting gold/silver (money). All these things are focused around luxury and pleasing the senses. The Ten Precepts effectively separate monks from others and prove they have renounced the world. Essentially, the monks are giving up all sensual attachments – the things we take for granted in daily life.

> **Activity**
>
> Use the answer starters to write strong answers to these questions:
>
> *Explain two ways in which a Buddhist might act in skilful ways. Refer to Buddhist teachings in your answer.* (5 marks)
>
> Buddhists follow the Five Precepts. The Buddha gave these five guidelines for living compassionately. Following these guidelines in a positive way is skilful means. First, they might ...... which keeps the _____ Precept (to abstain from _____) in a skilful way because ......
>
> Second, they might ...... which keeps the _____ Precept (to abstain from_____) in a skilful way because ......

> **Activity**
>
> **Show your understanding**
> 1 Come up with your own example of each of the Five Precepts followed in a skilful and an unskilful way.
> 2 How much more difficult is it for monks to keep the Ten Precepts than for the laity to keep the Five Precepts?

> **Revision tip**
>
> The opening sentence tells the examiner you know what is meant by 'skilful way' so sets up your answer. By giving an example, then naming the Precept, you are providing teachings as requested. By explaining how the action is skilful, you directly answer the question.

Influences

As a Buddhist, I start my day by reciting the Five Precepts. In the day I try to remain mindful of them as I go from task to task – I want to be aware of my impact on others, so that it can be positive. At the end of the day, I use the Precepts to think about how I could have done something better, and resolve to do so next time.

Answers at **www.hoddereducation.co.uk/myrevisionnotesdownloads**

Worship in Buddhism

Places of worship

There are a number of different names for places of worship in Buddhism.

Name	Use
Temple	Buddhist laity attend the temple whenever they wish to. Most attend every festival day. Temples include worship halls and shrines. Many have gardens for reflection and spaces for meditation. Many also have rooms for consultation with the monks based at the temple. Pujas (acts of worship) are held here daily.
	Many temples are built near stupas, which are relic houses (contain religious artefacts such as a tooth from the Buddha). Stupas are dome shaped.
	There are bodhi trees at many temples, reminding people of the Buddha's enlightenment. Many are said to be descended from the original tree.
Shrine	A shrine is a small or large sacred place dedicated to the Buddha; it can be at home. It is centred around at least one Buddha rupa (statue of the Buddha). Each temple has a shrine room as its most important place for worship. Acts of worship take place and offerings are made to the Buddha here.
Vihara (monastery)	All have a temple within their compound. Pujas (acts of worship, but NOT services) are held here daily. Since the monks live here, there will be living quarters, as well as kitchens, meeting rooms, etc.
Gompa (hall for learning)	This is the name given to Tibetan Buddhist shrine rooms. In Tibetan Buddhism there is a long tradition of training for monks to attain a degree in Buddhist philosophy, hence a hall for learning.

Some differences

Depending on the country, the name for the temple varies – a pagoda in China is a stupa in India is a wat in Sri Lanka.

In Theravada Buddhism, many temples are also homes to monks, that is they are also small or large monasteries. In Mahayana Buddhism, monasteries are less common and many temples have only a single religious leader based at them.

Revision tip

It is always easier to recall the elements of this page when we have a visual image. Collect images of all the things mentioned here and annotate them. The act of annotating helps your brain to take in and retain the information.

The importance of Buddhist places of worship

- Place of learning – laity or monk, anyone can learn more about the Dhamma from the religious leaders based there via lessons, individual discussions, or services (Dhammapada 276).
- Place for reflection/meditation – Right Meditation.
- Place to pay tribute to the Buddha – making offerings in thankfulness for his gift of the teaching of the Dhamma and for his example of attaining enlightenment – the act of dana (giving).
- Advice – many Buddhists will discuss personal and life issues with the monks to learn the correct Buddhist response (Dhammapada 276).
- Centre of the community.

Useful quote

'You yourselves should make the effort; the enlightened ones are only teachers'. Dhammapada 276

Key features of worship

The table shows the key features of worship in Buddhism.

Feature	About	Importance
Buddha rupa (statue of Buddha)	Can be sat in meditative pose, reclining, or standing. One focal Buddha rupa, usually centrally positioned (might be part of a trio). Often many rupas in a shrine room – different sizes, materials, etc.	Buddha is central to religion, so central to shrine. Symbols within rupa help worshipper to focus on spiritual truths.
Artefacts	Items of religious significance to aid worship or meditation, or to remind of Dhamma. Scriptures – may be only one sutra, e.g. Heart Sutra – representing the speech of the Buddha, i.e. all his teachings. Model of a stupa – representing the mind of the Buddha. Vajra – thunderbolt/diamond – symbolises five wisdoms and five kandhas/poisons. Instruments such as cymbals and bells are present to aid meditation/puja.	Aid to worship. Aid to meditation (as focus). Symbolic nature of each is important. Rupa, scriptures and stupa represent the Three Jewels, i.e. the Three Refuges (Buddha, Dharma, Sangha).
Offerings	Generally: ● Flowers = the beauty of enlightenment and a reminder of impermanence as they wither and die. ● Candles – light helps us to see where to go – the light of Dhamma in the darkness of ignorance. ● Incense – the sweet smell goes everywhere (no barriers) = Buddhism is fit for any place and any person. ● Food – gift of thanks to Buddha for the teaching of the Dhamma and to the monks for their religious devotion. ● In Mahayana, it is traditional to make seven offerings. Two bowls of water (washing, drinking) symbolise hospitality. Then five others – flowers, candles, incense, food, perfume – represent the five senses.	Dana (giving) is a key element of Buddhist ethics. It evokes Right Action. The symbolic nature of each item allows the worshipper to reflect on religious truths. Making the offerings is a way to focus on worship completely. Giving to the Buddha shows respect and thankfulness for his teachings/example.

Some differences

Mahayana temples usually have three Buddhas/bodhisattvas as the focal part of their shrine, known as a triad, which sit side by side. For example, it may be Sakyamuni Buddha (historical Buddha) with Manjushri (bodhisattva of wisdom) and Samantabhadra (bodhisattva of kindness). Theravada temples have one central rupa, but often have many other smaller rupa all around that one.

Theravadins make offerings of the four forms (flowers, incense, food and light) and can often buy these four items bundled together for them at the temple. In Mahayana, there are commonly seven offerings, with two water offerings and one of perfume additional to the Theravadin.

Worship – puja

What is puja?

Puja is a formal act of worship that takes place before a shrine. Before entering the shrine, or the shrine room if in a temple complex, the worshipper will have removed their shoes (humility; people sit on the floor, so this keeps it cleaner). In Buddhist puja, there are three core elements:

- Bowing to the Buddha – three times to represent the Buddha, Dhamma and Sangha (Three Refuges). This is often done from a kneeling position, with hands together in front of the chest, though it may be full prostration with the worshipper's head touching the floor. This reminds them of their commitment to the ideal set by the Buddha.
- Making offerings of incense, flowers, food and candles – each symbolic of key teachings. By making the offering, the worshipper becomes mindful of these and that they aspire to become Buddha themselves.
- Chanting – done when making offerings. It is often a recitation of a set scripture, dictated by the worshipper's form of Buddhism. It may focus on the example of the Buddha, or it may be about the symbolic nature of the offerings, for example.

> **Puja**: Buddhist act of worship.

Some differences

Tibetan Buddhists prostrate themselves fully before the statue, with arms stretched towards the statue. Theravada Buddhists kneel, put their palms together in front of their chest and bow three times to the Buddha.

The words recited will be fixed depending on which form of Buddhism the worshipper follows, for example Friends of the Western Buddhist Order (FWBO) recite about the offerings and what they symbolise.

Theravada Buddhists make four offerings; Mahayana Buddhists, especially Tibetans, make seven.

Why do puja?

Puja is an expression of devotion and thankfulness to the Buddha generally, but it may be for a specific purpose, such as becoming pregnant.

Through bowing and making offerings, the worshipper shows humility, which is crucial in the goal to enlightenment and demonstrates determination to achieve enlightenment.

Puja also shows Right Mindfulness as it requires a focus on what is being done and the symbolism behind it. The ritual of puja makes the worshipper engage actively and emotionally with the teachings – it is not enough to just understand the religion, Buddhism is about transforming a person entirely.

In Buddhist countries, most Buddhists attend temple, often daily. Many Buddhists also have home shrines (a space given over to a Buddha rupa, around which are placed items of significance to aid puja and meditation).

Useful quote

'Reverently, I prostrate with my body, speech and mind, and present clouds of every type of offering.' Tibetan prayer

Home	Temple
Done on own terms – when, how long, what is recited, etc.	Follows standard routine – enter, bow, make offerings, chant/recite
Effort goes into making shrine	Effort goes into attending temple
Study is personal and usually solitary, self-guided	Monks available to discuss issues, give advice, etc.
Shrine may be very small and simple	Shrines often full of artefacts, and ornate

Chanting

Chanting is a repetition of key scriptures/teachings and can be an aid to meditation. It must be conducted in a single-minded and sincere manner, though it can be done aloud/silently, alone/with others, with prayer beads or not, to music or not. It is always a demonstration of devotion.

Mantra recitation

This is a repetition of a set phrase in order to bring about a specific state of consciousness. Tibetan monks are often given **mantras** personal to themselves by their teachers. Om mani padme hum is a good example, the syllables of which represent the Six Perfections. It could be chanting to call upon the Buddha or a bodhisattva (as in Pure Land Buddhism where Amitabha is called upon). It always shows devotion but is also merit-making.

Use of malas

A **mala**, a string of prayer beads, is used to count prayers/recitations/mantras. There are 108 beads in total, representing 108 worldly desires and the means to overcome them. These aid focus, but also ensure the worshipper says the requisite number of prayers.

> **Mala**: Buddhist prayer beads.
>
> **Mantra**: set phrase, usually calling on the name of a Buddha/bodhisattva.

Now test yourself

TESTED ☐

1 What is puja? What three elements are there?
2 What do Buddhists chant at puja?
3 What are mantras?
4 What is a mala and why use it?

Answers at **www.hoddereducation.co.uk/myrevisionnotesdownloads**

Meditation

Meditation is mental concentration in order to achieve a state of mind from which one can eventually attain enlightenment. It is a physical and mental discipline. It is one of the elements of the Noble Eightfold Path, so most Buddhists meditate in some form.

Imagine the mind as a pool of water. Thoughts disturb the surface, so one cannot see clearly into it. Meditation aims to still the surface to allow clear sight and understanding.

How do we know meditation is important/ significant in Buddhism?

Right Concentration is one element of the Noble Eightfold Path, which is the Fourth Noble Truth (magga). Samadhi (meditation) is one element of the Threefold Way. It is considered crucial for attaining enlightenment. Meditation leads to mindfulness, which leads to detachment, which leads to nibbana.

The Buddha is most commonly seen seated in meditative pose in rupas/ images, hence implying its importance. He trained himself in meditation practices and then meditated until enlightenment, so this is his example.

The Buddha taught meditation, and from that so have Buddhist leaders throughout history. All Buddhists meditate.

Useful quotes

What the Buddha said

'Hard to restrain, unstable is this mind; it flits wherever it lists. Good it is to control the mind. A controlled mind brings happiness.' Dhammapada 35

'Though one may live a hundred years with no true insight and self-control, yet better, indeed, is a life of one day for a man who meditates in wisdom.' Dhammapada 111

'Not to do any evil, to cultivate good, to purify one's mind, this is the teaching of the Buddhas.' Dhammapada 183

'You yourselves should make the effort; the Enlightened Ones are only teachers. Those who enter this path and are meditative are delivered from the bonds of Mara.' Dhammapada 276

Reading these, it is clear that Buddhists should meditate. Meditation brings the mind under control, which helps a person eliminate unskilful thinking (and, in turn, unskilful words/actions). It brings non-attachment, and from being able to see things clearly, wisdom. Buddhism is a personal journey, and meditation is a crucial practice within that in order to bring success.

Types of meditation

For the course, you have to study four types of meditation.

Type	Information
Samatha (calm/ concentration and tranquility)	This aims to develop calmness and 'one-pointedness' of mind (mindfulness). Samatha trains the mind not to be distracted by thoughts.
	Eight 'trance' levels (jhanas) are recognised in samatha meditation, beginning with 'mindfulness of breathing'. This is about being 'in the present moment', still and calm. Each subsequent one is more complicated/refined. Nibbana cannot be attained from samatha, as the levels operate within the universe (so are part of conditioned existence).
	Buddhist texts list 40 meditation subjects, including, of breathing, on the Brahma-viharas (sublime states), and on the 32 parts of the body.
	Successful samatha leads to Right Mindfulness.
	Samatha changes a person's outlook and attitudes in daily life as well as while meditating.
Vipassana (insight)	This is specific to Buddhism, developed by the Buddha.
	Focus is on analysing the mind and body and interactions with the material world in order to break attachment. This allows insight to be gained into the true nature of reality, particularly the Three Marks of Existence. From that nibbana can be attained.
	It is a permanent solution to the problem of suffering, given the realisation of the Three Marks.
	Vipassana seems to be more connected to wisdom (panna) than concentration (samatha).
Zazen (meditation in sitting)	This comes from Soto Zen, Japanese Buddhism.
	The meditator sits in a meditative position in a quiet room and tries to attain a state of relaxed attention (no thoughts, no reasoning, no reflection). It is common for the meditator to have been posed a paradox – **koan** – the answer to which may come in these sessions. These are supposed to train monks to give up on logical reasoning and force sudden intuitive enlightenment.
	Dogen, the founder of Soto Zen, said that zazen in itself could constitute enlightenment.
Visualisation of Buddha or bodhisattva	This involves calming the mind and visualising Buddhas or bodhisattvas to develop compassion. It is common to Chinese (Chan) and Tibetan Buddhism.
	It may include trying to recreate an image in one's mind – of a mandala, a tangkha (image of a Buddha in their heaven, e.g. Amitabha), a Buddha, e.g. Guan Yin (bodhisattva of compassion), a Buddha heaven, or a mantra.
	The meditator is trying to see what it would be like to be the subject or in the place being visualised.

Now test yourself

TESTED ☐

1 What is meditation?
2 Why do Buddhists meditate?
3 What is the difference between samatha and vipassana?

Koan: statement/question intended to pose a mental dilemma ('What is the sound of one hand clapping?'), used in zazen.

Samatha: meditation for mindfulness, concentration.

Vipassana: meditation for insight.

Visualisation: use of images (actual or in the mind) to meditate.

Zazen: form of meditation used by Soto Zen practitioners.

Exam tip

A 'differences/contrasts' question on this topic might well be to explain different forms of meditation, rather than meditation done by different types of Buddhists.

Answers at **www.hoddereducation.co.uk/myrevisionnotesdownloads**

Death and mourning rituals in Buddhism

Buddhists contemplate death throughout their lives, not only before they are about to die. It was one of the Four Sights. It is just a stage in the cycle of samsara, and an example of anicca (impermanence) so a learning tool. Many Buddhists meditate on death and dying. It is common for Buddhist monks to meditate focused on a skull, reminding them that this is their future as well and that all things will pass.

Funeral rites emphasise the Three Marks of Existence (suffering, impermanence and no permanent self), the hope for a better rebirth, the showing of respect to the dead and to those choosing a religious path. Common to all funerals, monks will recite sutras to/for the dead. **Pamsukula robes** ('rag' robes) are given to the dead. Cremation is common. Families give alms to the local monastery/temple to transfer merit to the deceased for their rebirth. It is common to hold memorial services 3, 7, 49 and 100 days after the death.

Bardo: in Tibetan Buddhism, the state between death and rebirth lasting up to 49 days – a place of demons, ghosts and terror.

Butsudan: Japanese home shrine.

Matakabhatta: Food offerings given to monks on behalf of the deceased.

Pamsukula robes: 'rag robes' given to the dead (usually placed on the coffin).

Form of Buddhism	Process	Symbolism/significance
Theravada	Sutras recited to the dying/dead.	Trying to direct the thoughts of the dying/dead to the Buddha.
	The coffin with the body in it is surrounded by candles, incense and wreaths.	Tribute to the dead, but also reminders of the Three Marks of Existence.
	Monks visit to chant from Abhidharma scripture; food is given to monks (**matakabhatta**).	Transfer of merit to the dead from reading and giving of alms to aid rebirth.
	At cremation, monks sit facing the coffin; relatives bring lit torches made of candles, incense and a fragrant wood to put under the coffin and start the flames.	Watching death is a meditation on impermanence and no self. Monks are here to bless the dead. The elements of the torch remind of temple offerings.
Japanese	Funeral rites last several days.	Mark of respect.
	Procession to the temple. Coffin placed in front of items to invoke paradise. Mourners give money.	Hope for rebirth in a heaven. Dana.
	Priest kneels before the coffin and recites sutras. Family offer respect to the dead.	Reminding all of the Buddha's teachings on impermanence, and especially death.
	Body is burned, while a family meal takes place.	One willow and one bamboo chopstick, representing the bridge between this world and the next.
	Ashes/bones are placed into a box using special chopsticks. This is put out on the family shrine (**butsudan**) before internment in the family grave.	
Tibetan	Book of the Dead read to the dying/dead person to prepare them for **bardo**.	The reader gains good merit for themselves, and helps the recipient.
	In bardo for up to 49 days, beginning with a glimpse of enlightenment, their karma will then take them to it or pull them away from it to rebirth.	The 'being pulled away' is explained as the sense of 'I' being too strong to let go and so rebirth is inevitable.
	'Sky burial' – performed on a hillside. The body is dismembered while a scripture is recited.	Emphasises non-attachment – there is no 'I'. Buddha gave his body to feed starving animals in one rebirth.
	The parts are then left for vultures to eat.	This is a final act of dana by the deceased.

Festivals and retreats

Festivals specifically commemorate an event/person which is historically important. They could be seen as the religion's outward, public face. Retreats are a total focus on the religion, as if going inward away from the public gaze.

Retreats

During the three-month rainy season, the Buddha encouraged monks to seclude themselves in order to meditate more intensely. This **retreat** has been a practice of monks ever since.

The process involves taking oneself away from the normal concerns/demands of daily life for a period of time and leading a simple, focused life, during which time the main task is to study the Dhamma and/or meditate (i.e. develop one's spiritual practice or understanding).

In the UK this is a chance to fully relax but fully focus – away from busy Western society. It can be considered as a 'spiritual battery recharge'. Participants meet other people, so they can form a sense of community which lasts beyond the retreat.

> **Parinirvana Day**: commemorates Buddha attaining nibbana fully.
>
> **Retreat**: taking a break from society to focus on spiritual path.
>
> **Wesak**: festival commemorating full moon in May on which day Buddha was born, became enlightened and died.

Wesak

Wesak recalls the birth, enlightenment and death of the Buddha, each of which happened in May on the night of the full moon. The Buddha's teachings help everyone and the Buddhist path is seen as one of peace and so a boon to the world – hence the importance of this festival.

During the festival the laity follows Eight Precepts (the Five Precepts plus refraining from singing/dancing/wearing garlands and perfumes, eating after midday and sleeping in luxurious beds). They attend temple and make offerings to the temple, but also to the vulnerable of society (Giving), and restate their commitment to the Precepts (Virtue). They participate in chanting scriptures, listening to sermons, and in meditation (Cultivation), as well as doing good deeds (Merit-making). Some Buddhists wear white (novice) robes and spend the whole day/evening at the temple. Many pour water over statues of the Buddha, as if washing them, and put garlands of flowers over them.

Parinirvana Day

For Mahayana Buddhists, **Parinirvana Day** recalls the day that the Buddha died, so he reached nibbana. For most Buddhists this day is 15 February. It is important because it reminds of final death, ceasing to be reborn – the goal of all Buddhists. Buddhists should reflect on their future death and on any recent deaths.

The day involves attending temple and/or meditation. Some spend the day reading/reciting sutras (especially Parinirvana Sutra). Prayers will be said for the recently deceased to try to send them merit for their journey. Many Buddhists give money and items to support monks at monasteries. It is also a traditional day for pilgrimage in Asia.

> **Some differences**
>
> While Wesak is a social and joyful day, with activities for children and adults in the UK, Parinirvana is a solemn one requiring a certain level of understanding of the faith to be able to attend UK temples (effectively excluding children).
>
> Different countries celebrate the festivals differently. For Parinirvana Day, Buddhists in India may make a pilgrimage to Kushinagar; UK Buddhists will attend temple for an extended period.

Exam practice

What questions on this section look like:

Buddhism: Practices

This page contains a range of questions that could be on an exam paper. Practise them all to strengthen your knowledge and technique while revising. Check back to pages 13–14 to see the marking grids that examiners use: this will help you to mark your answers.

1 Which of these is not one of the Six Perfections?

   (a) Wisdom   (b) Generosity   (c) Not hurting   (d) Ethics   [1]

2 Which of these is a Buddhist festival?

   (a) Wesak   (b) Dharma   (c) Paramitas   (d) Tipitaka   [1]

3 Give two of the Five Precepts.   [2]

4 Give two forms of Buddhist meditation.   [2]

5 Give two elements of the Six Perfections.   [2]

6 Explain two similar features of Buddhist temples.   [4]

7 Explain two contrasting ways in which a Buddhist might meditate.   [4]

8 Explain two contrasting (different) forms of worship for Buddhists.   [4]

9 Explain two similar features of a Buddhist funeral in two Buddhist traditions.   [4]

10 Explain two ways in which Wesak is important in the life of a Buddhist. Refer to sacred writings or another source of Buddhist belief and teachings in your answer.   [5]

11 Explain two ways in which the Five Precepts are important to Buddhists. Refer to sacred writings or another source of Buddhist belief and teachings in your answer.   [5]

12 Explain two ways in which retreats might be important for Buddhists in Great Britain today. Refer to sacred writings or another source of Buddhist belief and teachings in your answer.   [5]

13 'Buddhists should always attend a temple for worship.' Evaluate this statement. In your answer you should:

- refer to Buddhist teaching
- give reasoned arguments to support this statement
- give reasoned arguments to support a different point of view
- reach a justified conclusion.   [12]

14 'Meditation is more important than good actions.' Evaluate this statement. In your answer you should:

- refer to Buddhist teaching
- give reasoned arguments to support this statement
- give reasoned arguments to support a different point of view
- reach a justified conclusion.   [12]

15 'Compassion without wisdom is not helpful.' Evaluate this statement. In your answer you should:

- refer to Buddhist teaching
- give reasoned arguments to support this statement
- give reasoned arguments to support a different point of view
- reach a justified conclusion.   [12]

ONLINE

Commentary

Grade 2 students make little use of quotations and/or teachings – 'limited reference to sources of wisdom and authority'. When used, they are the most common but often not the most appropriate for the question so the examiner is left trying to work out how they are relevant (they won't!). Those used are usually not applied to the question – they can just sit there, almost irrelevant. If this is you, get a stock of basic teachings for the religions you study and practise using them.

Grade 5 students use some quotes/teachings, but they can usually be more appropriate or better applied to the question. They are generally accurate, but could be sharper. If this is you, then you need to do more work on learning these teachings and making better use of them.

Grade 8 students make 'well-integrated reference to sources of wisdom and authority', in other words they use lots of quotes/teachings which are specific to the question and which they explain well in relation to the question. It is clear they have a deep understanding of the religion and this is evidence of that.

▶ 1.2 Christianity: Section 1 – Beliefs and teachings

The qualities of God   REVISED ☐

There are many qualities of God. This course seeks that you recognise and can explain a number of them, so questions could be asked specifically about these terms. The key qualities you must know are **omnipotence**, **all-loving** and **just**. If you know other characteristics that is good as you can use that knowledge in some of your answers.

Qualities of God evidenced in the Bible

1 Omnipotence means God is all-powerful. God can do anything because of this power. It does not mean God can do the impossible (such as create a mountain that God could not then move). Evidence includes:
   ○ the creation of the world (Genesis)
   ○ miracles performed by Jesus, for example calming a storm on the sea, raising Jairus' daughter from the dead
   ○ the resurrection of Jesus, which shows power over death.

2 All-loving means what it says – God loves all, without exception and without prejudice. Even a bad person is loved by God, which suggests that even bad people can be redeemed and reconciled to God. Evidence includes:
   ○ sacrificing His own son to make atonement for the sins of humans
   ○ parable of the Prodigal Son (Luke 15:11–32)
   ○ Jesus' teachings, for example Sermon on the Mount (Matthew 5:43–45, 48).

3 Just means that God is fair and will not act unjustly. God will give everyone equal value and rights, without prejudice or favour.
   ○ For Christians, it is important to believe God is just because they believe all will be judged after death. In the Parable of the Sheep and Goats (Matthew 25:31–46), Jesus talks about that just judgement.
   ○ In the Book of Job, it states that God will not act unjustly. 'God is fair and just' (Psalm 25:8).

Other characteristics

Other characteristics of God include that He is all-knowing (omniscient) – God is the supreme being so must be omniscient. St Anselm said that if God exists, He must be the 'greatest conceivable being', which means the most intelligent. He is also the creator because He is all-powerful and all-knowing.

God is also eternal – He created the world, so must have existed before it did, and is outside space and time, controlled by neither, so must be eternal as time does not impact on God. This also makes Him transcendent, which emphasises how different God is to humans and how humans cannot hope to really understand the nature of God.

Finally, God is immanent – involved in the world. Jesus is an example of this, as are miracles, which are a sign of God at work within the world.

> **All-loving**: God's love is without prejudice and without limit; the sacrifice made through Jesus evidences this love.
>
> **Just**: fair; God is always fair in His treatment, He will be fair at the Judgement.
>
> **Omnipotence**: all-powerful; God created the world, revealing His power. Nothing can ultimately defeat God's power.

> **Exam tip**
>
> Learn all key terms – you could be asked what they mean, or find a question which relies on you knowing one of them. There is a glossary on pages 109–110, which gives all the Specification key terms – the minimum you should know.

> **Activity**
>
> **Fix it!**
>
> A student wrote this answer. Improve it for them.
>
> *Explain how believing that God is omnipotent might influence a Christian today.*   *(4 marks)*
>
> They might say that it makes them feel safer because they know God loves them so much, He will look after them. In a difficult situation, they would know God was by their side and helping them.

> **Influences**
>
> As a Christian my belief in God influences my life because I know He has the ability to do anything so He can look after me in all situations and as He is all-loving I know He won't give me more than I can cope with and everything has a reason.

The Trinity

Like other religions, Christians believe there is only One God; however, Christians fundamentally differ from other religions in believing that God is revealed in three distinct ways ('Three Persons'). This is called the Trinity, or Godhead:

● God the Father – loving creator and sustainer of the universe.
● God the Son – saviour who became incarnate (human), lived, was crucified and then resurrected, namely Jesus Christ.
● God the Holy Spirit – source of strength which Christians find at work in their hearts.

The Trinity is referred to in all Christian ceremonies, for example baptism (I baptise you in the name of the Father and of the Son and of the Holy Spirit). It is part of basic statements of belief, such as the Apostles' Creed. Many hymns and prayers mention it.

Why is the Trinity important?

It is God, and the religion is based on that concept. Symbols, such as the shamrock and triskelion, demonstrate the concept in an easy way.

It helps Christians gain some understanding of God, who really is beyond the understanding of humans, and it makes best sense of what is written in the Bible.

Influences

As a Christian, believing in the Trinity influences my life because I have a way to visualise God in my mind when actually God is a really hard concept to describe. Also the act of God sending His son – showing this ultimate act of love encourages me to try to always show love to others even when it might put me at a disadvantage.

The problem of evil and suffering

What is the problem?

Christians believe that God is omnipotent, **omniscient**, **benevolent** and **absolute**. They believe this as a fact – God does exist. Christians, from their experience and knowledge, realise that there is suffering in the world. Some of the suffering is caused by humans (deliberately and accidentally), which is moral evil. Some is caused by nature – suffering is a fact of the world humans live in – which is natural evil.

The problem is why, if God exists, He allows humans, especially seemingly good and/or innocent ones, to suffer. He must know about it, has the power to prevent/end it, and loves humans unconditionally. So why does God allow the evils which cause suffering?

Absolute: unchanging, eternal.

Benevolent: all-loving; unconditional love.

Omniscient: all-knowing; knowledge without limits.

Some solutions

Some suggestions that have been offered up to explain this dilemma include:

● Moral evil: the devil tempts people (e.g. Adam and Eve); humans have free will, which they abuse and so hurt others.
● Natural evil: suffering is allowed as a punishment for wrong-doing; it is a test of faith, for example the story of Job; it is needed so that we can appreciate good, that is a balance; it is an education – we learn to help others and look after our world by seeing/experiencing suffering.

No attempt at a solution solves the problem fully. Most Christians say that humans must just accept the suffering, as humans cannot possibly understand God and His purposes. God is just, so the fairness of all will be made clear at the end of days. Most important is that humans respond positively to suffering, for example by helping others, as Jesus told in the Parable of the Sheep and Goats (Matthew 25:31–46).

Now test yourself

1 What is meant by the Trinity?
2 Why is it important for Christians?
3 Give two solutions to the problem of evil and suffering.
4 Explain two ways in which a belief in evil and suffering influences Christians today.

TESTED

Creation

Christians hold various beliefs about creation:

- God pre-existed the world, hence being able to create it.
- God is transcendent (outside space and time). As such He created the world and is not controlled by it.
- Genesis describes the creation: 1:1: 'In the beginning, God created the heavens and the Earth.'
- John 1:1–3 opens with: 'In the beginning was the Word, and the Word was with God, and the Word was God. He was with God in the beginning. Through Him all things were made; without Him nothing was made that has been made.'
- God created through His word – 'Let there be light', for example; 'Let there be space between the water and the heavens' and so on.
- The term Word has also been linked to Jesus: 'The Word became flesh and lived for a while amongst us.' This is the second person of the Trinity being referred to as both the Word and the Son of God (Jesus). Hence God and Jesus are ONE.
- The Trinity is also part of the creation: 'the Spirit of God hovering over the face of the waters.' This is the third person, the Holy Spirit. So God, Son and Holy Spirit are ONE.
- To conclude, therefore, all parts of the Trinity were involved in creation, so must have pre-existed it.

Genesis and its importance

The key points are that Christians believe the message within Genesis 1 is true. The world was planned, ordered and sustained by God. Human lives have purpose and meaning because God created those lives and humans are made in the image of God so all humans are of value.

Humans have a responsibility to treat each other equally. Humans were made stewards of the world to look after it.

Different interpretations

1 Genesis is literally true – every word is the word of God; God dictated the book and is totally correct. It happened as it says it happened. God is all-powerful and all-knowing, capable of doing all this in seven days.
2 Genesis does contain truth but it was not dictated. God inspired the writers – so if there are errors in the story, they are human errors. While generally correct, within the story, elements can be reinterpreted – does 'day' mean 'our day' or 'a period of time', for example?
3 Genesis was written by a person whose sense of God in the world inspired them to write. It is a man-made document. The point of the story is to give the messages that God is a loving God, we have a place in the world, and the world is a good place. It is a myth with an important message.

Each one of these has religious truths. Each way may influence a Christian slightly differently but essentially the messages are the same.

Influences

As a Christian, knowing that God created the world for us influences me to feel really special that He made me in His image. It also lets me understand my world is ordered and planned and I believe I have a purpose to being here and I must make the most of being here ... sort of making God proud of me.

Afterlife

Death separates life on earth (temporary) from life with God (eternal) – it is not something to be feared. Christians believe they will reunite with the dead, thus easing the pain of bereavement.

The Book of Revelations says God will wipe every tear – there will be no more death or crying or pain.

Afterlife for Christians

Belief in the resurrection is important to Christians. Resurrection means that the dead will be raised to life because of the teachings of Jesus and that he himself overcame death. St Paul said this was central to Christian belief.

What Christians mean by resurrection

Christians believe God will resurrect them before Judgement Day. Jesus told people that the new mode of existence would be different from the earthly one. On earth it is perishable; it is raised imperishable (a spiritual body). There is continuity between the person's earthly life and the resurrected life.

Roman Catholics believe in purgatory, a state between death and the afterlife. After death of the body, the soul goes to purgatory if it is destined for heaven, where it is purified enough to enter heaven.

There are different views about resurrection. Many Christians simply say humans have no answers – only to trust in God. Without scientific evidence it is all a matter of belief based in Bible teachings and Jesus' words.

Judgement

Jesus taught that God's love and mercy are unconditional. At the end of time on the Day of Judgement all souls (Christian or not) will be judged by Jesus. The parables – the Rich Man and Lazarus, and the Sheep and Goats – are Judgement teachings. Jesus will come to judge both the living and the dead.

Others reject the idea of a second coming of Christ. Jesus was just trying to express something that humans simply cannot understand. Humans will account for their actions, but no one knows how or when.

Heaven and hell

Christians use earthly images to explain their understanding of heaven. It is a state of being rather than a physical place; it is being with God outside time and space.

People often see heaven in a way they see their present lives. It is often described in a way that would appeal to them now, for example those in poverty describe it as a land of milk, honey and plenty.

The Bible paints a picture of hell via the metaphor of an unquenchable fire. This idea was historically used to frighten people into obeying Church rules. Hell is now seen as eternal separation from God. It is neither decided by God nor what God wants for us – humans choose it by turning away from God.

Some Christians embrace universalism – they believe everyone will eventually respond to God's love, having repented and been forgiven.

Influences

The afterlife for me as a Christian influences my life in that I know that God will be my ultimate judge. If I live a Christian life and believe in Jesus then heaven is open to me. Secondly, as there is an afterlife, it gives me hope and comfort that this life is not the end and God is waiting for me.

Now test yourself

1 How does belief in Judgement Day affect people in their lives today?
2 How might the existence of heaven and/or hell influence Christians in their lives?
3 Give two reasons why Christians might disagree about judgement.
4 What do Christians mean by the word resurrection?

TESTED

Jesus

His incarnation – Jesus the Son

Central to Christian belief is the idea that God took on human form as Jesus. John 1:14 says 'the Word became flesh and lived amongst us'. Christians believe Jesus was fully God and fully human – truly the Son of God. If Christians acknowledge Jesus as the Son of God, God lives in them.

Jesus: Son of God	Jesus' knowledge	Importance of belief in incarnation
● The title 'Son of God' is used about Jesus in the New Testament. ● Mary was a virgin who conceived through the power of the Holy Spirit. ● Some Christians accept the virgin birth as true whereas others suggest it is more a metaphor to show that Jesus was both human and divine.	● If fully divine, Jesus should have had full knowledge of what was happening, yet at times his knowledge was limited – e.g. he said he didn't understand fully about the end of the world. ● This can be explained by saying that to become fully human he had to give up most of his divine knowledge – a great sacrificial act. He came as a servant but was still fully God in his relationship with and understanding of God.	● It helps Christians understand the extent of God's love for humanity. ● It shows how Christians should live – as God so loved us so we should love one another (1 John). ● Many Christians have taken on this act of selfless love – consider Mother Teresa.

Crucifixion

- Jesus' work on earth lasted about three years, then he was arrested, tried and crucified.
- Convicted of blasphemy by the Jewish authorities, he was put to death for treason under Roman law.
- He was crucified at Golgotha – the place of the skull. It took six hours for him to die. Mark records that for three hours the earth was dark, perhaps symbolic of the judgement on Israel for its rejection of the Messiah.
- Jesus questioned: 'God, why have you forsaken me?'
- Mark says that at the point of death, the temple curtain tore in two – believed by some to show that Jesus' death had destroyed the barrier of sin that separated man from God, therefore making it possible to access God.

Why he had to die

- At the time – Jesus' teachings gave a new understanding of the Torah, which brought him into direct conflict with Jewish leaders.
- At the time – the Roman governor was under pressure to keep a peaceful land, so came down hard on any religious rebellion. When Jewish leaders implied Jesus was stirring up trouble, the governor had to act.
- In Christian thought – Jesus had to die to fulfil God's plan. Without his death humans could not be reunited with God and enter heaven. Jesus atoned for the sins of humanity, bringing God and man back together.

Salvation and reconciliation

- God gave His only son so that humans could be saved in eternal life (salvation).
- Jesus' death atoned (made up for) human sin.
- This was God reconciling with His people. He is so loving and merciful He made forgiveness possible through His own son.
- Christians work for reconciliation with others in the world today.

Now test yourself

1 What is the incarnation?
2 Why did Jesus have to die?
3 What is salvation?

Answers at **www.hoddereducation.co.uk/myrevisionnotesdownloads**

Resurrection

What happened to Jesus?

This is recorded in the New Testament in the Gospels of Matthew, Mark, Luke and John.

Joseph (of Arimathea) was given permission to take Jesus' body down from the cross. Joseph was allowed by Pontius Pilate (the Roman governor) to bury Jesus in a rock tomb he owned. However, the burial was delayed as it was the Sabbath day of rest. When the women returned on the Sunday morning, they found the stone rolled away. All three Gospel writers say that the body had gone and the women were told Jesus had 'risen'.

Mark says a man in white tells the women to return to Galilee to meet the risen Jesus.

John says a man reveals himself to Mary Magdalene as Jesus himself come back to life and she returns to the disciples to say 'she had seen the risen Jesus'.

All this is followed by 'resurrection appearances' recorded in Matthew, Luke and John only. During the next 40 days when he appeared he was not always recognised at first but the physical nature of his 'appearances' is always stressed.

The impact of the Resurrection

The disciples turned from men in hiding to going out spreading Jesus' message. This put them in great danger, indicating that something significant had happened. Peter, for example, went from denying he even knew Jesus to teaching his message openly. It was seeing the risen Jesus that caused these transformations.

What happened next?

On the 40th day after the resurrection some texts describe 'the Ascension of Jesus'. At Bethany, Jesus blessed his disciples before being taken up to heaven – 'a cloud received him from their sight' (Acts). This was the successful completion of his mission and return to God.

How does Jesus' resurrection influence Christians today?

It is the central element of Christian belief – if Jesus simply died then he is no different to others who may have died for their beliefs or as punishment for going against the authorities. Christians believe resurrection is the proof Jesus is the Son of God – showing how God triumphed over evil and death.

This victory over death opens up heaven for Christians. Jesus' sacrifice overcame sin, reconciled humanity with God and offered eternal life.

> **Exam tip**
>
> It is more important to know why the resurrection was important and questions raised about it than knowing the narrative. There is some debate about whether Jesus actually 'rose from the dead'.

> **Influences**
>
> This for me makes my faith complete. Jesus' resurrection makes him different to anyone else and so I know this is the true faith. I also know that if Jesus can overcome death as a human, like me, then so can I and I can enter heaven as Jesus did. Jesus showed us his Father's power by what he did.

Sin

The story of 'original sin' is in Genesis – Adam and Eve are tempted by the devil to eat from the tree of good and evil. Adam and Eve were evicted from the Garden of Eden as punishment.

Christians believe humans were all descended from Adam and Eve. Tainted by this act, all humans have an inbuilt tendency to disobey God.

Sin separates man from God, bringing eternal punishment. As humans are full of sin, so only God can rectify this problem. Christians believe God offered salvation through the sacrifice of Christ.

Most Christians do not take the Genesis story literally. To many, it conveys the message that humanity has the inclination to do what they are told *not* to (hence disobeying God), which damages their relationship with Him.

Salvation and what it means for Christians

Salvation means being accepted by God and having the assurance of eternal life.

1 Salvation through law:
   - In Jesus' time, the Jews thought that 'obeying the law' was the way to salvation.
   - Some Christians believe in salvation through works – the idea that a right relationship with God has to be earned.
   - Some Christians think salvation can be earned through obedience to God's laws; others take on Jesus' idea that God was more pleased with the thoughts in our minds and the love in our hearts for Him and others. Christians need to put these thoughts into action in their lives.

2 Salvation through grace:
   - Grace means the unconditional love that God has for us. God loves humanity regardless. God's love is there despite everything humans do – there is no need to earn salvation.
   - God shows His love in the gift of salvation to all who believe in Jesus as the Son of God.
   - Salvation through grace and spirit is made possible through Jesus' atoning death. Jesus' actions made possible the forgiveness for the sins of the world, leading to reconciliation.
   - Christians believe they receive God's grace through the presence in their hearts of the Holy Spirit. This allows them to try to show love as Jesus did.
   - Many people today believe that 'the grace of God' helps them every day and that 'acts of God's grace' are seen in the world daily.

Influences

I always know that God loves me, even though often I don't deserve it, and so I try and show love to others who may also not deserve it. I feel that I have the Holy Spirit within me and as such I try and demonstrate acts within my life that reflect I have this gift in me. But I know sin is so easy to do and often the right way is the most difficult so I have to be conscious of this.

Activity

Continue the answer

This is half of a 4-mark answer. Write the other half giving a second way. Use it as a model in answering these types of questions in your exam.

Explain two ways in which belief in 'salvation through grace' might influence Christians today. (4 marks)

One way that belief in salvation through grace could influence Christians today is to try and help others that are in need. For example, those who work for equal rights for others who are oppressed. This shows their love for others as Jesus showed his love for them. It is by the grace of the Holy Spirit in their hearts which enables them to carry out such actions.

Try another:

Explain two ways in which belief in 'sin' might influence Christians today. (4 marks)

Exam practice

What questions on this section look like:

Christianity: Beliefs and teachings

This page contains a range of questions that could be on an exam paper. Practise them all to strengthen your knowledge and technique while revising. Check back to pages 13–14 to see the marking grids that examiners use: this will help you to mark your answers.

1 What is meant by incarnation?

   (a) Fully divine   (b) Being born   (c) Returning to earth   (d) Embodiment   [1]

2 Which of the Gospels refers to the 'role of the word' in creation?

   (a) John   (b) Luke   (c) Mark   (d) Matthew   [1]

3 Give two reasons Jesus had to die. [2]

4 Give two Christian beliefs about heaven. [2]

5 Give two reasons Jesus' death is important for Christians. [2]

6 Explain two ways in which the resurrection of Jesus influences Christians today. [4]

7 Explain two ways in which a belief in the Trinity influences Christians today. [4]

8 Explain two ways in which a belief in the creation story influences Christians today. [4]

9 Explain two ways in which a belief in hell does not fit with the belief in a loving God. [4]

10 Explain two Christian teachings about salvation. Refer to sacred writings or another source of Christian belief and teachings in your answer. [5]

11 Explain two Christian teachings about the incarnation. Refer to sacred writings or another source of Christian belief and teachings in your answer. [5]

12 Explain two Christian teachings about the afterlife. Refer to sacred writings or another source of Christian belief and teachings in your answer. [5]

13 'Jesus did not rise from the dead.' Evaluate this statement. In your answer you should:

- refer to Christian teaching
- give reasoned arguments to support this statement
- give reasoned arguments to support a different point of view
- reach a justified conclusion. [12]

14 'God cannot be all-loving because evil and suffering exist.' Evaluate this statement. In your answer you should:

- refer to Christian teaching
- give reasoned arguments to support this statement
- give reasoned arguments to support a different point of view
- reach a justified conclusion. [12]

15 'Creation was so long ago it does not matter what actually happened.' Evaluate this statement. In your answer you should:

- refer to Christian teaching
- give reasoned arguments to support this statement
- give reasoned arguments to support a different point of view
- reach a justified conclusion. [12]

ONLINE

Commentary

Level 2 students write in a very limited way. They often write only a few words or a single sentence – no matter how many marks a question is worth. They also miss out questions. If this is you, then part of the problem is having too little knowledge – get notes which work for you, learn revision techniques which work for you, and use them. You will then have more to be able to say in the exam.

Level 5 students write in sentences and paragraphs. They usually try to extend their writing in all their answers. However, they may write less fluently than higher grade students and so the quality is not so good. If this is you, you need to learn and understand the topics better – that gives you more to write from, and when we have confidence in our understanding, we write better and fuller answers.

Level 8 students write fluently and in good, detailed English. Their work flows, using connectives and paragraphing well to give an impression of having good command of the subject.

Worship

REVISED ☐

There are many forms of informal worship across the different Christian groups.

Worship is an act devoted to God to show love and reverence for God. Most Christians hold acts of worship, or services, on Sunday of every week as a communal show of devotion. There are different types of worship.

What is liturgical worship?

Liturgical worship is found in the Roman Catholic, Orthodox and Church of England (Anglican) churches. The services follow a liturgy – a set pattern – usually from a printed book. The liturgy has an established structure (order) of set prayers and readings, with the congregation repeating key phrases.

Hymns are sung at set times (hymns vary) and a sermon (speech) is given. Some of the prayers, the hymns chosen, the Bible readings and the sermon differ from service to service.

The ordered nature makes worshippers feel comfortable and part of the process.

What is non-liturgical worship?

Non-liturgical worship is a more informal way of worship. It follows a pattern or order but the elements are tailored to each service. Prayers are often in the leader's own words, the sermon on a topical theme and Bible readings chosen to fit.

Without set words, worshippers feel it comes more from the heart.

What is charismatic worship?

Charismatic worship is a kind of informal worship. Evangelical worship is often in this style.

The service has recognisable characteristics (hymns, prayers, sermon, readings) but is very free-flowing. Charismatic is 'spirit inspired' – people often speak in tongues or feel the Holy Spirit at work within them.

How is the Bible used in worship?

The Bible is always the focus of any act of worship because it is considered either the 'word of God' or 'inspired by God'.

The Bible can be processed into church, many hymns are based on it, portions are often read out loud and the sermon often explains a Bible passage.

Useful quotes

'Humble yourselves in the sight of the Lord, and He will lift you up.' James 4:10

'But the hour is coming, and now is, when true worshippers will worship the Father in spirit and in truth, for the Father is seeking such to worship Him.' John 4:23

Charismatic worship: (informal) worship that is free-flowing and lacks structure.

Liturgical worship: worship that follows a set pattern (liturgy).

Non-liturgical worship: worship that follows a changeable structure.

Private worship

This is just as important as public worship for Christians. It can be liturgical – for example, Roman Catholics may say the Angelus (a series of short meditations performed three times a day) – or non-liturgical – for example, a simple prayer at a time of need. Worshipping alone allows the person to feel close to God in exactly the way they want. It is a time to 'be with God', say things from the 'heart' and build a 'relationship' with God.

A rosary is a set of beads on a string with a crucifix on the end. Believers thread the beads through the fingers while saying set prayers (the Lord's Prayer, the Hail Mary, etc.).

Meditation, meanwhile, is mainly silent thought. It could be reflection on a Bible passage or religious truth. A sense of peace and calm is a key characteristic, alternating with the hustle of daily life.

Prayer

Prayer is both talking and listening to God – to be open to guidance from the Holy Spirit. It should include praise, confession, thanks, prayers for others and then the self.

Jesus spoke about prayer – humility and honesty are essential. He stated that an all-loving God would always respond to sincere prayers. Outcomes are not always in the way Christians seek, however – God knows best.

Set prayers (e.g. the Lord's Prayer) are used both publicly and privately.

Why it is important to worship

God wants people to worship Him. Worship can bring a sense of connection/togetherness with God to a community and/or an individual. It is an external expression of internal faith.

Through worship people gain a deeper understanding of their religion or of their faith in God. It purifies the worshipper, making them spiritually fit for what they do.

The Lord's Prayer

This is important as it is the prayer Jesus taught his disciples when he was asked by them 'Master, how should we pray?'
1 Know what each line of the prayer means (find a copy and jot down notes against each line).
2 You don't need to learn it off by heart, as any questions based on this prayer should give you the part you need to comment on.
3 It has praise, thanks, confession and asking God for the things the worshipper and others need –so it's a 'perfect prayer'.
4 As it was given by Jesus, it links back throughout the history of Christianity.
5 It can be used in public or private worship, out loud or silently.
6 It is usually part of all types of worship.

> **Exam tip**
>
> Questions with 4 marks should focus on similarities/differences or contrasts in religious practice.
> Make sure you know the similarities/differences:
> 1 Between the different types of worship – liturgical/non-liturgical/charismatic or informal/formal.
> 2 Between public and private prayers – what they are/how they are done.
> 3 Between the importance for the believers of the types of worship/prayers.

Sacraments

Sacrament	Outward and visible sign	Inward and spiritual grace
Baptism	Water and the signing of the cross with the words – in the name of the Father, Son and Holy Spirit	Receiving the Holy Spirit The removal of original sin Entry into the kingdom of God/the Church
Confirmation	The laying on of hands by the bishop	Strengthening/sealing the gifts of the Holy Spirit in the person Becoming an 'adult' member of the Church
Eucharist	Bread and wine	Spiritual 'feeding' with the body and blood of Christ
Reconciliation	Words of forgiveness	The forgiveness of sins Rebuilding of bonds
Healing	Anointing and the laying on of hands	Spiritual and sometimes physical healing Preparation for death
Marriage	Ring(s)	The endless love between the couple
Ordination	The laying on of hands by the bishop	The special gifts of the Holy Spirit needed by a deacon or priest

Sacrament:
- The external and visible sign of an inward spiritual grace.
- Can be experienced with the senses.
- Has a deeper meaning which is not experienced through the senses.

Protestants acknowledge two sacraments: baptism and the Eucharist. They are known as Gospel sacraments because they were authorised by Jesus and there are many references to their use in much of the New Testament.

Roman Catholics, Orthodox Christians and some Anglicans have seven sacraments, all of which are implied through Jesus and the early church.

The importance for those who observe them

Christians believe God imparts gifts through the sacraments. They are offered at appropriate times in a person's life (like rites of passage) – baptism, confirmation and marriage.

In the Eucharist the bread and wine unites Christians with the risen Christ. Reconciliation helps Christians realise what they have done wrong, show penitence and then receive forgiveness through the priest's words.

Healing can be given during a long illness or when a person is near to death to give strength and peace of mind.

Ordination separates those who devote their lives to God in the priesthood, giving them gifts to carry out this role.

Why some Christians do not believe in sacraments

Quakers and members of the Salvation Army reject all sacraments – no direct reference is made to most of the seven in the Bible.

They believe Jesus did not intend either baptism or his words and actions over the bread and wine at the Last Supper to become prescribed rituals. They believe that God speaks directly to the believer's heart so there is no need of any form of 'go-between', and that symbols and ritual distract from true religion.

Exam tip

Definitions of these words could be required as a 1-mark multi-choice question.

For 2-mark questions you could be asked about reasons why certain Christians see the sacraments as important, or to name two of them.

There are many differences to refer to if you are asked about how different groups view the sacraments as a 4-mark question.

Some Christians do not believe in sacraments so this could be the focus of an evaluation ('The sacraments are not important'). Or it could focus on which is most important.

So this topic could appear in a variety of question types – it is worth learning carefully.

Baptism

John the Baptist was the first Jew to use baptism to symbolise the 'forgiveness of sins'. This prepared for a new way of life with the coming of the Messiah (Jesus). Jesus was baptised by John and experienced the Holy Spirit entering his life. Jesus' last instructions were to 'baptise them in the name of the Father, Son and Holy Spirit' (Matthew 28:18–19).

Baptism welcomes a person into the Christian community. It is practised by almost all Christian communities today.

Baptism ceremonies today

Baptism is important as Christians feel they are doing what Jesus did so it connects them to him. It welcomes a person into the Christian church. Baptism removes sin and enables spiritual growth.

Infant baptism

Actual ceremonies differ from one Christian group to the next. However, the services have core similarities.

Key elements used by Roman Catholics, Orthodox and the Church of England are:
- baptism of a baby
- use of holy water (blessed) from the font and poured three times over the forehead
- the sign of the cross made on the forehead in the name of the Father, Son and Holy Spirit.

Many baptism services also include promises made by parents/godparents on behalf of the child to reject evil, repent sins and turn to Christ; the lighting of a pascal candle, which symbolises receiving the light of Christ; the use of holy oils to symbolise strength (to fight evil) and salvation; and readings and prayers.

Believers' baptism

This is a ceremony for older children and adults, which takes places in a baptistery. The central rituals are the use of water and the Trinitarian formula (Father, Son and Holy Spirit).

The subject testifies to why they seek baptism, then declares the repentance of sin and their intention to follow a Christ-centred life, avoiding evil.

Walking down three steps symbolises the end of the old life of sin. Then there are three full submersions in the name of the Father, Son and Holy Spirit. The person then leaves by three other steps to start a new life as a Christian.

> **Exam tip**
>
> Know the basic elements of each baptism. You could be asked to explain two differences or two similarities between ceremonies. You could be asked to give two reasons why baptism is important or two **gifts given by the Holy Spirit**. Equally, a question option could be an evaluation based on baptism (which type is more important, whether baptism is necessary, is it the most important sacrament?).

> **Gifts of the Holy Spirit**: knowledge, courage, understanding, right judgement, wisdom, reverence, awe and wonder in God's presence – 1 Corinthians 12.

Support for infant baptism	Support for believers' baptism
Natural for parents to want to bring their child into the Christian faith	Only those old enough to understand should take this step – should be able to make their own promises
Gifts of the Holy Spirit to allow the child to grow up strong in God's love	A child might grow up to resent the promises made for them so they need to decide for themselves
Enables the child to receive the other sacraments	Jesus was an adult when baptised
Brings comfort to the family of an ill child that if it dies then it will be with God	God's love is not dependent on human actions – so baptism is unnecessary
Removes original sin and purifies the child	How can a child even have sins to remove?

The Eucharist

The Last Supper

The **Last Supper** is the basis of the 'bread and wine' service. Jesus took bread, broke it – 'This is my body which is given for you; do this in remembrance of me.' Jesus took wine – 'This is my blood, do this in remembrance of me.' This was a sign of a new **covenant** between God and all believers, established by Jesus' death.

Some say the Eucharist is a taste of heaven, unites the worshipper with Christ, and is food for the soul, giving strength to live every day as a Christian.

Christians today re-enact the Last Supper in different ways. It can be done daily, weekly or monthly, as part of, or in addition to, a normal service.

The Orthodox Divine Liturgy

'Divine' is a reminder of the sacred mystery of the service and 'liturgy' means 'work of the people' in the praising of God.

Bread and wine are prepared on the altar behind the iconostasis. It is divided into four – the Eucharistic prayer said to consecrate three of them so that they coexist with the actual body and blood of Jesus.

The service includes Bible readings, sermon, prayers and the Bible processed through the Royal Doors. The cherubic hymn is sung. The bread and wine are carried through the Royal Doors. The priest invites all baptised members to participate. From one chalice of bread soaked in the wine, spoonfuls are given. The fourth unconsecrated piece of bread is broken up to be taken home.

The Roman Catholic mass

In a Roman Catholic mass, worshippers confess sins and forgiveness is given. The service includes Bible readings, sermon and prayers, and the Nicene Creed is recited. Bread and wine are brought to the altar and the Eucharistic prayer is said to consecrate them.

The people stand before the priest to receive the bread, which is placed on the tongue or in their hands. Only the priest drinks the wine. The post-Eucharistic prayer and blessings are said.

> **Covenant**: an agreement made between man and God.
>
> **Elements**: bread and wine used in the Eucharist.
>
> **Last Supper**: the last evening meal Jesus shared with his disciples before he was arrested.
>
> **Transubstantiation**: the change in the bread and wine to become the body and blood of Jesus.

Anglican Holy Communion

This follows a similar pattern to that of the Roman Catholics. Wine is taken by the congregation from one single chalice and the bread is placed on crossed hands – all participate in both bread and wine.

The Lord's Supper – other Protestant groups

These tend to be much simpler services, with people gathering at the front of the church. The Last Supper story is read out and the bread and wine are shared. Often the wine is non-alcoholic and given in little individual cups. Hymns may be sung and the Lord's Prayer and additional prayers may be said by all.

The meaning and significance vary for different Christian groups:
- Orthodox: the consecration of bread and wine remains a mystery but they believe that Jesus is mystically present in the **elements**.
- Roman Catholic: believe in **transubstantiation** – the bread and wine are invisibly transformed into the actual body and blood of Jesus.
- Anglicans: some believe the same as the Catholics but most believe that the bread and wine hold the spiritual presence of the body and blood rather than becoming it.
- Other Protestants believe the bread and wine are purely symbolic of Jesus' death, which brought salvation.

Pilgrimage

A religious pilgrimage is a visit to a holy place. These places often have a feeling of spirituality and of closeness to God. The journey can be as important as the visit.

Lourdes (France) – history and significance

Bernadette in Lourdes	Pilgrimage to Lourdes	Healings in Lourdes
Here Bernadette claimed she had seen a woman, the Virgin Mary, in 18 visions.	Many pilgrims visit Lourdes today – taking part in processions, saying the rosary and mass, touching the walls of the cave (grotto).	Since the first cure in 1858, 69 more Lourdes healings have been declared miracles.
In a cave near the River Gave she was told to dig away the growth clogging the spring and drink the water.	Water is often taken home and statues of the Virgin Mary bought.	Most pilgrims not experiencing physical healing still feel as though they have been healed spiritually.
Her friend bathed her dislocated arm in the water and it was healed.	The sick or disabled go hoping for healing.	Pilgrims also describe feeling peace of mind.

Iona – history and significance

About Iona	Pilgrimage to Iona today
This is known as the cradle of Christianity in Scotland, as Columba, an Irish monk, settled there in 563CE.	Iona has a very long history, making pilgrims want to visit.
The Gaelic rulers of Ireland gave him Iona to build a monastery and spread the Christian message.	Individuals or groups often go home renewed in their faith to live and work in the modern world.
Columba died in 597CE but the monastery continued, leading to new monasteries in Ireland and Lindisfarne. Many came on pilgrimage via a system of Celtic crosses and processional roads which were built.	A stay at Iona means work as well as worship (and study).
The Book of Kells, an illuminated manuscript of the Gospels, was produced.	
Iona fell into disuse, but in 1938 George Macleod had the monastery rebuilt and set up the foundation of the ecumenical Iona Community – open to all Christian groups.	
Their way of life was founded in the Bible – daily prayer, Bible reading, stewardship of time and money, regular meeting with other members and the active promotion of justice, peace and the environment.	

Importance

A pilgrimage allows focus on faith and a renewed energy to cope with the demands of life, as well as offering time for spiritual growth. Some pilgrimages include very simple living, being closer to the way Jesus led his life. The experience might bring healing, either physical or spiritual.

However, the money could be better spent in helping others, and some people cannot afford to make a pilgrimage. The renewal while on pilgrimage quickly wears off when pilgrims return home. Spiritual development can be gained at home in prayer and reflection – prayers and healings can happen anywhere as God hears all prayers.

> **Revision tip**
>
> This is a good topic for evaluative questions. List reasons for and against the following:
> 1 Lourdes is the best place for pilgrimage.
> 2 Pilgrimage is the greatest act of devotion in the life of a Christian.
> 3 Pilgrimage is just an excuse for a holiday.
> 4 All Christians should make a pilgrimage to a holy site.

Festivals

Useful quote

For unto us a child is born, to us a son is given, and the government will be on his shoulders. And he will be called Wonderful Counsellor, Mighty God, Everlasting Father, the Prince of Peace. Isaiah 9:6

Christmas

Christmas celebrates the birth of Jesus. The specific date is unknown but the Western church chose 25 December and the Eastern church chose 6 January.

The story of Jesus' birth is found only in the Gospels of Matthew and Luke. These accounts are slightly different in detail if you read Matthew Chapters 1 and 2 and Luke Chapter 2.

The general outline of the story is that Jesus was born in Bethlehem (there because of the Roman census) in a stable as the town was overcrowded. Mary gave birth, laid him in a manger and he was visited by kings/shepherds who had been told that the new King of the Jews/Messiah had been born.

Christians disagree over the accuracy of what happened but the message is key – that the incarnation of God (Jesus) had humble beginnings, thus showing humility.

Celebration and importance

Christmas is a state holiday in the UK, showing the importance of this event in a 'Christian country'. It is celebrated in a secular way with cards, gifts, food and parties, and in a religious way with the four weeks of advent, the Christingle service, Christmas Eve mass and a Christmas Day service. Christmas carols are sung throughout the period, the birth stories are read and nativities are acted out. Believers often send religious cards (e.g. with a nativity scene, religious wording, etc.).

Christians thank God for his gift of Jesus. They focus on family, children, the poor and lonely to make Christmas a time of warmth, love and togetherness. It is common for churches to set up shelters, host meals and distribute gift parcels for/to the most needy.

It is a time of giving, receiving and of love to symbolise the love that God showed. It is also a time for hope – for peace, reconciliation, love to our fellow man – and for Christians to show their faith to the world.

Exam tip

Remember, you will not need to recall every detail of the Christmas story, just its key elements. Questions at 4/5/12 marks will focus around the symbolism, importance and influence of the festival, or an evaluation of it.

Revision tip

Read the stories and jot down some similarities and differences between the birth stories from the Gospels. Also look at the ways the birth stories are celebrated by different Christians today. A simple description of the festival stories or celebration is unlikely to be asked for, but knowing both will help make evaluations much easier to discuss. By writing notes, you are helping your brain retain the information, so it is easier to recall it later.

Activity

Fix it!

Read this answer and improve it.

Explain two ways in which the celebration of Christmas influences Christians today. (4 marks)

Christmas influences Christians to be kind to others (giving). It also influences them to be hopeful that things will get better for the world.

Answers at **www.hoddereducation.co.uk/myrevisionnotesdownloads**

Easter

Easter remembers the death and resurrection of Jesus.

Holy Week begins with Palm Sunday and ends with Easter Sunday. Each day remembers the events that led to Jesus' death, his actual death and then resurrection.

The stories can be found in Matthew Chapters 21–28, Mark Chapters 11–16, Luke Chapters 19–24 and John Chapters 12–21. From this you can see how much of each Gospel refers to this last week – thus its importance.

The key events are:
1 Palm Sunday – Jesus' entry into Jerusalem.
2 Maundy Thursday – the Last Supper and Jesus' arrest.
3 Good Friday – Jesus' crucifixion and death.
4 Easter Sunday – the resurrection.

Celebration and importance

Special church services run throughout the week remembering the lead-up to 'the greatest sacrifice ever made'. In a secular way people send cards, gifts, Easter chocolates and have family meals. In a religious way Christians see Palm crosses are given out, church services take place for each of the special days, including Easter vigils, and special Easter prayers and hymns are said. Believers send Easter cards.

Christians move from a period of great sadness to great joy knowing what God has done for them (sacrifice of His son to bring about reconciliation). The human suffering of Jesus and his obedience to the will of God are emphasised.

Christians believe that God reunited himself with humanity by the actions of Jesus so that they can once again be reunited with Him at death – the new covenant.

> **Exam tip**
>
> Remember, you will not need to recall every detail of the Easter story, just its key elements. Questions at 4/5/12 marks will focus around the symbolism, importance and influence of the festival, or an evaluation of it.

> **Exam tip**
>
> Festivals could be a topic for 5-mark questions, focusing on two ways in which a chosen festival is important to Christians. You need to be able to back up these ideas with Christian teachings as you have to refer to two of them in your answer.
>
> *Explain two ways in which Easter is important for Christians today. Refer to teachings in your answer.*

Now test yourself

TESTED ☐

1 What is a sacrament? Name two.
2 Why are sacraments important?
3 What is a pilgrimage? Name a Christian place.
4 Why is pilgrimage important?
5 Name a Christian festival. Say what it celebrates.
6 Name another Christian festival. Say why it is important.

Activity

Which bit of Jesus' life was the most important? Evaluative questions could easily focus on this, for example *'Christmas is more important than Easter'*. You would need to refer to the events of his life to answer this. Complete this chart to prepare yourself for any question like that.

Reasons why it is ...	Christmas (birth)	Easter (death)	Easter (resurrection)
Most important			
Not most important			

The role of the Church in the local community

Christians have always been involved in working to make communities better places to live. They work in support groups for the young and old, support charities that help the needy, welcome immigrants, and work as street pastors and at food banks.

The parable of the sheep and goats teaches that if people fail to help those around them, it is as though they fail to help Jesus himself.

1 John says, 'If anyone has material possessions and ignores his brother in need, how can he love God?' Also, 'Let's not love with words or thoughts but with actions and in truth'.

Jesus spent much of his time helping people in society who were needy or outcasts or simply those who were looked down on by others. He said, 'It is not the well that need a doctor but the sick', showing how we should help those that need help in any way possible.

Food banks and street pastors

At food banks people volunteer to collect and distribute food. 2004 saw the launch of the UK-wide network with a vision to end poverty and hunger, show compassion and give practical help.

Many food banks are centred in churches or church halls. People in need are identified by police, schools or social services and given vouchers to exchange for food parcels.

Street pastors are Christians who go out on city streets at night to care for the physical and spiritual needs of young people who might be affected by excessive drinking, drug use, fighting, etc. They care for, listen and try to help, regardless of the young people's behaviour. Following training, they ask for God's blessing on this difficult type of ministry.

Over 270 towns now have street pastors. Their governing body is the Ascension Trust, which works with local councils, the police and other official bodies. The work is based outside pubs/clubs/shops where there may be anticipated issues.

> **Exam tip**
>
> Knowing the religious teachings and examples on which Christians base their work will be useful for this topic. Also the emphasis here is on the value of Christians using their faith as a basis for action and the action itself showing that faith. High marks require the use of teachings in an answer.

The Salvation Army

Founded as a result of the deprivation people were living in and the apparent unconcern shown by many Christian churches, the Salvation Army works with the poor and disadvantaged, setting up, for example:
- food kitchens and hostels for the homeless, including emergency assistance
- toy collections at Christmas
- training and employment help and advice.

St Vincent de Paul Society

This is a Roman Catholic society whose aim is to provide for the great needs of people in society. Its motto is to help the homeless, visit the sick, befriend the lonely and feed the hungry. The society is involved in, for example:
- setting up support centres and counselling services
- providing work training
- helping refugees, released prisoners, the disabled and the mentally ill.

Evangelism

Church growth

Christianity has always been a missionary religion, spreading all over the world. African Christian membership is on the rise but in Europe it is in decline. In recent years there has been a renewed focus on preaching to make the Gospel relevant in a modern world. Many churches are trying to find fresh approaches to worship while maintaining their key beliefs.

The Church Army – committed to Christian mission

Church Army members are trained and licensed by the Church of England to work throughout the UK. They aim to help people find faith, showing their love of God as revealed through Christ. They focus their work on vulnerable and marginalised people in society – for example, providing projects for young children and families, working with drug addicts, as chaplains in prisons and hospitals, visiting the elderly, and providing access to worship outside of church.

SIM – Serving in Mission

SIM has a worldwide scope to follow Jesus' instruction to send people out on **mission**. Members work chiefly in areas where it appears Christianity is under attack – for example, in Nigeria where Christians are often the target for terrorist groups. Churches have been destroyed, vicars killed and people left traumatised by what they have suffered. SIM supports the rebuilding of these communities.

The Ichthus Fellowship

This is a group of new 'churches' linked to already established churches which are 'planted' so that the church continues to grow. They offer more **evangelical** than traditional worship, to appeal to a modern audience who are not enthused by traditional forms of worship.

Fresh Expressions

This organisation offers 'different churches', set up in pubs, cafés, schools and even skate parks or beaches. These gatherings take religion directly to people who would never think about going to church. They are all planted to suit the needs of that group and help them become and develop as Christians.

> **Evangelical**: spreading the word by way of preaching the Gospel of Christ.
>
> **Mission**: 'a sending' – being sent to do something.

> **Exam tip**
>
> Mission has become popular because there is a discussion as to whether religion can still be as relevant to people in a modern world as it was centuries ago. It is possible for evaluation questions to look at this issue with a statement to discuss, such as 'Religion is not relevant in the modern world'. Knowing examples of how people are making it relevant could help with such a question.

> **Activity**
>
> **Fix it!**
>
> Read the answers below, each of which is worth 2 marks, and improve each to 5 marks.
>
> *Explain two ways in which mission is important to Christians today.* (5 marks)
>
> *Mission is important to Christians today because in Matthew's Gospel, Jesus told his disciples to go and make everyone a Christian follower. It is also important because it means that people in non-Christian countries get to hear the Christian message.*
>
> *Explain two ways in which mission is important in showing faith in action for Christians today.* (5 marks)
>
> *Mission shows faith in action because a Christian knows Jesus told them to 'Go make disciples of all nations' (Matthew). They could just read the Bible and think about it, but this is an instruction, so they have to actually get out and do something active. In other words, they aren't just believing in their heads, but showing their belief by their actions (faith into action).*

Persecution and reconciliation

Persecution is hostility and ill-treatment, usually because of prejudice. It can be brief or long-term; it can be by one person or many; it can be by a government, or against the law in a country; it can be recently begun or historic in nature and spanning many years; it can be mild or life-threatening.

The Church has faced persecution as far back as Jesus himself. The Romans and the Jews persecuted him and his disciples. Many early Christians suffered death as a result of spreading the Christian message. For nearly 300 years after Jesus' death it was illegal to be a Christian, carrying a likely death sentence as punishment.

Christian reaction to this has been to trust God in times of need ('all things will pass', 'God knows best', 'blessed are the persecuted'), react with forgiveness and love rather than hate, and for those not suffering persecution to support the persecuted (irrespective of faith or no faith). This is still the case in the world today.

There have been individuals and organisations involved in support for the persecuted, from Brother Andrew who smuggled Bibles into communist countries, to James and Stephen Smith who set up the Aegis Trust, which encourages people to challenge all types of discrimination (now working extensively in Rwanda following genocide there), and the work of Open Doors, an organisation which fights for justice and freedom, raises awareness of persecution issues, trains people to work with those affected by persecution and offers practical help to rebuild communities.

Reconciliation means bringing people together to be friendly again. When Jesus reconciled the world through his death, it was the ultimate sacrifice. Christians should be able to reconcile with each other after dispute, whether as families, communities or nations.

Corrymeela in Ireland and the international Community of the Cross of Nails are two communities working for reconciliation. There are also individuals with similar aims, such as Archbishop Desmond Tutu in South Africa who has spent his whole life trying to reconcile the black and white communities there after years of discrimination. He has also worked with the Israeli and Palestinian communities.

The Quakers do not believe in the use of violence. Many Quakers have worked as mediators to bring reconciliation to opposing sides in the pursuit of peace.

> **Persecution**: hostility and ill-treatment, usually because of prejudice.
>
> **Reconciliation**: coming back together after a falling out, so that no grudge is held.

Exam tip

Reconciliation is a key Christian concept so make sure you: (1) know a clear definition; (2) can give examples of why it is necessary and examples of how it works; (3) know similar and different ways that Christian groups work to reconcile people; (4) can explain two ways in which reconciliation is important to Christians and two teachings to support this, and (5) can evaluate the need for reconciliation and the outcomes if the world was reconciled (and indeed even if this is possible).

Now test yourself

1 What are mission and evangelism?
2 Why do Christians evangelise?
3 What is persecution?
4 How have Christians fought persecution?

Why the need for help and the Christian response

LEDCs are the poorest countries in the world and the people suffer generally through no fault of their own. Often one or more of these contexts applies: they are at war, debt ridden, suffer natural disasters, have corrupt governments, have few natural resources, employment/pay is low, and they are exploited by rich countries. They are not in an economic position to raise the standard of living for all their people.

Christians have links to many countries and they are moved with compassion at media coverage of disasters and crises that some people face. Many see helping as putting their beliefs (faith) into action. In the poorest countries even the smallest response can make a massive difference. Jesus worked among the poor and so Christians are copying his example and re-enacting his work.

The Parable of the Sheep and Goats clearly states that whoever a believer helps, it is as if they are helping Jesus himself and that they will gain the reward of heaven.

The Parable of the Good Samaritan clearly shows the need to help where help is needed, regardless of who the victim is – this encourages Christians to help in all situations.

The Specification names three religious agencies at work in LEDCs – Christian Aid, CAFOD and Tearfund. You must study at least one. All three provide **emergency**, **short-term** and **long-term aid**. They are all part of the UK's Disasters Emergency Committee (DEC) and work with partner organisations when a disaster occurs.

All three work in the UK to campaign for the government to raise issues to secure justice for LEDCs. They increase public awareness through the media and educational programmes which keep the issues in the minds of the public. They all fundraise so that the public keep giving money, ensuring these charities can continue to meet the needs of many people in **poverty**.

All encourage Fair Trade. This means that producers get a fair amount for the goods produced and in turn can pay their workers fairly. It helps raise the economic status of people throughout the system, but crucially the producers who are usually paid least.

CAFOD

The Catholic Agency for Overseas Development has more than 500 partners in LEDCs. The organisation works in disaster areas providing relief and disaster risk reduction strategies. Long-term projects are carried out with local groups. It is essential that the communities themselves see the value of what is being done.

The idea is that projects can breed self-belief and self-reliance, which often then lead to much greater change, as communities gain confidence and see more ways to develop and improve what they have.

Christian Aid

This organisation was set up to deal with the refugee crises in Europe after the Second World War, but since then it has extended its work worldwide, providing a response to disasters and promoting long-term

Emergency aid: immediate response to a disaster with urgent medical and survival provisions.

LEDC: less economically developed country.

Long-term aid: development of communities to become self-sufficient, through projects which usually last for at least a year.

Poverty: the absence or paucity of the basic needs of life – food, water, shelter, healthcare, education and employment.

Short-term aid: start of the rebuilding process after emergency response, or development projects which usually last a few weeks or months.

Revision tip

Notice the similarities here in reasons to help and the way that help is achieved. As there are plenty of religious teachings that cover the requirement to help, this lends itself to a 5-mark question. It is also good to have in mind a couple of real examples of what has been done in aid projects.

development. It works with partner agencies and will support all of them, regardless of race, religion, etc. It assesses projects in a country, then supplies experts and materials for the projects to be completed.

The key focus since 2012 has been to see an end to poverty and to generate global justice by empowering those who are currently exploited and disadvantaged.

Every year 'Christian Aid Week' envelopes are delivered to all households to collect money to continue the organisation's work.

Tearfund

This began as a fund collected for the 40 million refugees caused by wars worldwide. The money was given to evangelical agencies caring for such refugees.

Prayer is key to the organisation's work, as well as the principle of following Jesus to where the need is greatest. Money is raised from evangelical churches and young people are encouraged to join projects in gap years or on mission trips.

All types of aid are given but Tearfund does emphasise people's spiritual as well as physical needs – 67,000 churches have been created or helped in the past five years. The agency claims to have changed 15 million lives.

It promotes self-help projects so that people are empowered to help themselves out of poverty, for example loans given for small business start-up, meaning that money is community produced rather than received as charity.

Activity

Support or challenge?

'Religious people should make helping the poor out of poverty their most important duty.' Evaluate this statement. Refer to Christianity in your answer. You should agree and disagree, and come to a justified conclusion.

Use the list of arguments below to help you write a strong answer to the question. They are mixed up though, so first you need to work out which ones agree (support) and which disagree (challenge) with the statement. You may have other arguments as well. Remember that a conclusion should not just be repeating what you have already said, so it is worth keeping back one argument to use as your reason for agreeing or not.

Argument	Support statement in question	Challenge statement in question
Jesus said people should give up all they owned to the poor and follow him.		
Religious people should worship God as their priority.		
Religious people need to look after themselves and their families before they look after anyone else.		
Most Western Christians can afford to give to those in poverty, so they should.		
Love thy neighbour – the Good Samaritan helped.		
Money is no good when we die, but using money to help others now might help us on Judgement Day.		

Exam practice

What questions on this section look like:

Christianity: Practices

This page contains a range of questions that could be on an exam paper. Practise them all to strengthen your knowledge and technique while revising. Check back to pages 13–14 to see the marking grids that examiners use: this will help you to mark your answers.

1 What does the term 'eucharist' refer to?
   (a) Thanksgiving   (b) Praise   (c) Last meal   (d) Bread and wine ceremony   [1]
2 Which of the following remembers the resurrection of Jesus?
   (a) Christmas   (b) Palm Sunday   (c) Good Friday   (d) Easter   [1]
3 Give two types of Christian worship.   [2]
4 Give two reasons why Christians believe they should evangelise.   [2]
5 Name two types of prayers.   [2]
6 Explain two similar ways that Christian Aid and Tearfund help the poor.   [4]
7 Explain two similar beliefs found in the idea of Christian evangelism.   [4]
8 Explain two different ways of worship found in the Christian church.   [4]
9 Explain two contrasting beliefs about whether baptism is necessary or not.   [4]
10 Explain two ways in which the Eucharist is important to Christians. Refer to sacred writings or another source of Christian belief and teachings in your answer.   [5]
11 Explain two ways that food banks demonstrate 'faith in action'. Refer to sacred writings or another source of Christian belief and teachings in your answer.   [5]
12 Explain two ways in which pilgrimage is important for Christians today. Refer to sacred writings or another source of Christian belief and teachings in your answer.   [5]
13 'Worship should always be liturgical.' Evaluate this statement. In your answer, you should:
   ● refer to Christian teaching
   ● give reasoned arguments to support this statement
   ● give reasoned arguments to support a different point of view
   ● reach a justified conclusion.   [12]
14 'The sacraments are just excuses for celebrations.' Evaluate this statement. In your answer, you should:
   ● refer to Christian teaching
   ● give reasoned arguments to support this statement
   ● give reasoned arguments to support a different point of view
   ● reach a justified conclusion.   [12]
15 'The churches should focus on the worship of God rather than helping the community.' Evaluate this statement. In your answer, you should:
   ● refer to Christian teaching
   ● give reasoned arguments to support this statement
   ● give reasoned arguments to support a different point of view
   ● reach a justified conclusion.   [12]

ONLINE

Commentary

Level 2 students answer questions simply and not always in the way asked. They mix up the 'command words', which are the key instructions of a question. They also fail to provide required information, especially the religious teachings. If this is you, you need to practise so that you are really clear on what the questions are asking. You also need to have a few teachings which you can use – don't bother learning them word for word, an approximation is usually good enough.

Level 5 students do as the questions ask but often not in enough detail and also without providing enough teachings. This course demands them all the time, so you have to know some. If this is you, get a teacher to help you rewrite the teachings in a way that you can understand and learn, then learn them. Write them on the front of the exam paper before you start answering to help you as you do the exam.

Level 8 students know and use a lot of teachings. This is part of how they demonstrate their very good subject knowledge and why they are worth the highest grades.

1.3 Islam: Section 1 – Beliefs and teachings

Six Articles of Faith (Sunni)

What	Importance
The Oneness of Allah – Allah is One, eternal, the absolute creator	If Allah has absolute power, then Muslims will live according to His will
Angels – do the work of Allah and record all words and actions	Angels making records affects how Muslims live their lives to earn a place in paradise
Holy books – sources of authority in written form	Holy books allow Muslims to know and understand the right path for life
Prophets – deliver messages from Allah to guide humanity	If Muslims listen to the words and examples of prophets, they will follow the right path
Day of Judgement – Allah judges Muslim actions to decide on heaven or hell for eternal life	The whole of this life is a test for the life to come and facing Allah's judgement
Al-Qadr – Allah's will is supreme so everything is ordered by Him	Allah determines everything and even with human free will Allah knows the choices before humans make them

Five Roots of Usul ad-Din: the five beliefs that underpin the faith for Shi'a Muslims.

Shi'a: the second largest Muslim group following a line of leaders from Muhammad's family.

Six Articles of Faith: the six key beliefs that are the foundations of faith for Sunni Muslims.

Sunni: the majority group within Islam following the 'way of the prophet' – the Sunnah.

Five Roots of Usul ad-Din (Shi'a)

What	Importance
1 Tawhid (Oneness) – Allah is One, eternal, the absolute creator	One God, one power, no confusion, a single path for Muslims to follow
2 Nubuwwah (Prophethood) – Allah has sent prophets to advise and guide mankind on how to live according to His ways	Provides the guidance for life from the past (prophets) and present (Qur'an)
3 Adalat (Justice) – Allah is supremely fair	All life has a purpose, sometimes beyond understanding, but Muslims have faith that all Allah's ways are right
4 Imamate (Leadership) – the imams are earthly leaders of the faith	These leaders protect the Muslim religion and continue to guide Muslims in the modern world
5 Al-Ma'ad (Resurrection) – humans will live again after death	Muslims face judgement and need to live with good intentions and actions to pass the test

Revision tip

Use cue cards to create visual diagrams for these beliefs so that they are easier to remember. And make sure you learn the key terms.

Now test yourself

1 How many Articles of Faith are there? Can you list them?
2 How many Roots of Usul ad-Din are there? Can you name them?
3 Can you give two reasons why lists of beliefs like these might be important to believers?
4 Explain the similarities between the Six Articles of Faith and the Five Roots of Usul ad-Din.

Answers at **www.hoddereducation.co.uk/myrevisionnotesdownloads**

The nature of Allah

Oneness of Allah – Tawhid	Beneficent and merciful
One God, absolute, ultimate power, indivisible, eternal, unborn, nothing is like Him, beyond understanding, He know and sees all, He cannot be questioned but provides everything for us and is the ultimate source of compassion. For Muslims believing this develops humility, modesty, courage and determination to live as Allah wants.	Allah is kind, compassionate and merciful, He sent prophets to guide people, His rules are just and compassionate, He forgives those who repent and He loves His creation. Suffering is a test of faith. Muslims are imperfect so need Allah to be like this. Suffering always has a purpose even when they don't understand why things happen, so this belief helps them cope with human life.
Omnipotent	**Fair and just**
All-powerful, humanity always needs Him, sees all actions and knows all innermost thoughts and desires. He hears all calls/prayers to Him and there are hidden blessings to all things. Given this, Muslims are encouraged to submit to His will totally.	Allah always does what is right, He is fair in His creation, His divine justice rules the universe. Humans are not able to understand the justice of the world as they cannot fully understand Allah. Muslims are commanded to be fair and just in action or words. Muslims strive to do the best they can in the fairest way as they will face justice for their actions on the Day of Judgement.
Immanent	**Al-Qadr**
Allah is vital to human existence, closer than the jugular vein (if this is cut we die) so life without Allah is worse than death. He is in this world to help and guide, to provide a purpose to life and the ability to live it. If Allah is in this world then humanity is not alone; Muslims must believe He acts in their lives.	Allah decrees everything that happens in the universe. Humans do have free will to make choices, including the wrong choices, but Allah knows these before they are made. It is important for their faith to know that Allah controls the universe and at the same time that they have free will in their lives. Knowing Allah knows wrong choices are made helps Muslims ask Allah for His mercy.
Transcendent	**Key quote**
Allah is outside this created world, outside time so not affected by it, has no beginning/end, beyond all human understanding, limitless and separate to the world, He can act in the world and not be affected by it. Being greater than the world itself He can affect it in any way, without limit.	Say: He is Allah; Allah, the Eternal, Absolute; He begetteth not, nor is He begotten; And there is none Like Unto Him (Surah 112).

Exam tip

Examiners are impressed by inclusion of religious teachings/quotes, so learn one for each of these qualities. If you are able to explain the quote then this is an easy way of accessing marks in the 4-, 5- and 12-mark questions – your work will stand out.

Risalah

- Risalah = the different ways Allah communicates with humanity; guidance.
- Allah uses different means to communicate a message of guidance to humans. This guidance leads them to follow the right path, which means they can have a good afterlife. Allah gives the guidance from His all-loving nature.

- After the creation of humankind Allah, being fair and just, had to provide guidance for His creation as to what He wanted from them.
- The guidance was a path to be able to return to Allah at the end of time.
- Humanity is tested by Iblis on how they follow the code of behaviour Allah sent.

Risalah: simply means 'communication between Allah and humanity'. Allah has sent guidance in three key forms – through books (e.g. the Qur'an), through angels (delivering his messages) and through prophets (warning and advising the people of what Allah expects).

- Risalah allows Muslims to know what Allah wants from them.
- This enables Muslims to have a purpose in life now that they know what Allah wants from them.
- Which enables them to know the right path in their lives.

- Allah sent messages in three ways: books, Prophets and angels.
  - Through Prophets like Adam, Ibrahim, Musa, Isa and through his last Prophet Muhammad.
  - These individuals set examples to follow and wrote texts to guide humans in the form of holy books (the Suhuf, the Tawrat, the Zabur, the Injil and the Qur'an).
  - In this world, angels guide people and the Prophets, and also have special roles to do with eternal life.

Figure 3 Risalah

Activity

Support or challenge?

'Allah has given humans all the guidance they need.' Evaluate this statement. Refer to Islam in your answer. You should agree and disagree, and come to a justified conclusion.

Use the list of arguments below to help you write a strong answer to this question. The arguments are mixed up though, so first you need to work out which agree (support) and which disagree (challenge) with the statement. Remember that a good conclusion does not just repeat points made already, so you might like to keep back one argument for that. You might also have your own different arguments to use.

Argument	Supports statement in question	Challenges statement in question
Allah has given books, angels and prophets – that is a lot!		
The Qur'an says Allah has given guidance, and it is the truth.		
The guidance isn't about everything, and especially not modern life.		
The guidance was in different places at different times, so some people had no chance to be guided.		
There is no other proof – except from the guidance itself – that Allah sent this guidance.		
The guidance is about behaviour and this applies to everything, so it does show us how to be a morally good person.		

Prophets

Prophets are humans who were chosen by Allah to carry out specific roles on earth. These included taking Allah's guidance to humans and warning humans of the consequences of their behaviour. Many have also been great leaders of their communities. There have been 124,000 of them – Adam was the first, Muhammad the last.

The life of Adam

● Adam was the 'caretaker' of the earth. He was taught everything by Allah – the ability to learn, to reason, to evaluate and make choices.

● He was given Hawaa, a woman, for company. But they disobeyed Allah, failed the test from Iblis and were banished to earth instead of living in the Garden of Eden. They asked for forgiveness and Allah was merciful. Adam taught people about Allah.

● He is the Father of humankind, a prophet until his death. He built the Ka'aba and taught that life here was temporary and next was the life eternal.

● Adam did wrong but repented and was shown mercy and salvation – a message for all Muslims.

The life of Ibrahim

● Ibrahim believed in one true power – Allah – and rejected the idea of idol gods/statues.

● He preached this message but was often rejected. Allah sent a miracle to save Ibrahim when people tried to burn him and then people started to follow him.

● He married Sarah, who couldn't have children, and then Hajar, with whom he had a son called Ismail.

● Allah tested Ibrahim's faith by asking him to sacrifice his son. Ibrahim was willing, so Allah was pleased and sent a ram for sacrifice instead.

● Allah then allowed Sarah to have a son, Ishaq. Sarah and Hajar then became jealous of each other and so Hajar and Ismail left to live in the desert. They ran out of water, but Hajar never gave up looking to save her son and eventually Allah gave them the Zamzam well. To thank Allah for saving Hajar and Ismail, Ibrahim rebuilt the Ka'aba with Ismail, who later led the community to Makkah.

Now test yourself

TESTED

1 What is Risalah?
2 What are the three means of guidance?
3 Name two books.
4 Name two prophets.

Activity

Fix it!

Read the answer to this question. Work out how it can be improved and then rewrite it.

Explain two Islamic beliefs about Risalah. (4 marks)

Two beliefs about Risalah are that it means guidance from God, and that God has spoken to humans (not directly) to tell them how they should be behaving.

Influences

As a Muslim, the fact that Allah has given me all these sources of guidance tells me He loves me and wants me to succeed and attain paradise. I am thankful for this, and worship Him to show that. I also try to follow the guidance, so I try to live as a good Muslim.

Prophet Muhammad

Prophet Muhammad was the final prophet, the 'seal of the prophets' who gave the message of Islam and ensured it was unchanged thereafter. It is Prophet Muhammad's Sunnah (example) which Muslims follow today.

Why was Muhammad chosen as a prophet? He had the personality and qualities to deliver a message, convert people, organise a new community and do all of this under difficult situations and in personal danger.

His calling? Muhammad's calling is a well-known story of the Qur'an being revealed to him in a cave on Mount Hira by Angel Jibril. But why at this point in time?

- First, it was part of Allah's plan at this time.
- Second, people were becoming too distant from Allah and needed guidance to be brought back.
- Third, previous holy books had been lost.
- Finally, Muhammad was the perfect example to carry out Allah's plan.

What did he do? He first went to Makkah (**Hijrah**) to try to preach the message. However, the message of the Qur'an was rejected there and his life was in danger so he had to escape to Madina. There he was welcomed and became the political and religious leader. He set up a belief system with the Five Pillars, set up community rules and delivered the Qur'an. This was the first Muslim community; it is where his tomb is. Following three decisive battles, he returned to Makkah victorious and set up the Ka'aba for the worship of Allah alone.

His **Sunnah** and **Hadith** (written accounts of Muhammad's sayings, customs and traditions) provide guidance for everything in life in any era in a way that is easy to understand and follow.

The importance of Muhammad

As an individual:

- He was the perfect example of a man who served Allah for Muslims to aim to emulate.
- He showed many qualities that would serve Muslims well in their lives today – determination, patience, courage, humility and modesty.
- He rejected all immorality, and had a sense of duty and community.

As a leader:

- He was charismatic and a good leader of men.
- He was an excellent political and religious leader.
- He allowed religious freedom, rights for women, the elderly, sick and strangers.
- He created rules which benefited everyone.

As a family man:

- He saw the family as the basic unit for society.
- He was a good husband and father.
- He made good marriages for his children and was a good grandfather.

As a teacher:

- His words made him a great teacher and he lived the life he preached.
- He spoke with authority, which made people listen.
- He sought ways for everyone to be able to learn – if the method is right and patience is shown, anyone can learn anything.

Key quote

Surah 96:1–5 – Read In the name Of thy Lord and Cherisher, Who created – Created man, out of A clot Of congealed blood: Proclaim! And thy Lord Is Most Bountiful – He Who taught the pen – Taught man that Which he knew not.

Hadith: the written sayings of the Prophet often used as they are easier to understand than the Arabic Qur'an.

Hijrah: Muhammad's journey from Makkah to Madina in 622AD, which allowed a Muslim community to begin and so the faith to build.

Sunnah: the practices, customs and traditions of Muhammad.

Now test yourself

1 What happened when Muhammad was chosen to be Prophet?
2 How do the responses of the people of Makkah and Madina differ?
3 What are the Sunnah and Hadith?

TESTED

Exam tip

Make sure you know the details of Muhammad's life as this will make it far easier to answer questions that focus on his impact at the time he lived and for Muslims today. Focus on his example in the four areas to show how he is the perfect example today.

The Qur'an

The Qur'an is the holy book of Islam, considered to be the actual word of Allah in its original Arabic form. 'Qur'an' means 'recitation'.

Revelation of the Qur'an:

● The Qur'an was first revealed to Muhammad on the Night of Power. Angel Jibril told him: 'Recite! In the name of your Lord, Who created all that exists.'
● It was a direct message from Allah.
● What was revealed was the will of Allah. Muhammad did not see Allah Himself.
● Muhammad recited the revelations in public and used one lead scribe.
● Sunni and Shi'a believe the revelations were complete by the time of Muhammad's death.

Compilation of the Qur'an:

● There is disagreement about how and when the full book was compiled. However, it was put together in a single book after Muhammad's death to ensure the message would be preserved.

Authority of the Qur'an:

● The Qur'an may be important because of where it comes from (Allah), or what it contains (guidance).
  ○ It comes directly from Allah and has His authority. It is without error in its original form. It supersedes other holy books. Muhammad was illiterate (could not read or write) so the Qur'an is seen as a miracle; greater than any book that man could produce.
  ○ It covers every aspect of life, influencing a person throughout their lives, personally and spiritually. It contains basic worship developed by Muhammad, and the Shari'ah system of law. It explains ultimate questions such as creation and the afterlife, and is compatible with all scientific developments.

The Qur'an as a basis for Shari'ah:

● The Qur'an contains direct guidance from Allah. Where there is no guidance already, scholars make judgements based both on the Qur'an and Sunnah, for example some modern issues such as social media did not exist when the Qur'an was revealed. However, teachings from the Qur'an and Sunnah can be considered and applied (a 'what would Muhammad do?' way of thinking).
● The laws of Allah are always superior to the laws of man as they are fairer and based on what Allah knows and understands to be best.
● There are a number of groups of scholars, known as 'schools', which study the Shari'ah and rule on it. Sunni Muslims accepts four schools of Islamic Shari'ah, and Shi'a Muslims accept one school, but in all cases the start point is the Qur'an.

Influences

As a Muslim, I believe the Qur'an in its Arabic form is the original words of Allah – I must follow its teachings. As a child I began to learn the words by heart, and now I can recite the whole Qur'an. The recitation and sound give me great comfort and strength in my daily life to face any difficulties.

Other holy books within Islam

The Torah (Tawrat)

These are the revelations given to Musa (Moses) by Allah and are now lost, no longer existing in their original forms. It is believed the Tawrat was put together by Moses' followers after his death using parts of the original text but adding their own. Some Muslims believe that Allah preserved the books. The fact that Muhammad still believed them to be reliable in his time suggests an importance. The Tawrat is talked about in the Qur'an as 'guidance and light', revealed by Allah and taught by all prophets and priests and not just Musa. It is not now considered the direct word of Allah.

Suhuf (the scrolls of Ibrahim)

Prophet Ibrahim is always called the 'upright one', always faithful to Allah. It is believed he received revelations on the first day of Ramadan and they came in parable-like stories. They cover issues of worship, reflection and building livelihoods. Muslims do not think they were ever in one single book.

Psalms (Zabur)

These are collections of prayers and poems by Dawud the great King. Allah gave them as a form of guidance, which Dawud then recited as songs and poems. A version is found in the Psalms of the Bible. The idea of the Messiah is found in the Zabur, whom Muslims believe to be Isa (Jesus), and who will return to the world at the end of time, bringing hope to all that they can enter paradise.

Gospel (Injil)

Isa (or Jesus) is an important prophet in Islam. The Gospels were the account of Jesus' life and death written by his followers after he died. Muslims believe that they may contain mistakes as they are not the direct word of Allah.

What about the authority of these books for Muslims today?
- The Qur'an refers to all four of these books so they must be important.
- Muhammad learned and taught from them so this gives them importance.
- They are connected to well-respected prophets, thus giving them authority.
- They give Allah's guidance, even if not perfectly.

At the same time though:
- Some are lost now and no one knows what they actually said.
- Some have been changed so might this take away some of their authority?
- If important, as they were given by Allah, why were they not preserved?
- The Qur'an has more authority than all of them together as it is the word of God, unchanged.

Activity

Fix it!

Below are two answers to the same exam question. Neither is perfect, so what is wrong each time? Remember the key rules of needing two teachings and having to explain. Then write your own perfect answer.

Explain two Muslim teachings about the Gospels.

Answer A:

They teach that Jesus is the prophet who will return. They also teach that there are many mistakes in them.

Answer B:

They teach that there are many mistakes, and the form we have is not truthful because of that. This was because they were written many years after Jesus' death by people who hadn't fully understood Jesus' message in the first place.

Answers at **www.hoddereducation.co.uk/myrevisionnotesdownloads**

Angels

What are they?

- Angels are made of elements of light, have wings and move at the speed of light.
- They can appear in human form but they are not like humans, have no gender and are part of the unseen world.
- They always complete Allah's task. They always obey Allah as they have no free will.

What is their role?

- They watch over humans, bringing peace to believers and fear to non-believers.
- They record all thoughts and actions for Judgement Day.
- Angels deliver all of Allah's messages at His command.
- The Angel of Death takes the soul at death; others question each soul as it waits for Judgement Day.
- Angels greet those in paradise and punish those in hell.
- The angel will blow the horn to signify the end of the world.

There are many angels who have specific roles, including guardian angels, angels who lead the army of Allah, angels who protect people from death until the right time, angels who carry Allah's throne, angels who bestow blessings, angels who give the foetus its soul and angels who travel the earth finding those who worship Allah.

Angel Jibril

Who: the name means 'God is my strength'. Jibril is known as the spirit of holiness as he always brings good news. He was the first thing given life by Allah and sent to see paradise and hell. He knows the beauty of paradise but also how hard it is to get there. In hell he saw how no one would want to be sent there but that it was very easy to end up there because humans are surrounded by desires and lusts.

Role: Jibril delivered many messages to prophets and is mentioned in both the Qur'an and the Hadith. Examples of his work include helping Ibrahim when he was thrown into a fire; opening up the Zamzam well for Hajar; telling Maryam she would have Isa; dictating the Qur'an to Muhammad and teaching him the way of Allah and the Five Pillars.

Angel Mika'il

Who: known as the giver of rain and sustenance, Mika'il has also seen hell and how easy it is to get there and how hard it is to get into paradise. He is the friend to humanity. He was one of the first to bow to Adam and it is believed he provides spiritual help to the soul and material help to the body.

Role: Muslims believe Muhammad went on a night journey to the seven heavens and the throne of Allah. Before this Mika'il had to prepare him by providing the water for Jibril to purify him. He also helped Muhammad at the Battle of Badr in the fight for Makkah.

On Judgement Day both Jibril and Mika'il will help with the weighing of people's actions.

Now test yourself

TESTED

1 Name two angels.
2 Why are angels important?
3 What tasks do angels carry out?

Influence

Believing in angels means I know I am watched and my actions recorded. I am more conscious of doing right and wrong – after all, I want Judgement Day to go well for me! I am also grateful to Allah for providing guidance through them – I know Jibril and Mika'il will help me, for example. I show my gratitude through worship.

Akhirah (life after death)

Akhirah (life after death) definitely exists – the Qur'an (as the word of Allah) says it does. Akhirah explains why we are here in this short existence on earth – it is a test from Allah. Muslims face the test of life, with the end result being Akhirah.

The prophets say humans are accountable for their actions, with rewards and punishments as a result. Those rewards are hell and paradise. Guardian angels keep a record of our behaviour in this life to use on Judgement Day in the decision for/against our soul.

The Grave and Barzakh

At death the soul is taken by Azra'il, who is the Angel of Death. The soul watches the burial, seeing everything but unable to communicate. Those attending a funeral should make a statement about the person, so the soul has to listen to this.

Two angels ask questions: Who is your Lord? What was your life like? Who is your prophet? If answered correctly the soul waits comfortably in sleep for the Day of Judgement. If not, the soul is tormented – 'the punishment of the grave'. The soul will be taken through its whole life to see its good and bad actions. The torment is greater when reviewed actions were bad.

This waiting is known as **Barzakh**, meaning 'barrier'.

The end of the world

Angel Israfil sounds the trumpet, the sky will split and the light will be blinding, the earth will be destroyed, with oceans boiling over with fire. Earth will be transformed and the dead raised up. The living will die instantly.

The **Mahdi** (the guided one – prophesied redeemer of Islam) will come to earth, Isa will return to help the Mahdi fight false prophets. He will rule before the Day of Judgement and rid the world of evil. The Qur'an will be taken to paradise and no one will remember the words. Smoke will cover the world and 40 days later the dead will rise to face judgement in their physical body.

Akhirah is eternal, gives life its purpose and affects actions because what is on offer at the end are the two extremes of paradise or hell.

Akhirah II – Al-Qadr

Al-Qadr = 'predestination: everything happens according to Allah's will.'

Think about it: if everything that happens is known to Allah already, is there a point to human life? Why might Allah have designed humans with the capacity to do wrong? Why does Allah not just punish humans while they are alive on earth? If there is Al-Qadr, do humans really have free will?

According to Islam:
- Humans control themselves – thoughts and actions, choices and decisions. Humans are responsible for all their actions and will be held accountable for them.
- Some things are uncontrollable, for example when we are victims of a natural disaster, or have an illness, but we can control our reactions to these things. We can also control our reactions to the suffering of others.

Akhirah: belief in life after death.

Al-Qadr: predestination of the will of Allah – He decrees all that happens in the universe.

Barzakh: place of waiting for the soul after death.

Mahdi: the guided one or the Messiah who will return to earth at the end of the world.

Answers at **www.hoddereducation.co.uk/myrevisionnotesdownloads**

- Our reactions are 'human free will'. We should use it to do good. Those reactions should be positive/constructive (e.g. staying strong in difficult times, helping others when they are in need, etc.).
- Allah knows the choices, however. He controls the boundaries of life, but each person has control over the part they play.
- Humans do not know their destiny, Allah does.

Responsibility and accountability

Muslims often say 'inshallah – if Allah wills'. But humans can also play their part by behaving positively and responding positively.

Muslims have to take responsibility for their actions as they will be judged on them, but they can also put their trust in Allah – for example, that He will not test them beyond their limits.

If humans are responsible they are also accountable, as they will be questioned about 'what they did' and the answers will equal paradise or hell.

Now test yourself

1 What is Akhirah?
2 What is Al-Qadr?
3 What happens at death?
4 What will happen at the end of the world?

TESTED ☐

Activity

What's the question?

Your exam answers have to be clear, making it easy for the examiner to credit them fully. Read these two answers. The first isn't great – what makes it difficult for the examiner? The second is good.

A good rule of thumb about how clear an answer is is to check whether you could work out what the question was by only reading the answer. In each of these answers, can you work out what the question was?

Answer A:

The Qur'an says Allah will judge people for their actions. Prophet Muhammad told people to keep the Five Pillars if they wanted to please Allah, so they could go to heaven.

Answer B:

One way in which belief in the afterlife influences Muslims today is that it makes them think about how they behave towards other people in everyday and one-off situations. They know that Allah will judge them on this behaviour, so have to be just, compassionate and kind all the time.

A second way in which belief in the afterlife influences Muslims today is that it reminds them they have to obey Allah in keeping the Five Pillars. They will be judged on this on Judgement Day. This means they do go to mosque regularly, they do read the Qur'an, and so on.

Influences

Believing in Akhirah to me means I know this world is a test, and that Allah will use that test to decide if I should be allowed into paradise. Both good and bad is part of the test – so I should view things in that way of thinking. How I respond to the test is important, so I must always respond by following the Qur'an, and by being fair and compassionate to others.

Day of Judgement

What will happen on the Day of Judgement?
- People will be raised from the grave.
- People will be grouped together for 'the sorting'.
- Each person will hold a book called 'Your Record'. For some, Allah will show mercy; others will face punishment.
- A set of scales will balance good deeds and bad deeds.
- Bad people will be thrown in the gates of hell, unable to escape.
- A bridge over the pit of hell called the As-Sirat will reach over to paradise. It will have glass shards all over and is as thin as a human hair.
- Those who cross safely will reach paradise.

> **Revision tip**
>
> Think of an image for each of these so you remember the order by images in your mind. Then you just put the images into sentences in the exam.

Paradise and hell (Jannah and Jahannam)

Jannah (paradise)

How do people get there?
- A person must have been religious.
- They must have asked for Allah's forgiveness.
- They should have shown good beliefs and actions.

What kind of place is it?
- It is a reward from Allah.
- Wishes and desires are fulfilled; there are pleasures and delights.
- There is no illness/pain/worries or dying.
- Families are reunited amid stunning beauty.

How do people enter?
- By invitation from Allah.
- Via the As-Sirat bridge.
- There are eight gates representing good actions.
- Two angels welcome people.
- People say, 'Praise be to Allah who has fulfilled His promise.'

Jahannam

How do people get there?
- They will have lived a wicked life.
- They have rejected teachings of the Qur'an.
- They have taken no responsibility for their actions/blamed others.

What kind of place is it?
- A place of punishment – which differs dependent upon the sins committed.
- Fire is 70 times hotter than any place on earth.
- There is extreme pain through fire and boiling water.
- There is no escape.
- There are seven levels – some go for a set time, others for ever.

How do people enter?
- They are cast into hell directly for certain sins.
- They are judged and sent there on Judgement Day.
- Some fall from the As-Sirat bridge.

> **Activity**
>
> Use the information about Akhirah on the previous pages and your own knowledge to add detail to the spider diagram in Figure 4.
>
> Al-Qadr and human freedom — Jannah and Jahannam — Akhirah — End of the world — Judgement Day
>
> **Figure 4 Akhirah**

> **Exam tip**
>
> Make sure you know how these beliefs in paradise and hell would influence Muslims in their lives today. In other words, how does believing in life after death make people behave differently?

> **Influences**
>
> Believing in paradise gives me a great incentive to obey Allah in my life, and to do good. Believing in Jahannam makes me very fearful of Allah's punishment, so I avoid evil actions. I am always mindful of my actions, that they follow the Qur'an and Sunnah.

Exam practice

What questions on this section look like:

Islam: Beliefs and teachings

This page contains a range of questions that could be on an exam paper. Practise them all to strengthen your knowledge and technique while revising. Check back to pages 13–14 to see the marking grids that examiners use: this will help you to mark your answers.

1 What is meant by Akhirah?
  (a) Justice   (b) Prophethood   (c) Life after death   (d) Oneness   [1]
2 Which of the following is a belief only for Shi'a Muslims?
  (a) Jihad   (b) Imamate   (c) Akhirah   (d) Sawm   [1]
3 Name two words used to describe the nature of Allah.   [2]
4 Name two angels of Allah.   [2]
5 Give two reasons Muhammad is important to Muslims.   [2]
6 Explain two ways in which a belief in Risalah influences Muslims today.   [4]
7 Explain two ways in which a belief in angels influences Muslims today.   [4]
8 Explain two ways in which a belief in the Five Roots influences Shi'a Muslims today.   [4]
9 Explain two ways in which a belief in Jannah influences Muslims today.   [4]
10 Explain two Muslims teachings about the Day of Judgement. Refer to sacred writings or another
   source of Muslim belief and teachings in your answer.   [5]
11 Explain two Muslims teachings about the immanence of Allah. Refer to sacred writings or another
   source of Muslim belief and teachings in your answer.   [5]
12 Explain two Muslims teachings about Al-Qadr. Refer to sacred writings or another source of Muslim
   belief and teachings in your answer.   [5]
13 'The Qur'an is not more important than other Muslim holy books.' Evaluate this statement. In your
   answer, you should:
   ● refer to Muslim teaching
   ● give reasoned arguments to support this statement
   ● give reasoned arguments to support a different point of view
   ● reach a justified conclusion.   [12]
14 'Allah cannot be all-powerful with the suffering in the world today.' Evaluate this statement. In your
   answer, you should:
   ● refer to Muslim teaching
   ● give reasoned arguments to support this statement
   ● give reasoned arguments to support a different point of view
   ● reach a justified conclusion.   [12]
15 'Sunni and Shi'a should unite together as one.' Evaluate this statement. In your answer, you should:
   ● refer to Muslim teaching
   ● give reasoned arguments to support this statement
   ● give reasoned arguments to support a different point of view
   ● reach a justified conclusion.   [12]

ONLINE

Exam tip

Grade 2 students often write very little in the exam. This makes it difficult for them to build high scores. It starts from not knowing enough of the course content. If this is you, make sure you always ask for explanation when you need it, and make sure you have notes which make sense to you so that you can revise from them effectively.

Grade 5 students often write lots, but the clarity of what they write, and its precise match to the question, can be off. This is one reason why they don't get higher marks. If this is you, make sure your notes are clear, which will help you learn them more effectively and so be clearer in your answers.

Grade 8 students answer in good detail because they have a very good understanding of the content studied.

The Five Pillars

These are five 'pillars' on which the religion is built. The five key practices or duties are kept by both Sunni and Shi'a Muslims. They are all equal in importance and if carried out they make people servants of Allah. The first is always Shahadah as this is a belief and the other four are all actions that Muslims carry out because of that belief.

Pillar 1: Shahadah – the declaration of faith

'There is no God but Allah

Muhammad is His messenger'

Shi'a Muslims add:

Ali is the beloved of Allah and rightful trustee

Of the Prophet, and his immediate successor.'

Muslims reject anything other than Allah as their focus of belief. Muhammad's role is the perfect example to follow – if a Muslim follows the Sunnah, they will also believe in Risalah and Akhirah.

The Shi'a additions clearly show the place Ali has in history.

The words must be said from the heart.

When is the Shahadah said?

It is said every day as part of the Adhan (call to prayer), so Muslims hear it five times. It is said every evening before sleep.

It is also whispered into the ear of newborn children and uttered at death.

Why is it important?

It is important for a faith to have a clear statement of belief. The fact that it is so concise allows every Muslim to know it (even if they cannot translate it) and repeat it. It unites Muslims all over the world, prevents any confusion due to its simplicity, and focuses all Muslim thoughts on Allah and the example of the life of Muhammad. For the Shi'a it emphasises the clear historical differences between themselves and the Sunni with their reference to Ali.

Activity

Read the question and the start of the answer to it. Then use your own knowledge and information from page 74 to develop the answer and complete it to a high level. There are clues following to help you.

'Muslims should recite the Shahadah daily.' Evaluate this statement. Refer to Islam in your answer. You should agree and disagree, and come to a justified conclusion.

I think they should as this is the statement of belief for Muslims. It is the most basic belief they have. It says there is only one God, and if they remember that every day, they will behave better.[1] It also says Muhammad is the Prophet, so they know to follow his Sunnah.[2] It is an easy phrase to say – aloud or in your head any time.[3] However, if they love God they can show that in their behaviour.[4] Just saying something doesn't make a person better.[5]

[1] Why? How?

[2] What are they? Why follow them? How?

[3] Example?

[4] Such as?

[5] Give an example.

Exam tip

Beware of questions which try to suggest that one pillar is more important than the others – frequency of carrying them out or position in the five are irrelevant: they are all equal. However, when faced with an evaluative question about that, you have to make a case for why each is especially important. For example, Shahadah is important because it is the start point, sawm because of the effort it can take, and so on.

Pillar 2: Salah – prayer

REVISED

The words of the Adhan are said by the Mu'adhin from the minarets. Men go to the mosque (women may, but pray separately), while the women stay at home.

Shoes are removed and wudu, or the washing process, is carried out for purity of body and mind. The head is covered by a scarf or topi.

Muslims stand shoulder to shoulder facing the Mihrab in the Qiblah wall (which signifies the direction of Makkah). They then make their intention to pray (Niyyat).

Rak'ahs and recitations

These are carried out five times every day at set times for Sunni Muslims; the Shi'a have prayer three times daily.

Both Sunni and Shi'a Muslims total 17 sequences of prayer each day by way of rak'ahs (set movements) and recitations (set words). Each rak'ah (sequence of prayer) has a number of different physical positions. One of them, sujud, means kneeling down with the forehead touching the floor (a wooden block for the Shi'a), showing total submission to Allah – the idea of 'bowing down' or 'prostrating'.

Sunni and Shi'a have slightly different ways of carrying out the positions. Each physical position includes saying aloud a Qur'anic recitation.

The importance of salah

The following explains why Muslims pray and why they pray so often.
- It is prescribed in the Qur'an: 'prostrate and draw near to Allah.'
- It is believed that whoever prays will enter paradise.
- Prayer brings knowledge and more awareness of Allah as the heart is open.
- Prayers are spread through the day so Allah is never forgotten.

- Prayer prevents bad/wrong thoughts/actions.
- Prayer in the mosque brings rewards far greater than those for praying alone. Muslims believe these rewards will help tip the scales in their favour on Judgement Day.

Visible benefits

- Salah reminds each person praying of the 'greatness' of Allah.
- It reminds them of their insignificance as they pray with a sea of others.
- The comparison between the greatness of God and the insignificance of humans leads to humility and modesty.
- It encourages positive and respectful behaviour, which brings a sense of peace and community.
- It brings discipline and order to people's lives and the preparation for prayer calms the mind.
- It benefits an individual's character by reminding them of God's mercy, grace, etc.

Activity

Fix it!

Read the question and both answers. Which answer is better? Use a highlighter and annotation to show why it is better.

Explain why Muslims pray.   *(4 marks)*

Answer A:

They pray because they have to in the Pillars. If you are a Muslim, you have to pray. Prayer is called salah. Muslims go to the mosque and they wash first, then go into the prayer room. They bow down and kneel down, and prostrate whilst saying the Qur'an. Then at last they greet other worshippers and go.

Answer B:

One of the Pillars is salah – prayer is a duty which all Muslims have to keep. They also pray because Prophet Muhammad did. They also pray because they want to have a good Judgement Day.

Some differences

- Shi'a pray at three times, Sunni at five each day.
- Shi'a make different positions, for example touching the head to a block of wood, not the floor (as Sunni do).

Now test yourself

TESTED ☐

1 How many Pillars of Islam are there?
2 How many times a day should a Muslim pray?
3 Why is it important to pray?
4 How does a Muslim benefit from prayer?

Answers at **www.hoddereducation.co.uk/myrevisionnotesdownloads**

The mosque, Friday prayer, prayer at home

Jumu'ah prayer – Friday prayer

These are congregational prayers at the mosque on a Friday at noon. They are the best attended of the week as it is believed great rewards come from such attendance. Men are expected to attend as missing four Fridays is considered to make them less of a believer.

The adhan is called, then wudu is performed, and often Muslims make **du'as** as they wait for the sermon.

The **khatib** delivers the first part in the language of the community as a teaching tool, perhaps about issues in the community or wider issues. It is really important in those parts of the world where few people can read. The imams should be responsible and not use this to promote radical ideas. The second half is done is in Arabic and is a set speech.

The Iqamah is then read and two rak'ahs are performed. Often Muslims do four rak'ahs by themselves before the two compulsory ones and then two after – copying Muhammad.

Prayer at home

For women, salah prayers are often done at home (although they can attend the mosque as there is a separate area set aside for them). They are performed in exactly the same way, with washing, facing Makkah and the use of a prayer mat. The expectation to carry out salah is the same for men and women and the same rewards are granted by Allah.

Prayers can be done at home at any time in the day. They are more personal and a time Muslims can open up to Allah, who is always there to hear prayers. These could involve asking for help/support for themselves or others or for forgiveness.

No rak'ahs are involved so words are freely used.

Du'as are often said by families before mealtimes, to break fasts or on special occasions such as Eid.

Muhammad said prayers at night called Tahajjud, so those who are especially disciplined say these still.

> **Exam tip**
>
> The mosque is not on the Specification so cannot be directly asked about but you can refer to it in your answers and gain credit. If you know the design, for example, with the key features of the minaret, dome, Qiblah, **Mihrab** and Minbar, you can refer to it while explaining prayer, or knowing what the mosque is used for explains how the Muslim community works.

> **Du'as**: Private prayers often said after set prayers in the mosque at home.
>
> **Khatib**: the imam who delivers the sermon at the Friday prayers.
>
> **Minbar**: the raised platform used by the imam to deliver the Friday sermon.

> **Exam tip**
>
> Prepare ideas about the following before your exam so that you have something to work with, especially for evaluation questions:
> - Are prayers at the mosque more important than those done in the home?
> - Are prayers for men and women equally important or not?
> - Is there a need for prayer to be done so often? Are prayers too repetitive?
> - Are Jumu'ah prayers more important than prayers on other days?
> - Are salah prayers more beneficial than du'a prayers?

> **Some differences**
> - Men must go to the mosque; women need not.
> - Some Muslims do the required prayers; others do extras to copy Muhammad or for their own reasons.

Pillar 3: Sawm – fasting

REVISED

The Prophet Muhammad told Muslims to fast during the hours of daylight during Ramadan, the ninth month of the Muslim calendar, the month that the Night of Power took place (the call of Muhammad, the first revelations of the Qur'an).

Successful fasting means mind over matter, the spiritual over the material. Allah must be at the forefront of people's minds, not just fitted around normal life and material issues. Ramadan reminds them that Allah comes first.

The main idea is to aim to be better Muslims, not just for this month but for their whole lives. Ramadan provides this time to refocus on one's good moral and spiritual behaviour. It is said to be a shield against the fires of hell as it puts lives back on track here and now.

Ramadan can be harder depending upon which time of year it occurs – longer daylight hours in the summer, for example, mean longer periods to fast.

So what does fasting involve?	Who is exempt?	Benefits of fasting
No eating and drinking from dawn to dusk.	The young and the elderly as they need nourishment.	Brings Muslims closer to Allah as it removes worldly distractions.
No sexual relations during these hours.	The ill – they need medication and nutrition.	Reminds people of the hungry poor – reminder to give zakah.
No TV or video games (as these are purposeless).	Pregnant women – both woman and child need nutrition.	Builds personal qualities such as self-discipline, determination, piety, humility and courage.
Considerate behaviour to others, more time spent in the mosque, reading of the Qur'an.	Travellers and menstruating women can make up the fasting days later.	Builds sense of community as everyone is fasting and facing hardship together.

Pillar 4: Zakah – alms giving

REVISED

Zakah is charity, a directive from the Qur'an. Wealth is on loan from Allah, so some should be used to help others. A sum of 2.5 per cent is paid on income and savings to the mosque for distribution for community causes.

To help each other is to help Allah and giving should be done willingly as Allah knows all intentions.

The benefits of giving zakah include:
- to purify and cleanse – giving makes the remaining money 'clean'
- sharing the blessings of wealth with others prevents greed
- money benefits both giver and receiver – the giver will receive a 'hundred-fold' back in the afterlife and they should also feel the satisfaction of giving
- if everyone gave zakah then there would be no poor in the world.

Now test yourself

TESTED

1 Name the Five Pillars in Arabic and English.
2 Why are the Five Pillars important?
3 What is sawm?
4 What is zakah?

Some differences

Sawm: not all Muslims fast for the same number of hours each year – it depends on where in the world they are as it is based on daylight hours. Men will go to the mosque to break their fast each day; women do not.

Zakah: children do not have to give zakah, but many still do; all adults who meet the criteria must give. In Muslim countries, Muslims pay zakah as Shari'ah law proscribes; Muslims in the West usually have to give a cash equivalent.

Pillar 5: Hajj – pilgrimage to Makkah

Place visited/actions done	Significance of the place	Significance of the action
On the journey to Makkah – *Ihram*	Ihram (two white cloths) put on and saying of the Talbiyah prayer.	Shows all Muslims stand equal before Allah with no material/worldly differences – just as they will stand before Allah on Judgement Day.
Great Mosque – *Circle it seven times*	Tawaf is performed at the holiest shrine to Allah on earth where Muhammad set it up for the worship of Allah.	The circling shows a Muslim's love for Allah – it fulfils the desire to personally see the Ka'aba in its magnificence.
Zamzam well – *Drink/take water from the well*	Remembers Hajar, Ibrahim's wife, searching for water for her son Ismail. The well spring was seen as a miracle from Allah.	Demonstrates Muslim dependence on Allah – Allah is vital for spiritual life and will reward determination.
As-Safa and Al-Marwa – *Walk seven times between the two small hills*	This is the place where Hajar ran frantically searching for water for Ismail.	Shows that Muslims will never give up in their determination for Allah.
Mt Arafat – *Pray from noon til sunset*	This is the place Adam and Hawaa were reunited and Muhammad gave his last sermon.	Muslims hope to be forgiven for their sins after meditating and praying.
Mina – *Throwing of pebbles at the three jamarat*	Ibrahim was prepared to do as Allah asked (sacrifice his son).	Muslims show their own rejection of Shaytan, hoping to pass any test Allah asks of them.
(Mina) Eid ul Adha – *Feast of sacrifice*	Ibrahim and Ismail sacrificed sheep/goat as Allah rewarded their obedience.	Celebrated by all Muslims (on Hajj or not) showing their responsibility and commitment to the poor.
Madina – *Praying at the Prophet's mosque*	This is the place of the first mosque and Muslim community set up by Muhammad.	All prayers made here will be heard and accepted by Allah.
Great Mosque – *Tawaf*	The holiest shrine to Allah on earth.	To see the holiest shrine for one last time – perform tawaf to show they are committed to Allah.

How does Hajj influence the lives of Muslims today?

While there:
- Muslims feel part of a united ummah, something special that is achieved only while they are there.
- The sense of equality is a humbling experience.
- It is very emotional to actually see the Ka'aba and this would make prayer in the future far more meaningful.
- It affects how Muslims think about life and what is really important.
- Having sins forgiven allows a clean start with far more of a focus on the faith.

On returning home:
- The pilgrims are more respected members of the community.
- People seek advice from them.
- People see them as more spiritual and more understanding of the religion.
- People's reactions make individuals try to live up to what respect others give to them so their life is more Allah-centred.

Exam tip

'Influence' and 'importance' are often answered by the same ideas. If something influences me, then it must be important in the first place; if something is important to me, I will be influenced by it. Remembering this should help you in answering questions.

Shi'a Islam

Where:
- 10–15 per cent of Muslims are Shi'a. Iran is the main Shi'a country and leads Shi'ism.
- Shi'a is the majority religion in Iran, Bahrain, Lebanon, Iraq, Lebanon and Azerbaijan.
- Shi'a is split into a number of groups – this course focuses on Twelver Shi'a.

Ten Obligatory Acts of Shi'a Islam

There are Ten Obligations for Shi'a Muslims. Laws come from Muhammad and the 12 imams. Today there are clerics who are seen as guardians of Islamic law, basing their decisions in the Qur'an and Hadith in responding to modern-day issues. These are called Ijtihad. Clerics such as ayatollahs (religious leaders in Iran) make such decisions.

What are these things that Shi'a Muslims should believe and do?
- Obligations 1–4 – the first four are the same as those for the Sunni – salah, zakah, sawm and Hajj.
- 5 = Jihad – faith struggle (this actually applies to all Muslims).
- 6 = Khums – an extra tax to be paid on business profits.
- 7 = Amr-bil-Maroof – directing others towards good.
- 8 = Nahi Anil Munkar – forbidding evil.
- 9 = Tawalla – to express love towards Allah.
- 10 = Tabarra – to express hatred towards those who oppose Allah.

Obligations 6–10 are what make the Shi'a different to the Sunni. They aren't easy to keep but people must strive for them.

Salah

The Shi'a have prayer three times a day (at dawn, in the afternoon and in the evening) but in total complete 17 sequences of prayer (the same as the Sunni).

For Shi'a Muslims, wudu is an integral part of prayer, not just preparation for it. It shows Allah who obeys Him, purifies a person and makes them alert. For the actual prayer it (1) cancels out sin, (2) affirms Allah as Almighty, (3) affirms the insignificance of humans, and (4) restates a person's obedience to Allah in submission. It makes prayers valid by creating a level of humility and discipline.

Sawm – the point for Shi'a

Two purposes of fasting for Shi'a Muslims are to realise the struggle many face and then to make them think about what awaits them on Judgement Day.

Fasting helps Shi'a grow spiritually. It will make them stronger in rejecting evil (munkar) and doing what is good (maroof) – both Obligations.

Zakah – for Shi'a?

Imam Ali said the purpose of zakah was to test the rich and provide for the poor. The law prescribes tax on a list of specific things – anything else is not obligatory as the law did not name anything else. The list does not relate well to modern business, so it is difficult to apply.

Many Shi'a give an equivalence in money.

> **Exam tip**
>
> In the exam, if asked about different practices for salah, sawm or zakah, use this to give a Shi'a perspective and contrast with the information learned earlier.

Khums

Khums is a 20 per cent tax on annual surplus income (after expenses). It is split, being used for Allah, Muhammad and relatives of Muhammad, orphans, the needy, and people away from home who cannot pay to return.

The first three portions of khums can now be given to religious teachers/preachers (as it is impossible to give them to those originally intended). There will always be orphans, poor and stranded people so it is easy to fulfil this portion.

The value of Hajj for Shi'a Muslims

Hajj unites all Muslims, giving them all the same purpose and the same value from participating in it.

Anyone who visits Arafat (the Mount of Mercy), according to Imam Sadiq, gains forgiveness for themselves or their family.

Imam Abedin said that performing the Hajj sees bodies become healthy, sustenance expanded and faith improved. For Shi'a Muslims, Hajj is important in their spiritual lives and moves them forward in their personal struggle for Allah.

Jihad: how is this term to be understood?

Jihad is a struggle for faith.

Greater jihad	Lesser jihad
Jihad is about striving or making effort (juhud) to be a good Muslim.	This means defending Islam – some take up arms against any enemy of Islam as they see it. Many Muslims, though, say the actions of extremists claiming holy war are a wrong understanding of lesser jihad.
It equates to following a moral and virtuous life – following the Five Pillars, forgiving others, working for social justice, etc. It is a duty and act of worship (notice there is no reference to holy war here).	Rules exist about how lesser jihad/holy wars can be carried out – in defence of Allah, seeing no harm done, restoring peace, showing mercy, respect and protection and allowing freedom.

Amr bil Maroof and Nahi Anil-Munkar – the effect on the lives of Muslims

Maroof refers to anything approved by Shari'ah law, while munkar is anything not approved.

Muslims should promote what is good, speak out about what is wrong, disapprove of wrong in their hearts and stop the wrongs that damage society.

Tawalla and Tabarra: what do these mean?

This is to love those in Allah's path and express hatred for those who oppose Allah.

Some Shi'a see the first three Caliphs as their enemies as Ali was the rightful Caliph and they believe the Sunni have persecuted them throughout history.

Sunni Muslims reject Tawalla and Tabarra as they cause divisions. They see Shi'a love of Ali or the imams or their shrines as blasphemy. The Shi'a would say the Sunni misunderstand their beliefs – they are showing only great respect in their actions.

> **Exam tip**
>
> For the exam you need to know what 'Ten Obligations' means and what they are. You also need to know the influence of believing in them for the Shi'a – in effect, they govern much of their thinking and hence their lives. Six of them make Shi'a very different to Sunni – remember that.

Festivals Eid ul-Fitr

Eid is celebrated at the end of Ramadan, beginning at the start of the new moon. Ramadan is a hard month, with a focus on the spiritual side of the religion like a renewal of faith, so all Muslims welcome Eid.

They make preparations for the day, such as sending cards, decorating houses, buying food, and organising gifts and sweets for the children. They make joyous greetings of Eid Mubarak as the fast is broken by the simple eating of dates.

In the morning, men attend Eid prayers at the mosque, including two sermons explaining the rules for paying Zakat. Then the day is a family day, visiting friends and relatives, visiting cemeteries to remember the dead, exchanging gifts for the children, with new clothes and a special meal in the evening.

Muslims in Britain are allowed the day off work and school and in Muslim countries it is a public holiday.

Why is Eid so important?

The importance of the Eid festival is the same for Sunni and Shi'a Muslims. By fasting, Muslims have felt how hard life is for fellow Muslims who regularly go hungry.

This is the day zakah becomes due. Often mosques put up boards showing the families that attend and names are crossed off when zakah is given, though what they give is not written up.

Eid is important because Muslims reflect on the previous year and look into the future for the next year in terms of how they live up to the Prophet's example.

Reflecting on Ramadan, Muslims see the role religion should have in their lives: that Allah needs to be the focus of everything; that the Qur'an and prayer should dominate time; that behaviour should be modest, polite, peaceful, showing kindness to others; and that their wealth is not their own and it should be used as Allah would want – to benefit the community.

Those who have fasted should have been more obedient Muslims during this month – the hard thing being to maintain this throughout the next year and in future years.

Eid celebrates achievement and betterment so these ideas should continue so as to make the community a better ummah and improve each Muslim's prospects for a good afterlife.

Now test yourself

TESTED

1 What is Eid?
2 Why is Eid celebrated?
3 How does Eid affect the attitude of Muslims?

Some differences

Eid prayers vary slightly for Sunni and Shi'a in the number of rak'ahs, positions and prayers.

Shi'a pay khums as well as zakah; Sunni pay just zakah.

Eid ul-Adha

REVISED

This recalls Ibrahim and his resistance when Shaytan tried to get him to disobey Allah's test to sacrifice his son Ismail. Ibrahim threw stones to make Shaytan leave.

It is celebrated by the sacrificing of a lamb called qurbani. The meat is split three ways – the family, relatives and then the poor. Many families pay charity money instead of sacrificing a lamb.

Muslims complete Eid prayers, dress in new clothes, listen to an Eid sermon, exchange gifts, visit relatives and enjoy special meals.

Ashura

REVISED

Ashura simply means 'tenth'. Both Sunni and Shi'a observe this festival on the tenth day of the Muslim month of Muharram; however, their reason for and way of celebrating are very different.

Sunni

- Muhammad saw the Jews fasting on the tenth of the month of Muharram. They explained to him that it was a day to remember when the Israelites were saved from the pharaoh and that Musa fasted on this day. He replied that 'we are closer to Musa than you'. So he adopted the practice and told his people to fast.
- Ramadan was established later to replace the fast in Muharram.
- Many Muslims remember Ashura as a Day of Atonement, when sins are forgiven if repented. Many fast, often on the eighth, ninth and tenth of Muharram.
- Sunni Muslims do not accept the whipping of their bodies because the body should not be harmed. This used to be a common practice for Shi'a Muslims.

Shi'a

- For Shi'a Muslims this is a significant festival based in sorrow.
- It remembers the martyrdom of Hussein, the grandson of Muhammad who was killed in the battle of Karbala on the tenth day of Muharram, 680AD, along with 72 members of his family.
- He was killed by Yazid, a Muslim leader, who had demanded Hussein give him his allegiance. Hussein had refused.
- Trying to escape, Hussein and his family were intercepted. They were all were murdered on Yazid's command and no respect was shown to the dead.
- Shi'a Muslims learn first, that Hussein and the imams should never be forgotten, and second, that Muslims must stand up for justice to make society better. Love of the imams reflects Shi'a love of Allah.

How do the Shi'a observe Ashura?

They regard it as a festival of sincere sadness and many wear black for grief. Black cloths are hung in mosques.

After the afternoon prayers poems about the tragedy are read and people will cry.

Less commonly now, some Shi'a gather to beat themselves with whips and chains in sorrow, especially in Karbala itself.

Some differences

The reasons behind celebrating Ashura are different for Sunni and Shi'a.

The mood generated by Ashura differs – Shi'a feel sadness and grief; Sunni remember a great prophet and his practices – so it is about reflection and spirituality.

Now test yourself

1 Name two Muslim festivals.
2 Why do Muslims celebrate these festivals?
3 How do Shi'a and Sunni Muslims celebrate festivals? What are the similarities and the differences?

TESTED

Exam practice

What questions on this section look like:

Islam: Practices

This page contains a range of questions that could be on an exam paper. Practise them all to strengthen your knowledge and technique while revising. Check back to pages 13–14 to see the marking grids that examiners use: this will help you to mark your answers.

1 What is meant by Shahadah?

    (a) Call to prayer   **(b)** Prayer   **(c)** Belief in Allah   **(d)** Declaration of faith   [1]

2 Which of the following is the festival that follows Ramadan?

    (a) Eid ul-Fitr   **(b)** Eid ul-Adha   **(c)** Ashura   **(d)** Eid Mubarak   [1]

3 Give two ways that Shi'a and Sunni prayers are different.   [2]

4 Give two reasons why Muslims fast.   [2]

5 Name two holy sites visited on Hajj.   [2]

6 Explain two similar ways in which all Muslims observe Hajj.   [4]

7 Explain two similar ways in which all Muslims perform prayer.   [4]

8 Explain two contrasting ways in which zakah can be given.   [4]

9 Explain two contrasting Muslim understandings about Ashura.   [4]

10 Explain two ways in which Ramadan is important to a Muslim's life. Refer to sacred writings or another source of Muslim belief and teachings in your answer.   [5]

11 Explain two ways in which Arafat is important in the Hajj pilgrimage. Refer to sacred writings or another source of Muslim belief and teachings in your answer.   [5]

12 Explain two ways in which maroof and munkar are important to Shi'a Muslims. Refer to sacred writings or another source of Muslim belief and teachings in your answer.   [5]

13 'Shahadah is far more important than the other Four Pillars.' Evaluate this statement. In your answer, you should:
- refer to Muslim teaching
- give reasoned arguments to support this statement
- give reasoned arguments to support a different point of view
- reach a justified conclusion.   [12]

14 'Jihad should not be understood in terms of holy war.' Evaluate this statement. In your answer, you should:
- refer to Muslim teaching
- give reasoned arguments to support this statement
- give reasoned arguments to support a different point of view
- reach a justified conclusion.   [12]

15 'Ramadan is not necessary as Muslims should always live an Allah-centred life.' Evaluate this statement. In your answer, you should:
- refer to Muslim teaching
- give reasoned arguments to support this statement
- give reasoned arguments to support a different point of view
- reach a justified conclusion.   [12]

ONLINE

Commentary

Grade 2 students usually only express opinions in the evaluation questions. They don't develop their reasoning, so answers can be a series of loose comments. If this is you, ask your teacher for examples of statements and go through them to really understand them.

Grade 5 students can argue for and against statements. Their range of arguments may be limited, or the depth with which they argue them is limited. If this is you, is it depth or range? Practise by targeting whichever the weakness is.

Grade 8 students not only give a range of arguments to support different viewpoints, they also develop and explain those arguments to give good depth and make convincing arguments.

The nature of G-d

REVISED

G-d as One and as creator

The Shema (statement of belief) affirms belief in One G-d. Monotheism separated the Jews from others who were polytheists. Belief in One G-d means belief in One Creator G-d who is indivisible and complete.

G-d made the world – ex-nihilo (from nothing) in His way and not dependent. The Jewish story of creation is found in the Book of Genesis describing the six days of creation and G-d resting on the seventh (hence the Shabbat day of rest).

The world exists because G-d wills it to, He existed before anything else and is eternal, and the world continues to exist because He wills it to.

G-d revealed Himself through His creation but remains incomprehensible.

Law-giver and judge

Having created the world G-d wants humanity to live a certain way and if they do, they will be serving G-d.

G-d has given many laws (mitzvot), the first to Adam (not to eat from the tree) and the second to Noah after the flood. These laws are a spiritual and ethical code of practice.

G-d gave 613 laws, which combine the Seven Laws of Noah, the Ten Commandments given to Moses and others. They cover all aspects of life, both spiritual and material actions.

The Tenakh gives examples of people disobeying G-d's laws, and how G-d punished them. Jews believe that G-d will judge everyone, resulting in punishment and reward.

Shechinah – the Divine Presence

This expresses how G-d is involved in the world. Humans cannot see G-d but people have said they have felt His presence. It has been described as a light created to connect G-d and the world or as 'the glory of G-d' surrounding people.

Phrases such as 'the earth shone in His glory' or as 'a pillar of cloud by day and fire by night' or 'clouds covering something to be filled with G-d's presence' or reference to 'G-d dwelling' in places all refer to this idea of Shechinah.

How the nature of G-d influences Jewish people

Jews believe that following the law is to please and serve G-d.

All aspects of their lives are ruled by G-d, including family, food, clothing, business, interaction with others, worship, etc. Religious clothing like the tallith (prayer shawl) is a constant reminder of G-d's laws.

G-d has and will punish people for not following His laws.

Exam tips

● Make sure you can outline the creation story – you can use it to exemplify your answers.
● Learn some examples of people G-d has punished in the past, and how, so that you can refer to them in your answers.
● Revise the laws of Noah, the Ten Commandments and some examples of the kinds of things the 613 laws apply to in daily life.
● Learn some of these phrases so that you can refer to them, showing how the scriptures describe how G-d is present in the world today.

Now test yourself

1 Give two names for G-d.
2 What are mitzvot?
3 What is the Shechinah?
4 How does belief in what G-d is like influence Jewish people in their lives?

TESTED

Covenants

The Chosen People of G-d

Out of all of earth's people the Lord chose the Jews as His treasured possession. Jews believe the offer was made to all peoples but was taken up only by the Jews.

The idea of being chosen brings with it responsibility. The job is to serve G-d though the laws, rather than being chosen giving people privilege.

Jews believe others have responsibilities to G-d too, just different ones to theirs. They will always be the chosen people – an everlasting **covenant**.

> **Covenant**: an agreement between G-d and mankind.

Abraham (formerly Abram)

Who was he?

Abram's father believed in many gods but Abram believe the world was created by One G-d.

He was married to Sarai and told by G-d to go to the Promised Land where He would make them a great nation and Abram the Father of it.

Abram had no children so he took another wife (who gave him a son), then Sarai bore a son too – Isaac (which means 'laughter'). Abram was renamed Abraham (father of many). Sarai became Sarah (princess).

The covenant

G-d promised Abraham land and descendants (hence he is seen as the father of the Jewish nation).

Abraham would only ever worship One G-d and be obedient to Him. The symbol was the circumcision of male babies.

Why is Abraham so important?

This first covenant connected the Jews to G-d before the Torah was written. Abraham had his faith in G-d tested ten times (the last being the sacrifice of his son Isaac). Both he and Isaac passed the test so G-d knew Isaac would carry on his father's work.

Abraham was the founding father of Judaism, and the circumcision of all males unites the children of Israel. For G-d this begins the idea of the 'Promised Land', so giving the Jewish nation a homeland.

For Jews, Abraham is a role model of belief and worship of their One G-d.

> For this course you need to know about **the covenants** with Abraham and Moses. For each covenant, there is a promise made by G-d to His people, a promise made by humans to G-d, and each has a physical sign to seal the agreement.
>
> A covenant (berith) creates a permanent link between the past, present and future that will never be dissolved. G-d needed a people to 'dwell' in, who would serve Him and prepare the world for a future time when all humans would know G-d. If the Jews did this, G-d would never abandon them.

Moses

Who was he?

Moses was born into slavery in Egypt. He was saved from the Pharaoh's order to kill all Israelite babies by being placed in a reed basket in the river. He was found by an Egyptian princess who brought him up. Later he had to flee Egypt after he attacked an Egyptian guard who had attacked an Israelite slave.

Moses was ordered by G-d to set the Israelite people free, and with G-d's help (the Ten Plagues) they were released. He was given the Ten Commandments and the Torah by G-d and led to the Promised Land.

> ### Influences
>
> If I believe G-d set up covenants with my people, then I have to keep to my side of that agreement; following the mitzvot does that. I also feel I have good role models in Abraham and Moses, so can look to their tenacity, humbleness and devotion to G-d and try to also be like that.

The covenant

Moses was given the laws as well as their interpretation. His people promised to follow the laws (the Ten Commandments and the mitzvot). G-d would continue to give the people His blessings as His chosen people. The Sabbath day of rest was the physical symbol.

Why is Moses so important?

Moses freed the Israelite people from slavery. He led the chosen people to the Promised Land so that they were no longer a nomadic people.

He laid down the laws that bind all Jews to G-d and so by their observance Jews continue to serve G-d.

Key quote

Genesis 12:1–3 – The Lord had said to Abram, 'Leave your country, your people and your father's household and go to the Land I will show you. I will make you into a great nation and I will bless you; I will make your name great, and you will be a blessing. I will bless those who bless you, and whoever curses you I will curse; and all peoples on earth will be blessed through you.'

Activity

Support or challenge?

'Covenants do not mean anything in the modern world.' Evaluate this statement. Refer to Judaism in your answer. You should agree and disagree, and come to a justified conclusion.

Use the list of arguments below to help you write a strong answer to the question. They are mixed up though, so first you need to work out which ones agree (support) and which ones disagree (challenge) with the statement. Remember that a conclusion should not just be repeating what has already been said, so it is worth keeping back one argument to use as your reason for agreeing or not. You may have other arguments to use as well.

Argument	Supports statement in question	Challenges statement in question
They were made centuries ago – they are pre-scientific.		
They are eternal because they were made with G-d.		
G-d does not renege on his promises, which is what the covenants are.		
Jews still manage to keep them and observe the outward symbols (circumcision, Sabbath, rainbow) so they are still valid.		
Torah teachings are absolute and eternal, making the covenants relevant for all time.		
Most people are not Jewish and do not recognise these covenants, so they are no longer valid.		

Laws (mitzvot) and reasons for observance

The mitzvot total 613 laws given to Moses. They are the rules of G-d found in the Torah. They govern every aspect of Jewish life, covering rituals of worship and ethics to do with morality. Jews agree to follow them as part of the covenants.

Some laws are judgements, such as 'thou shall not kill'. These are called mishpatim. Some are statutes, that is, laws testing faith. The reasons for these laws and this type of law are known only to G-d.

These laws bind the Jewish nation; the well-being of the nation depends on keeping these laws. Observance of the laws separates Jews from non-Jews, making them a distinct group.

The Ten Commandments

The Ten Commandments are found in Exodus 20:1–17 and repeated in Deuteronomy 5:6–21.

These ten laws are found in the Torah, directed at people for ever. They are a condensed version of the 613 mitzvot written on tablets of stone by G-d for Moses. They are essential to Jewish life to serve G-d and together with the Torah they form the sources of authority for Jewish life.

They are depicted over the ark in the synagogue and are a standard feature of all synagogues, as well as quite often being depicted additionally elsewhere.

Following the Ten Commandments builds society, as it sets a baseline of moral behaviour which, if everyone followed it, would mean harmony and respect from/to/by all. Four of the laws concern G-d and six concern our relationships with each other.

613 mitzvot

Of the 613 laws, 356 are commands to 'not do' and 248 are commands 'to do'. They are listed in the Mishneh Torah written by Malmonides.

These laws are religious laws encompassing all aspects of daily life to build a better person and more harmonious society. The mitzvot cover areas such as food, business practices, punishments, agriculture, clothing, wars, the poor, G-d, rituals, the temple and many more aspects of life.

> ### Influences
> If I believe G-d has given these laws, then I should follow them. By following the laws, I 'walk the right path' and will be rewarded. These laws give structure and security to my actions, which I find comforting.

> ### Activity
> Exodus 20:1–17 is the content of the Ten Commandments. Look it up and make notes.

Now test yourself

1. What are mitzvot?
2. What are mishpatim?
3. Where would you find the Ten Commandments?
4. Why are the Ten Commandments an important set of rules?

Mitzvot between humans and G-d

The mitzvot show G-d reaching out to His people and vice versa.

Jews believe G-d also gave Moses the **Halakah** (an interpretation of the laws). The Halakah is 'the path that one walks' and by following the laws they are doing as G-d wants. Rabbis add to it to keep Jewish life up to date in the modern world.

> **Halakah:** Jewish law – 'the path that one walks'.

There are six constant mitzvot – to know there is a G-d, to not believe in other gods, that G-d is One, to love G-d, to fear G-d and not to be misled by your heart of eyes.

Jews are encouraged not just to believe in G-d but also to know Him (by study) in mind and to love Him (in their hearts). All mitzvot bring Jewish people 'closer' to G-d and so they underpin the whole of Judaism.

Mitzvot between human and human

These laws relate to action towards others – family and neighbours – creating a code of ethics. Each law is also a guiding principle.

If Jews act in a responsible way, G-d is pleased, His goodness flows through people, so G-d and humans are closer. This means the act of serving G-d is fulfilled.

Following the law is 'walking in the path', fulfilling one's part of the covenant and bringing G-d's holiness to the world ready for the time when all humans will know G-d.

Free will and the 613 mitzvot

Free will is having the ability to make decisions and to choose right from wrong. Without free will, actions have no religious or moral value. In the Torah G-d has a role in determining what humans do, but it is also clear that humans choose what to do.

Rewards and punishments follow choices. The 613 mitzvot tell Jews how to do good and avoid evil – humans have the power to do either.

Sometimes humans cannot control what happens but they can control their reaction to it, for example responding to suffering by showing compassion or helping, responding to persecution by standing up against it, being strong rather than giving up in the face of difficulty.

Free will: how do Jews know humans have it?

Genesis says that humans know good from evil. However, knowing good is not a guarantee that humans will do good; punishment follows evil acts. If a person can be punished, then by definition they have had free will to be able to do the punishable act.

Orthodox Jews follow the mitzvot strictly, so their free will is directed to obeying; Reform Jews say some of the mitzvot are open to interpretation, so they use their free will to decide whether to obey.

Activity

Fix it!

Read the answer to this question. Work out how it can be improved.

Explain two Jewish beliefs about the mitzvot. (4 marks)

Jews believe G-d gave them these rules to follow all their lives. They also believe the laws bring a person closer to G-d.

Key moral principles

Tikkun olam – healing the world

Mankind has a responsibility to heal or restore and change the world. On a fundamental level, people do it through keeping Shabbat. This is a day when Jews renew their efforts to bring about a better world. Found in the Mishnah (the first writings of the oral laws by rabbis) it teaches doing actions not because holy texts say so but rather because it helps create social harmony.

Ethical mitzvot show that to be a Jew is to live and work as a collective to create a better world. If these laws are followed then the world will be repaired. The more people who do this, the more the world is repaired and the nearer it is to the **Messianic Age**.

The Aleinu prayer (said three times a day) implies that Jews should heal the world so that the goodness of G-d can shine through. Many Jews pray for the harmony of nations, uniting of people, no more hatred, where the sick are healed and the damage done by humans to humans ends. Through this desire to heal the world Jews hope that their actions will be an inspiration to others to follow suit, whether they are religious or not.

Orthodox Jews believe **tikkun olam** comes from following the mitzvot; Reform Jews believe it needs to be done in a practical way.

> **Chesed**: Hebrew word for loving kindness.
>
> **Messianic Age**: a time on earth with peace and togetherness.
>
> **Tikkun olam**: Hebrew term meaning to repair or heal the world.
>
> **Tzedakah**: charity and giving to the poor, bonded together with justice.

Justice and charity

Micah says G-d requires them to 'only do justice, love kindness and walk humbly with G-d'.

Jews believe their wealth is on loan from G-d. By helping the less fortunate through the means of charity, this brings justice to the poor.

Jewish people believe that giving **tzedakah** brings the power to change the world. This is because when you help people they become more able and empowered, and the injustice they are subject to is made a little less.

Jews support many areas that promote justice – social justice for different races/sexes/disabilities/sexualities. They work for religious freedoms, women's rights, the rights of people to live in a safe world, for example street children in poverty, or the need for American gun laws.

> **Exam tip**
>
> Make sure you know the work of Tzedek as this will give you some practical examples of how Jews work for justice through charity.

Now test yourself

1 What do we mean by 'moral principles'?
2 What is tikkun olam? Give examples.
3 What is tzedakah? Give examples.
4 Why is it important to follow such moral principles as these?

Loving kindness

'The world is built on chesed.' (Psalm 89)

This virtue also contributes to tikkun olam, because out of kindness we try to heal the world. It is central to the commandments as it focuses on people's relationships with each other.

Jews believe that G-d's creation was a clear act of **chesed** and he sustains the world through chesed. The Pirkei Avot states the world stands on the Torah, service of G-d and acts of chesed. The world will always be difficult but chesed can make many situations better. It is the loving intention behind these acts, rather than just doing these acts, that is important.

Chesed is about personal service, personal attitudes and efforts of the heart and includes all aspects of life – people, animals and the environment. Chesed can be done for rich and poor, the living and the dead, and with money and actions. No one should harm another, or take advantage of others' misfortune. This would be the opposite of chesed.

Activity

Read the question and both answers. Which answer is better? Use a highlighter and annotations to show why it is better.

Explain how belief in Tzedakah influences Jews in their lives. (5 marks)

Answer A:

They treat other people with justice. They give money to charity.

Answer B:

'Do only justice' it says in the Book of Micah. So Jews believe that everything they do must be done with fairness, not being unkind or discriminating against anyone. For example, if they owned a shop, they shouldn't cheat their customers by charging unfair prices.

Influences

I believe that tzedakah is a really important attitude to have. It isn't just about charity – believing in justice means I want to help as by giving charity I restore some element of justice. This world, which G-d created, needs to be looked after – tikkun olam – so I try to live in a way which contributes to looking after it.

Activity

Support or challenge?

'The key moral principles are nothing to do with religion.' Evaluate this statement. Refer to Judaism in your answer. You should agree and disagree, and come to a justified conclusion.

Use the list of arguments below to help you write a strong answer to the question. They are mixed up though, so first you need to work out which ones agree (support) and which disagree (challenge) with the statement. Remember that a conclusion should not just be repeating what has already been said, so it is worth keeping one argument back to use as your reason for agreeing or not. You may have other arguments to use as well.

Argument	Supports statement in question	Challenges statement in question
The Jews would disagree as they have religious teachings and duties about them.		
The Jews believe G-d has given humans these as duties, so there is religious motivation in carrying them out.		
Really they are about being a decent person – no religion needed.		
Most humanists would agree with these as basic principles for living.		
By keeping tikkun olam, they believe the Messianic Age comes closer, so are motivated by that.		
Justice is what all modern societies work towards – few of them are religiously motivated.		

The Messiah

What does Messiah mean?

- Not G-d as he will be born of human parents.
- The Hebrew Moshiach means Anointed One.
- Will be a descendant of King David (second king of Israel).
- The term is used in the books of the Torah.

How will the age of the Messiah happen?

- Will be announced by Prophet Elijah.
- Graves will open and the dead will rise.
- A human figure will be sent by G-d to bring in a new era of peace – the Messianic Age.

When will this happen?

- Some Jewish scholars believe G-d has set aside a specific date ... so when G-d decides, really.
- Others say society's conduct has to improve before a Messianic Age can happen.
- Two options: (1) when humans deserve it the most as beliefs and behaviour are better; or (2) when life is so terrible that humans need it the most.

What are Jews told he will be like?

- Will be a great political leader descended from King David who fully understands and keeps Jewish law.
- Will be a charismatic leader who inspires people to follow him.
- Will be a military leader and a righteous judge ... but not a G-d or supernatural.

What will he do?

- He will bring political and spiritual peace to Israel and Jerusalem will be restored.
- A government will be set up in Jerusalem for all peoples of the world.
- He will rebuild the Temple and set up worship as it should be.
- Jewish law and the religious court system will be re-established as the law everywhere.

What will the Messianic Age be like?

- People will live together in peace, with no hatred or intolerance or sin.
- Animals will no longer prey on each other and crops will be plentiful.
- All Jews will return to Israel and all people will recognise the Jewish G-d as the true G-d.
- All people will understand religious truths so religion will no longer divide people.

Note: it is a bit like what people generally believe heaven to be like!

Figure 6 Messiah

Activity

Look at the following exam answer: can you spot the problems with it?

Explain how a belief in the Messiah influences Jews today. [4 marks]

Jews believe that by behaving better, making the world a better place, then the Messiah will come. Others believe that it will happen when the world is so bad G-d will know we totally need his help.

Influences

I believe in the Messiah. His coming depends on us – so I follow the mitzvot, and try to do my bit for making the world a better place. I always live with hope that I will see the Messiah in my lifetime.

Life after death

The is a very difficult topic in Jewish belief as it is clear we know nothing about death and we cannot explain rationally what will happen after death. Life after death is also not a central belief for Jews and there are many different views. But what Jews do agree upon is that this life is not the end of everything.

So, what do Jewish holy books say?

The Torah says nothing about an afterlife; it focuses more on this life now (**Olam ha-ze**). There are references to the righteous being reunited with loved ones and that the not so righteous will not.

Later prophets like Daniel discuss the afterlife in terms of the body being created from dust (so it will decay) but the soul comes from the presence of G-d (so it will live on).

Resurrection

The **resurrection** of the dead is a key belief, though it is not discussed in the Torah. Masorti Jews believe this but say our understanding is too limited to know clear details. Reform Jews believe this too but 'this life now' is more important.

Efforts to repair the world are a way to a good afterlife.

Resurrection will happen in the Messianic Age – the righteous dead will rise and evil people will not be resurrected.

Reincarnation

Some people believe **reincarnation** is happening all the time – souls are reborn to continue tikkun olam (repairing the world) so this should be their focus.

Reincarnation allows the soul to fulfil the mitzvot, showing a compassionate G-d giving the soul a second chance to get it right.

The world to come – Olam ha-ba

Olam ha-ba is like a perfect version of the world that will exist at the end of days after the Messiah has come and G-d has judged the living and the dead. The righteous will rise to Olam ha-ba (the spiritual realm where souls go at death).

Olam ha-ba has to be prepared for by good deeds and knowing the Torah (like the perfect Shabbat). This can be seen in two ways: first, as life after the Messiah, or second, as a place where souls go at death or in the future.

Gan Eden

There is no clear picture as to what this is and how it fits into the afterlife. Some say it's a good place people go when they die.

All nations sit and eat in **Gan Eden** when the peaceful Messianic Age comes.

Gehenna

Gehenna is associated with hell, but it is more a place of cleansing of the soul for less than 12 months, then people move to Olam ha-ba. It is a place to recognise and be remorseful for wrong-doings, not a place for eternal punishment. Anyone who does not live by the Torah will spend time there.

Some Jews think the soul of an evil person ceases to exist after 12 months whereas others believe the soul remains in a state of remorse.

Gan Eden: a place good people go when they die.

Gehenna: a place associated with hell.

Olam ha-ba: the world that is to come.

Olam ha-ze: life in the present, here and now.

Reincarnation: the rebirth of the soul.

Resurrection: a physical coming back of the body to life after death.

Influences

I am not sure what will happen after death, so I live now as if something will! I worship G-d my Creator, I treat others with respect and kindness, I live by the commandments. It is important to be a good person, but also to show devotion to G-d.

Pikuach nefesh

REVISED

This is the belief that the saving/preservation of human life takes precedence over everything because 'life is sacred'.

The sanctity of human life

G-d made humans special – He breathed life into them, gave them free will and gave them a soul. The human task was to carry out tikkun olam and to work for a close relationship with G-d. The human soul is made in the image of G-d.

Life is sacred even beyond the law, so rules can be broken to save it – even Shabbat rules!

Each Jewish person has a purpose – to live as G-d wants through the Torah and the mitzvot. Their aim is to change and repair the world from evil and horror to peace and harmony. They have a duty to make the most of the gift of life.

No human can take life, unless in self-defence, state punishment or war.

So how does pikuach nefesh work?

In the Talmud there is the idea that people 'live' by the law – it protects life and helps them survive. So where laws may cause harm (for example, by a doctor not helping someone because the Shabbat laws do not allow him to work), the law must be set aside because 'saving life' is more important.

Jews are required to break the law in cases where life is at risk, whether it is animal or human. If it is unclear whether life is actually at risk then action should be taken as if it is because waiting might cause more harm.

> **Exam tip**
>
> It is not always easy to apply this law in the modern world. For your exam you can use these beliefs in topics about life/death but you have to balance them out with the idea that sometimes taking life can prevent far more suffering in the long term. Think about the four ethical themes you have studied – there is no harm in using these ideas with those topics. It will show you have the ability to apply connections and show how beliefs affect decisions people make.

> **Revision tip**
>
> Try using mind-mapping diagrams as a way to remember all the topics. Look at the simple one in Figure 7, covering all the Judaism beliefs topics. As the diagram becomes wider, more information is added. The law section has been started for you. Try your own as all our minds work differently – use the words/colours that will help *you*.
>
>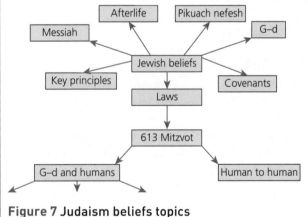
>
> **Figure 7 Judaism beliefs topics**

It also applies to occasions where life-shortening issues occur – organ donation is allowed to continue the life of the patient (as long as the giver's life is not at risk). Autopsies can also be done if the knowledge gained from them helps saves lives in the future.

In the world today Jews are involved in pikuach nefesh – as health workers, aid workers, environmental campaigners, police and fire services, and peacekeeping soldiers, for example.

> **Now test yourself**
>
> 1 What does 'pikuach nefesh' mean?
> 2 Explain the Jewish concept of sanctity of life.
> 3 How does pikuach nefesh impact on daily life for Jews?
>
> TESTED

Answers at **www.hoddereducation.co.uk/myrevisionnotesdownloads**

Exam practice

What questions on this section look like:

Judaism: Beliefs and teachings

This page contains a range of questions that could be on an exam paper. Practise them all to strengthen your knowledge and technique while revising. Check back to pages 13–14 to see the marking grids that examiners use: this will help you to mark your answers.

1 What is meant by chesed?

  (a) Justice   (b) Charity   (c) Loving kindness   (d) Repairing the world   [1]

2 Which of the following means 'the world to come'?

  (a) Tikkun olam   (b) Gehenna   (c) Gan Eden   (d) Olam ha-ba   [1]

3 Name two prophets G-d made covenants with.   [2]

4 Give two types of mitzvot.   [2]

5 Give two reasons Jews believe tikkun olam is important.   [2]

6 Explain two ways in which a belief in the law influences Jews today.   [4]

7 Explain two ways in which a belief in 'loving kindness' influences Jews today.   [4]

8 Explain two ways in which a belief in pikuach nefesh influences Jews today.   [4]

9 Explain two ways in which a belief in G-d as creator influences Jews today.   [4]

10 Explain two Jewish teachings about Shechinah (the Divine Presence). Refer to sacred writings or another source of Jewish belief and teachings in your answer.   [5]

11 Explain two Jewish teachings about G-d as law-giver and judge. Refer to sacred writings or another source of Jewish belief and teachings in your answer.   [5]

12 Explain two Jewish teachings about the importance of the covenants. Refer to sacred writings or another source of Jewish belief and teachings in your answer.   [5]

13 'Mitzvot between man and G-d should the most important mitzvot for Jews today.' Evaluate this statement. In your answer you should:
- refer to Jewish teaching
- give reasoned arguments to support this statement
- give reasoned arguments to support a different point of view
- reach a justified conclusion.   [12]

14 'Life here and now is more important than the afterlife for Jews today.' Evaluate this statement. In your answer you should:
- refer to Jewish teaching
- give reasoned arguments to support this statement
- give reasoned arguments to support a different point of view
- reach a justified conclusion.   [12]

15 'It is impossible to repair the world so the Messianic Age will never happen.' Evaluate this statement. In your answer you should:
- refer to Jewish teaching
- give reasoned arguments to support this statement
- give reasoned arguments to support a different point of view
- reach a justified conclusion.   [12]

ONLINE

Commentary

Grade 2 students have limited knowledge of the content of the course. They struggle to recognise key terms and so find some questions difficult because they don't understand the central term. If this is you, learn key words to begin to help yourself.

Grade 5 students have general knowledge of the topics, so they recognise most of the key terms. Their understanding of them may be limited, so they don't go into detail often enough. If this is you, practise by making yourself explain everything, which comes from understanding the content better.

Grade 8 students have a strong understanding of the content and know the key terms well. They use more than just the obvious terms and use them showing good understanding and application. Their answers are detailed and clear.

1.4 Judaism: Section 2 – Practices

The law

REVISED

Judaism governs all aspects of life via the TeNaKh (**Torah**, **Nevi'im** and **Ketuvim**) plus the **Talmud**. TeNaKh is the name for the full set of holy scriptures of Judaism: the law, Prophets and the Writings.

The Torah

The Torah is the religious law of Judaism. It has divine origins as it was given by G-d to Moses on Mount Sinai. The Torah links G-d and humanity. It is is absolute (never-changing) and eternal (forever valid).

The mitzvot 'separate' Jews from others as they are part of the Covenant. They contain two types of laws: mishpatim (judgements) and chukim (statutes).

During a year in the synagogue the whole Torah will be read in 54 portions. Study of the Torah is essential and many Orthodox Jews devote their lives to this.

Purpose for today: Torah means 'guidance' or 'instruction' – by following its rules Jews stay close to G-d.

The Ketuvim

The 'writings' are unconnected books, containing poetry, historical stories, songs and philosophical debates.

Five of the books are used at five festivals – Pesach (Song of Songs), Shavuot (Ruth), Tishah B'Av (Lamentations), Sukkot (Ecclesiastes) and Purim (Ester).

Purpose for today: the underlying theme shows people commitment to G-d through endless difficulties and hard work.

The Nevi'im

This consists of books containing the stories and teachings of the prophets. Prophets are chosen by G-d to guide people and warn about their behaviour.

Purpose for today: they provide the historical story of early Judaism, religious interpretations of the events and revelations from G-d. They also allow people to see the character of G-d through reading the stories.

The Talmud

The Torah is timeless but difficult to apply throughout time. The Talmud relates today's problems to Torah law, interpreting the laws so they are more easily understood and followed.

Talmud means 'study' – greater study brings greater understanding, allowing Jews to follow the laws better. It has been called an endless conversation through time about the law.

The Talmud has in it the **Mishnah** (a study of the law) and the **Gemara** (a commentary on the Mishnah). The Mishnah sits in the centre of each page, flanked by sections of commentaries to help understanding. There are also Torah references so the reader can see what the study is about. The variety of commentaries and references show how Jewish thought and understanding have developed through time.

The Talmud keeps Jewish law and understanding up to date and applied to modern issues. Hence the Jewish Torah is always applicable and relevant.

> **Exam tip**
>
> Make sure you can give reasons for:
> - why each of the Torah (and its parts) and the Talmud could be said to be the most important texts for Jews
> - why either may be all that is necessary to understand what G-d wants humans to do
> - why/how holy books written years ago are relevant to believers in the modern world.

Jewish dietary law (1)

Kashrut means people and actions that cover Jewish religious requirements. The requirements are laid down mainly in Leviticus 11 and Deuteronomy 14.

Jewish people must keep kosher – a set of rules about animals that are 'fit' or acceptable to eat. Food not fit to eat or unclean is Treyfah. Acceptable animals must be slaughtered in the correct way to maintain kosher, but not all parts of kosher animals are kosher to eat.

The basic principles are that animals that have both split hooves (feet) and chew the cud (eat grass), fish with fins and scales, clean birds (poultry), that is those which do not consume other creatures, are acceptable. The pig is considered unclean. Any animal that has died naturally cannot be eaten (as it will not have been ritually slaughtered). Eggs also have to be checked as some have a blood spot in them.

Vegetables are a neutral food (parev) so after being washed clean they are fine to eat with anything. There are rules about not eating milk and meat products together, and rules covering food preparation and use of cooking implements.

Dietary laws are observed in a variety of ways today, with some Jews following them loosely, others taking a stricter approach.

Jews often have separate sinks, fridges, cupboards, pans and utensils to keep meat and milk apart. This in effect means a double kitchen which many Jews cannot afford or fit in their house, but many strictly Orthodox Jews do this to the letter of the law.

Keeping kosher is part of being Jewish, reminding them of their connection with G-d, who is their creator.

> **Gemara**: a commentary on the Mishnah.
>
> **Ketuvim**: Books of Writings.
>
> **Mishnah**: a study of Jewish law.
>
> **Nevi'im**: Books of the Prophets.
>
> **Talmud**: written interpretation of all Jewish civil and religious laws.
>
> **Torah**: law consisting of five Books.

> **Kashrut**: term used to denote Jewish food law.

Activity

Support or challenge?

'It is not important to keep kashrut for Jews today.' Evaluate this statement. Refer to Judaism in your answer. You should agree and disagree, and come to a justified conclusion.

Use the list of arguments below to help you write a strong answer to that question. They are mixed up though, so first you need to work out which ones agree (support) and which ones disagree (challenge) with the statement. Remember that a conclusion should not just repeat what has already been said, so it is worth keeping back one argument to use as your reason for agreeing or not.

Argument	Supports statement in question	Challenges statement in question
Kashrut is commanded in the mitzvot.		
Kashrut is part of the covenant with G-d.		
It is more important to live by the moral principles of Judaism in today's world.		
The laws are so old that they should be ignored today.		
Many Jews do not keep the food laws, or keep them only partially, or are selective about when they keep them.		
Keeping kashrut reminds a Jew at every contact with food (buying, preparing, eating) of their connection to G-d.		

Jewish dietary law (2)

Ritual slaughter
- There are two key criteria – the animal must be one allowed by scripture *and* have been slaughtered in the right way.
- An animal must have been killed by the **shochet**, using a sharp blade to cut the neck with one stroke of the blade. This causes quick blood loss and death, which is humane for the animal.
- Kosher butchers are regulated by the **Bet Din**.

Draining of blood
- Blood is the life of the animal (Leviticus 17:11) and is forbidden to Jews.
- The shochet will remove most of the blood from the meat.
- Within 72 hours of slaughter the rest of the blood is removed by **broiling**, soaking or salting.
- Most meat has had this done by the butcher, but many Jews still salt meat before cooking.

Meat and milk
- The Torah commands: 'Do not boil a kid in its mother's milk.'
- The Talmud explains this as no cooking or eating the mixture of meat and milk.
- There should be no meat and milk in the same meal or within six hours of each other.
- It is believed this act shows compassion as to have a mother seeing their child, or vice versa, being cooked/eaten would be cruel, hence this provided dignity and sanctity to both lives.

Jewish cuisine
- Cuisine varies according to region and is influenced by the culture within which it develops.
- Ashkenazi Jews based in north-eastern Europe have food that is very distinctive from that of Sephardi Jews based in Spain and the Mediterranean.

> **Bet Din**: rabbinical court, the remit of which includes checking kosher butchers and awarding kosher status.
>
> **Broiling**: cooking something by direct heat.
>
> **Shochet**: a qualified kosher slaughterer.

Issues of living in a non-Jewish country

Most Jews live outside Israel so it is not surprising that in other countries they often live in large Jewish communities, making it possible to access kosher foods. Nevertheless, there is still the issue of non-kosher meat/foods on display and being served.

Some differences
- Many Jews keep a strict kosher diet, using Jewish butchers and shops, for example; many Jews only lightly observe kashrut though, for example not scrutinising packets to check the contents are kosher, or even eating non-kosher foods.
- Some Jews will have one set of dishes and kitchen utensils, which they ritually clean for Pesach; most have two sets (one just for Pesach).
- The cuisine of Ashkenazi Jews is quite different from that of Sephardi Jews.

> **Exam tip**
>
> Remember that there are no 'describe' questions in your exam so you need to know the above information and be able to apply it – to show the impact it has on Jewish life. For example, to explain two ways in which keeping kosher is important in a Jew's life. The answer would focus on why kosher is important, not what it is.

Synagogue and worship

Why is the synagogue important?

Synagogue means 'bringing together', emphasising community worship of G-d. It is a house of worship, a place for specific prayers to be said. It is also a place to study the word of G-d, so it is known as shul.

Jews have always had a 'special place' to worship – Moses built a tabernacle, Solomon built a temple. The last temple was destroyed in Jerusalem in 70CE. Away from Jerusalem, Jews worship in synagogues, which are representative of that one temple.

A minyan (ten members) must be present for worship to take place. A synagogue has a community use and links the faith now to Jewish history and traditions.

A synagogue has various key features. On the outside there is the Star of David (a five-pointed star) symbol and the menorah (the seven-branched candlestick). On the inside are the following:

- Aron hakodesh – Ark of the Covenant, housing the Torah and other scrolls. This represents the Holy of Holies, the most sacred part of the temple when it stood and before that the tabernacle.
- A cupboard in the Eastern Wall facing Jerusalem covered by a curtain (parokhet) to safeguard and glorify its contents. Lions of Judah holding the Ten Commandments are above it.
- Ner Tamid – this represents the ever-burning lamp in the tabernacle, showing that the Torah should always have meaning – a light in the world's darkness. Traditionally an oil lamp, it is seen as a symbol of Israel as the 'light of nations'.
- Bimah – this is a raised platform from which the Sefer Torah is read. It represents the sanctuary in the temple and that the teachings should go out to the entire world.

Worship

It is important to worship as it:
- forms part of the covenant, is a mitzvot and so a duty
- keeps people mindful of G-d and shows their devotion
- shows G-d worship and praise
- brings the community together.

Worship is important both in the synagogue and in the home. Synagogue worship includes Shabbat services, daily services, festivals, rites of passage, study, holocaust memorials, etc. Worship at home includes Shabbat meals/prayers, study, circumcisions, variety of prayer and thanksgivings, etc.

Key elements include:
- Dress:
  - Orthodox males wear kippah, tallit and tefillin, whereas Reform Jews usually wear just a kippah.
- People:
  - The rabbi is the spiritual leader, a learned man of scripture and law who has attended Yeshivah. Reform allows women to this role too.
  - The cantor sings prayers and often leads worship.
- Structure:
  - The synagogue is centred around different prayers from the siddur (prayer book) and chamash (printed Torah).
  - Key prayers are the Shema, the Amidah, the Kaddish and the Aleinu.
  - On Shabbat, both Torah and prophecies will be read.

Influences

When I worship, I do so with others – this reminds me of our link to and need for others in our lives. The synagogue is a community – I can always find help, which makes me offer help to others as well.

Some differences

- Orthodox Jews use the name 'shul', Reform Jews use 'temple' and Masorti use 'synagogue'.
- Seating: Orthodox – women sit separately, all face the Bimah, which is central to the room; Reform – all sit together, all face the Ark and Bimah at the front of the room.

All about prayer

The Hebrew word for prayer is tefillah. It is a time for reflection on a person's relationship with G-d and each other and on how they are following their duties. Prayers are found in the Siddur (prayer book) and along with teachings of rabbis and minhagim (traditions) prayers have been shaped over the centuries.

Prayers

Shema

- Jewish declaration of faith: *'Hear O Israel, the lord your G-d is One G-d.'* Must be recited three times daily.
- Taken directly from verses in the Torah.
- Three sections follow the statement – about G-d and religious duties, accepting and keeping the law, and then keeping the mitzvot to wear tzitzit.
- Reform Jews do not include the last two of those sections.

Amidah

- Amidah means 'standing'. It is said stood facing Jerusalem.
- 19 blessings: 3 for praise, 13 requests and 3 thanksgiving.
- Spoken with the movement of lips rather than out loud – the sound comes from the heart.

Kaddish

- Kaddish means 'holy' – a hymn of praise to G-d.
- Can only be recited if there is a minyan; said each prayer time each day in the synagogue. It begins 'May His great name be exalted ...'.
- There are different kaddishes for different occasions.

Aleinu

- A prayer to praise G-d and restates a Jew's dedication to G-d.
- Reminds them that G-d's rule is eternal.
- Reminds them that they are the chosen people and that choosing brings with it difficulties.
- Said at the end of services.

Clothing

Prayer is done at home as well as in the synagogue. At home prayers are more personal and do not require a minyan. People must be in the right mindset (kavanah) and dressed in a respectful way for G-d.

A kippah, also called a yarmulke, is a small cap worn by Jewish men. Women also cover their heads, as a sign of respect.

A tallit is a prayer shawl worn around the shoulders. It has four corners for the four corners of the world. Each corner has tzitzit – fringes tied with five knots in them (5 + 5 on each side representing the Ten Commandments). Fringes hang loose to represent the 613 mitzvot. All are reminders of G-d's law being all around them and not to be forgotten.

Tefillin are two small leather boxes with straps, one on the forehead, one on the arm. Each contains a passage of scripture. As the items are put on, prayers are said to focus the mind. The box on the arm points to the heart, reminding of G-d's love, and the one on the head is symbolic of being aware of G-d.

When to pray

Minchah is the afternoon prayer following Isaac's timing of prayer. Maariv is the evening prayer following Jacob's timing.

It is a mitzvot, shows devotion, sets people up for the day in the right way, and links Jews to their history. It is a cleansing act and a channel of communication with G-d.

Exam tip

There is a lot of key language in this topic that could feature in the 1/2-mark questions. Make sure you know of each item and why each is important.

Shabbat

Shabbat is the Jewish day of rest, beginning at sundown on Friday and ending on Saturday evening. It is a commandment to keep it holy, part of the Jewish covenant with G-d. It is a reminder that G-d created the world and copying G-d's example of resting from work.

What does no work mean?
- The Talmud forbids 39 areas of work on Shabbat.
- Work covers melachah tasks (those which are creative or change one's environment).
- Remember, the principle of pikuach nefesh overrides Shabbat rules for work.

The order of Shabbat

Getting ready:
- The house is tidied, food is already made, table set.
- Arrangements have to be made to ensure no work need be done.

Shabbat begins:
- No later than 18 minutes before sunset, before the meal, two candles are lit. The mother passes her hands over her eyes and recites the blessing to welcome Shabbat.
- Two candles are zakhor and shamor (remember Shabbat and observe Shabbat).
- The family attend synagogue (mostly the men only in Orthodox and Masorti traditions), Shabbat prayers are said (Kabbalat – six chapters from Psalms, then the maariv prayer and seven Amidah blessings – 12 petitions are omitted as Shabbat provides for all).
- The family return for a family meal during which children are blessed, **Kiddush** is recited and prayers are said over the wine to make Shabbat holy. The bread (challah) is blessed and songs are sung. It ends with a blessing.
- The rest of evening is for family time.

Kiddush: a blessing/ritual using wine.

On the Saturday:
- The whole family attend the synagogue after the rituals of Kiddush and the two challah have been repeated.
- The reading of the Torah is central to this service after having been paraded around the synagogue from the Ark to the Bimah.
- The message of the part read from the Torah is the theme of the sermon.
- The service is from the Siddur so everyone can follow it.
- Kiddush is shared at the end of the service, usually wine and cake.
- Orthodox Jews may spend the day in study of the Torah; for others it is family time.
- Shabbat ends with the Havdalah blessings recited over wine, candles and spices. Lighting candles is an act of work so indicates the separation of the Shabbat from other days.

Importance

This is a sacred time for all the family. It is a day of rest, separating this day from the other six in the week – a day to be 'right with G-d'. Religion is the focus of the day, giving time to study and reflect.

Shabbat brings the family and community together, and shows respect, devotion and duty to G-d. It also shows that all Jews are bound by the covenant promises, and honours tradition (minhag).

Now test yourself

1 Describe what happens at Shabbat.
2 Explain at least two differences in practice between Jewish groups in the way they celebrate Shabbat.
3 Explain two ways that Shabbat is important for Jews today.
4 Explain why in Judaism it is necessary to have this separate day.
5 Explain the influence Shabbat celebration has on the lives of Jews.

TESTED

Rites of passage

Jews mark certain stages in life with a special celebration. They all have religion at the centre of those celebrations. The celebrations unite the religion in its past, present and future.

Birth ceremonies

For boys, the **brit milah** ceremony happens eight days after birth. It takes place at home or in shul as soon as morning prayer is done and a minyan can be present. The boy is circumcised as a sign of the covenant and the way in which the male becomes part of the Jewish faith.

A **mohel** attends the home. The father wears his tallit and tefillin as a symbol of the commandments. The boy is given to a **sandek** (special male) who holds the child while the circumcision is carried out. Candles are lit to remember the room being lit up when Moses was born.

The mohel blesses the child, the father reads a passage from the Torah and then, on completion of the circumcision, the boy's name is announced. The boy is then fed by his mother and a celebratory meal is enjoyed.

In Sephardic and Italian communities the tradition of welcoming girls is called zaved habit (gift of a daughter). It is customary to name the girl in the synagogue after the father has been called to the Torah on the first Shabbat after her birth. The congregation sings to welcome her; the family provide Kiddush in celebration.

Reform Jews take the girl to Shabbat services but in other communities she stays at home where a rabbi will come to bless her.

> **Brit milah**: birth ceremony for a boy in Judaism.
>
> **Mohel**: man trained to carry out circumcision.
>
> **Sandek**: male person, specially chosen to hold the boy in the brit milah ceremony.

Bar mitzvah:
- Means 'son of the commandment' – it recognises that the boy has reached the age by which he is religiously responsible = a 'coming of age'.
- Boy reads the Torah in the synagogue on the Shabbat after his 13th birthday.
- He is now regarded as an adult, using tefillin in prayer, and can be counted in a minyan. His father no longer has the responsibility to bring up his son religiously.

Bat mitzvah:
- Usually takes place at 12 years of age; means 'daughter of the commandment'.
- For Orthodox Jews it takes place at home, with the girl reciting a blessing.
- For Reform Jews the girl may read from the Torah in the synagogue.

These ceremonies are important because the child consciously steps into the responsibility of being one with G-d's chosen people and confirms their wish to carry on in the religion. They also reinforce the togetherness of the community.

Now test yourself

TESTED

1. List the differences in the ceremonies for boys and girls.
2. Give two ways in which the birth ceremonies are important.
3. Give two reasons why a bar/bat mitzvah is important for the individual.

Answers at **www.hoddereducation.co.uk/myrevisionnotesdownloads**

Marriage

Marriage is a blessing from G-d. It is the most elaborate ceremony, full of custom and tradition. It fulfils the commandment in Genesis to 'be fruitful and multiply'.

Jews believe that marriage is the natural state for humans and the place to bring up children. So it is an expectation of all Jews to marry and have children. It helps an individual to overcome loneliness and is seen as the 'completion' of each other for the couple.

The marriage ceremony in brief

The ceremony takes place under a wedding canopy (huppah). The bride and groom recite blessings over wine and give/exchange rings. The ketubah (marriage contract) is signed before witnesses, then the rabbi gives a speech about marriage, followed by further blessings.

After sharing a glass of wine, the groom crushes a glass underfoot. Finally, the couple share some private time.

There are different cultural traditions:
- Before the ceremony: Orthodox couples do not see each other for a week before marriage, whereas for other Jews it is just the day before that they do not meet.
- Aufruf: on the Shabbat morning before the wedding, Orthodox grooms are called to read the Torah in the synagogue. They are showered with sweets and nuts to symbolise that their sins are forgiven and all is good.
- Kabbalat Panim: Orthodox Jews have separate receptions before the wedding for men and women. The groom is toasted for health and happiness. The bride sits on a throne to greet guests. The mother-in-law breaks some pottery to show damage cannot be repaired so marriages must be worked at.
- Veiling the bride: Ashkenazi brides are personally veiled by the groom until after they reach the huppah. This recalls two stories – first, that Rebecca was veiled before marrying Isaac; second, that Jacob was tricked into marrying Leah when he should have married Rachel because she was veiled and so he could not see her. In Reform and Masorti traditions, the bride places a kippah on the groom's head or cloaks him with tallit.
- Circling the huppah: Orthodox do this seven times, others three times.

Activity

Which is better?

Explain two contrasting rituals which Jews celebrate during the marriage ceremony.   (4 marks)

Read these answers. Decide which is better, and why. Then write your own better answer.

Answer A:

Some Jews walk round the huppah seven times; some do it three. Some Jewish grooms cover the wives' faces while they walk to the huppah because they want to be sure who they are marrying. Really they do know – it is just a tradition dating back to when Jacob married the wrong sister because she was covered up before he saw her.

Answer B:

Orthodox Jews walk around the huppah seven times, whilst Reform Jews walk around it three times. Orthodox Jews also have aufruf, which is where the groom goes to the synagogue to recite from the Torah before his marriage; others don't.

Death and mourning

1. *The person dies.* Their eyes are closed to close off this life, allowing them to see the next life. The body is covered and placed on the ground. Candles are lit and placed at the head so that the body will be watched until burial when the soul departs. No one knows when the soul leaves, hence the kindness of sitting with the body. The body is prepared for death by the Hevrah Kadishah, washed and dressed in white linen. Men are wrapped in their tallit, with the tzitzit removed (they are no longer bound by the mitzvot).	2. *Burial.* This happens as soon as possible after death. The body is interred in a wooden casket. The keria'ah ritual sees the mourners' garments torn or a strip of black ribbon worn. The casket is carried to the grave with seven stops along the way. It is lowered into the grave, with the head facing east (towards Jerusalem). The prayer of mercy is recited. The grave is filled by those present to show service and love. The men form lines for the bereaved to pass through. A meal is provided by friends/neighbours as a form of comfort.
3. *Mourning (aninut).* This comes between death and burial. The bereaved are excused from all religious duties. Shiv'ah lasts for seven days after burial for parents/children. They sit on low stools and are not allowed to work. Aninut still applies. People visit after three days to comfort, bring gifts and say prayers. It is common to take food to the bereaved – the community looks after them. During the 30 days of Sheloshim (including the seven of Shiv'ah) some restrictions are lifted and work can be resumed. Avelut is the next 11 months during which mourning continues for a parent. Kiddush is recited at the synagogue, helping the dead be released from any sins.	4. *Remembering the dead.* Families must buy a gravestone so that the dead cannot be forgotten. Yahrzeit is the anniversary of the death of a parent. Fasting is done. A memorial candle is lit for 24 hours. Donations of tzedakah are made. The Yizkor memorial prayer is recited by mourners on special days in the year.

For Jews, the mourning period is very much about supporting the bereaved, making them see they are not alone. While a person mourns, their community rallies round.

Some differences

- Funerals can take place at the grave, at a synagogue or at the funeral home.
- Those in attendance at the funeral will make a tear in clothes (Orthodox), or wear a black ribbon (Reform).

Activity

Support or challenge?

Read the answer to this question and improve it, including by adding more arguments.

'Jewish mourning rituals are more about the bereaved than the dead.' Evaluate this statement. Refer to Judaism in your answer. You should agree and disagree, reaching a justified conclusion.

Some might agree because the community looks after the bereaved.[1] The bereaved are sad and need the comfort and help of others, but this isn't true of the dead.[2] Also the rituals are mainly to do with the bereaved doing things and following rules.[3]

However, others would disagree. They sit with the body until it is buried.[4] They wash and prepare the body.[5] All the rituals are designed to remember the dead and show respect to them.[6]

In conclusion, I think that because the dead person is the centre of everything – it is done to or about them – then it is the dead, not the bereaved, that these rituals are for.

[1] How?

[2] Explain this.

[3] Examples?

[4] Why?

[5] Expand this.

[6] How?

Answers at **www.hoddereducation.co.uk/myrevisionnotesdownloads**

Rosh Hashanah (Jewish New Year)

This is the High Holy Day on the first day of the month of Tishri and begins a ten-day period of reflection and repentance, during which focus is on individuals' behaviour on earth (their keeping of the commandments).

The festival represents the day of creation. Jews believe all people will stand before G-d to be judged on their actions in the past year. Hoping to receive mercy, the next ten days are a chance to make sure of it.

Jews believe the righteous gain another year, the wicked do not, and others have the chance over Rosh Hashanah to make repentance and secure another year.

Key customs

There is a special midnight service on the Shabbat before Rosh Hashanah, involving the blowing of the shofar – a call to repentance – and reciting the Tashlich – casting of sins into the water in the hope that G-d will forgive.

The first night is totally dedicated to prayer, meditation and soul-searching. Celebration meals take place using sweet foods like honey.

Key beliefs and importance for Jews today

Jews are seeking repentance and mercy for lapses of faith/behaviour to show they deserve more time on earth as their lives are productive and their actions good. No one is so far away from G-d that they cannot find their way back to Him.

Rosh Hashanah highlights that deeds on earth are very important, rather than focusing on an afterlife. Carrying out tikkun olam and keeping the commandments are essential deeds.

Yom Kippur

This is the Day of Atonement, referred to in Leviticus 'to cleanse from sins'. It is a day of confession, to cast out sins and make heartfelt resolutions to sin no more.

The day brings pardon from G-d; forgiveness comes only if there is an attempt to repair any damage.

Key events

The Kol Nidre service takes place and the prayer asks for release from all pledges to G-d in recognition that not all promises made can be kept.

There is a day of fasting (25 hours) which can be difficult but people should remain cheerful. White garments are worn.

On this day the book of life closes so people gain another year – they thank G-d for being loving and merciful for releasing all their sin.

All synagogue services have the theme of confession and repentance.

Key beliefs and importance for Jews today

This is the completion of a year, like a new start. It shows that everyone can find their way back to G-d, but being truly repentant is important.

The atonement on this day is about sins between man and G-d rather than sins between each other (these have to be put right before Yom Kippur).

Some differences

- Orthodox Jews observe Rosh Hashanah for two days; many Reform observe it for just one.
- While it is common to eat challah bread or apples dipped in honey before the Rosh Hashanah meal, some Jews also eat pomegranates (the seeds reflecting the number of good deeds to be done in the next year).

Activity

Fix it!

Read the question and both answers. Which answer is better?
Use a highlighter and annotations to show why it is better.

Explain two ways in which Jews celebrate Rosh Hashanah. (4 marks)

Jews go to the synagogue and a shofar is blown. This is a ram's horn. It sounds sad, so is showing repentance – being sorry for what you have done wrong. That also means you want to be forgiven by G-d.

Pesach

Pesach is a festival of joy. All Jewish traditions celebrate in the same way. It is one of the three pilgrim festivals where a Jew had to attend temple for sacrifice. It is celebrated for seven days in Israel, or eight outside Israel. The festival today reinforces key customs which have enriched home life, as well as emphasising the religion and its links with history.

Origins

- Pesach remembers the Israelite people taken out of slavery in Egypt 3000 years ago.
- The belief that G-d will always come to the rescue is essential, Pesach being an example.
- Jews appreciate that the freedoms they have today were given by G-d, and that they should fight for freedom for all.
- There is the hope of 'next year in Jerusalem' – the hope that Jerusalem will be rebuilt as the spiritual centre of the world.

The seder meal – key points

The seder meal is held on the first or second night of Pesach following instructions from the Haggadah book, which tells the story of the Israelites and the Passover. This provides readings, hymns of thanks, symbolic explanations of scripture and a song of divine retribution which G-d brings for the mistreatment of the Israelites.

The leader of the meal wears a kittel (a white linen gown), which celebrates freedom from the Egyptians. The table is set with three matzah, wine and seder plates. The matzah is unleavened to remember the Israelites not having time to bake bread before they escaped Egypt.

On the seder plate the maror represents the enslavement of the Israelites, karpas (vegetables) represents the tears of the slaves, charoset represents the mortar made by the Israelite slaves, the shankbone represents the mighty arm of G-d and the pascal lamb sacrifice, and a roasted egg represents the temple sacrifice.

Preparing for Pesach

- On the morning before Pesach, the first-born son attends synagogue to study a portion of the Talmud.
- Most Jews give to charity (maot chitim).
- Chametz is removed – ten pieces of bread, which had been hidden round the house to be collected the previous evening by the father and children, are wrapped and burned before Pesach starts.
- Homes are spring cleaned, new clothes bought, special meals prepared so that the occasion is joyful.

Wine is drunk and ten drops are spilled, representing the ten plagues. An extra cup is set for Elijah (to be used if a stranger turns up). Elijah is a reminder of the Messianic Age.

The door is opened twice at the end of the meal to show the belief in the protection of G-d from harmful forces.

Key concepts of Pesach

The key concepts of Pesach are:
- memory: the past gives Jewish lives purpose/ meaning and a better future
- hope: without it the Israelites would not have survived
- faith: the Jews are blessed with support from a caring G-d, giving optimism for self, now and the future
- family: learning about the past strengthens the sense of belonging to the faith
- responsibility to others: the experience of the Israelites shows Jews need to care for those in need.

Exam practice

What questions on this section look like:

Judaism: Practices

This page contains a range of questions that could be on an exam paper. Practise them all to strengthen your knowledge and technique while revising. Check back to pages 13–14 to see the marking grids that examiners use: this will help you to mark your answers.

1 What is meant by kosher?
   (a) Lawful   (b) Forbidden   (c) Blessing   (d) Legal document for marriage   [1]

2 Which of the following is the Oral Law?
   (a) Torah   (b) Tefillin   (c) Talmud   (d) Tenakh   [1]

3 Give two rules about milk and meat.   [2]

4 Give two things that Jews do on the Friday Shabbat.   [2]

5 Name two prayers used by Jews.   [2]

6 Explain two similar features of Jewish synagogues.   [4]

7 Explain two contrasting ways in which a boy's bar mitzvah and a girl's bat mitzvah are carried out.   [4]

8 Explain two contrasting features of a Jewish wedding in two Jewish traditions.   [4]

9 Explain two similar Jewish rituals about the burial of the dead.   [4]

10 Explain two ways in which Shabbat is important in the life of a Jew. Refer to sacred writings or another source of Jewish belief and teachings in your answer.   [5]

11 Explain two ways in which the Talmud is important in Jewish life. Refer to sacred writings or another source of Jewish belief and teachings in your answer.   [5]

12 Explain two ways in which prayer is important for Jews. Refer to sacred writings or another source of Jewish belief and teachings in your answer.   [5]

13 'Jewish mourning is more about supporting the living than remembering the dead.' Evaluate this statement. In your answer you should:
- refer to Jewish teaching
- give reasoned arguments to support this statement
- give reasoned arguments to support a different point of view
- reach a justified conclusion.   [12]

14 'Pesach is more important than Rosh Hashanah.' Evaluate this statement. In your answer you should:
- refer to Jewish teaching
- give reasoned arguments to support this statement
- give reasoned arguments to support a different point of view
- reach a justified conclusion.   [12]

15 'Rites of passage in Judaism are outdated.' Evaluate this statement. In your answer you should:
- refer to Jewish teaching
- give reasoned arguments to support this statement
- give reasoned arguments to support a different point of view
- reach a justified conclusion.   [12]

ONLINE ☐

Commentary

Grade 2 students have a weak knowledge of the similarities and differences within a faith. Questions asking about these are very difficult. If this is you, make some notes about two similarities and two differences for each element and then learn them.

Grade 5 students can point out similarities and differences within the faith, although their answers will lack depth. It is often the case they know 'some', so the exam can be very testing if it doesn't fit what they know. If this is you, then you need to do more work on learning these aspects.

Grade 8 students know about a religion in depth. They can write easily and clearly about similarities and differences within the faith.

Key terms from the Specification

As you worked through the guide, you met lots of key terms. A good idea is to go back and create an RS dictionary of your own. On the exam, if asked to define a word, it must come from the Specification, so these are those words/phrases.

Buddhism

REVISED

Ascetic: a life spent in extreme self-discipline and denying oneself any indulgence.

Buddha: Siddhartha Gotama; means 'awakened one'.

Buddha nature: idea that all beings have the potential within them to become Buddha.

Buddha rupa: statue of Buddha.

Dhamma: the teaching of the Buddha.

Dhammapada: collected sayings/teachings of the Buddha.

Enlightenment: Nirvana – ceasing to be bound by the wheel of samsara; full realisation of the true nature of things.

Five Moral Precepts: five guiding principles for Buddhists to follow. They can be followed in skilful (upaya kausala) or unskilful ways.

Four Noble Truths: the four central beliefs which contain the essence of the teaching of the Buddha: dukkha (suffering), samudaya (causes of suffering), tanha (ending of craving) and magga (Noble Eightfold Path).

Four Sights: illness, old age, death, holy man: seeing these made Siddhartha begin his search for enlightenment.

Human destiny: the potential we all have; in Theravada to become an arhat (perfected being), then achieve Buddhahood (full enlightenment); in Mahayana, to become a bodhisattva (an enlightened being who has chosen to put off full enlightenment in order to help others), or to achieve enlightenment.

Karma: energy created by intentional thoughts, words and actions which shapes lifetimes.

Mahayana: major tradition within Buddhism (53 per cent), mainly found in China and the Far East.

Mala: prayer beads, used to aid meditation.

Mantra: short religious phrase which should be repeated.

Meditation: practice of focusing; samatha (concentration), vipassana (achieving insight); includes zazen form (self-focus) and visualisation exercises.

Mourning rituals: practices carried out after someone has died to remember them or to deal with the body.

Parinirvana Day: festival to celebrate the enlightenment of the Buddha.

Paticca samuppada: concept of dependent arising; belief that causality underpins existence.

Places of worship: temple, shrine, vihara (monastery), gompa (hall for learning/meditation.

Puja: act of worship.

Pure Land: form of Buddhism found in Japan, which includes the concept of a heaven.

Rebirth: belief that the skandhas are reborn into new lifetimes, shaped by the karma of previous ones, until enlightenment is achieved.

Six Perfections: Mahayana tradition; six qualities Buddhists (especially bodhisatvas) should try to cultivate within themselves.

Skandhas: the Five Aggregates which make up each person (form, sensation, perception, mental formations, consciousness).

Sunyata: emptiness, void, calmness.

Theravada: oldest form of Buddhism, based around the Sangha.

Three Marks of Existence: three aspects common to all existence – anicca (impermanence), anatta (no fixed self), dukkha (unsatisfactory nature of life, suffering).

Three Poisons: the three causes of suffering: ignorance, greed and hate.

Threefold Way: a way to develop one's spiritual self, through sila (ethics), panna (wisdom) and samadhi (meditation).

Wesak: main Buddhist festival celebrating the birth, enlightenment and death of the Buddha.

Christianity

REVISED ☐

Ascension: Jesus being taken up to heaven on the 40th day of Easter.

Atonement: the action of making amends for wrong doing. The idea of being at one with the self.

Baptism: sacrament; a ceremony to welcome a person into the Christian religion.

Believers' baptism: a ceremony to welcome an adult into the Christian religion using full immersion.

Cafod: a charity: Catholic Agency for Overseas Development.

Christian Aid: a charity working in the developing world providing emergency and long-term aid.

Crucifixion: capital punishment used by the Romans which involves nailing a person to a cross to kill them; Jesus died this way.

Denomination: the names for the different branches of the Christian church.

Eucharist: bread and wine ceremony in the Anglican church.

Evangelism: preaching of the faith in order to convert people to that religion.

Food banks: charity groups collecting donated food to distribute to the poor in Britain.

Genesis: first book of the Bible; means 'beginning'; includes creation story.

Grace: unconditional love that God shows to people who do not deserve it.

Holy Communion: the bread and wine ceremony in the Church of England.

Incarnation: God in human form; Jesus.

Infant baptism: ceremony to welcome a child into the Christian religion.

Iona: an island in Scotland with a fourth-century monastery, used by Christians today as a place of pilgrimage.

Liturgical worship: a church service with a set structure of worship.

Lord's Prayer: the prayer Jesus taught his disciples to show them how to pray.

Lourdes: a town in France where the Virgin Mary appeared; now a place of pilgrimage.

Messiah: the anointed one who is seen as the saviour by Jews and Christians.

Mission: an organised effort to spread the Christian message.

Non-liturgical worship: informal structure found in some church services.

Omnipotent: the idea that God is all-powerful.

Oneness of God: the idea that God is 'One'.

Original sin: belief that everyone born carries the sins of their forefathers.

Orthodox Church: a branch of the Christian church with its origins in Greece and Russia.

Protestant: a branch of the Christian church that broke away from the Roman Catholic Church.

Reconciliation: the process of making people in conflict friendly again.

Resurrection: the physical return of Jesus on the third day after he died.

Roman Catholic: the largest Christian group based in Rome, with the Pope as its leader.

Sacrament: the external and visible sign of an inward and spiritual grace.

Salvation: the saving of the soul from sin; includes through grace and spirit.

Street pastors: a Christian organisation of people working on the city streets at night caring for people who are drunk or involved in anti-social behaviour.

Tearfund: a Christian charity working to relieve poverty in developing countries.

Trinity: the belief in God the Father, God the Son and God the Holy Spirit.

Islam

REVISED

Adalat: justice in Shi'a Islam.

Akhirah: belief in the life after death.

Beneficence: characteristic of Allah; all-loving.

Hajj: pilgrimage to Makkah and the Fifth Pillar of Islam.

Imamate: leadership in Shi'a Islam.

Immanence: the belief that God is closer to us than our heartbeat and is involved in the world.

Jihad: the greater or lesser striving for the way of Allah.

Jummah: Friday prayers where the khutbah (sermon) is read.

Justice: characteristic of Allah; being fair.

Khums: welfare tax in Shi'a Islam.

Makkah: holy city of Islam in Saudi Arabia with the great mosque housing the Ka'aba.

Merciful: characteristic of Allah; forgiving.

Night of Power: the night Muhammad received the first revelations of the Qur'an.

Omnipotence: the belief that God is all-powerful.

Predestination: Al-Qadr; the idea that everything that happens has been decided already by God.

Psalms: the books written by David.

Rak'ah: a sequence of prayer containing actions and recitations.

Ramadan: the holy month of fasting for 30/31 days.

Risalah: communication between man and God in the form of books, angels and prophets.

Salah: compulsory prayer five times a day and the Second Pillar of Islam.

Sawm: month of fasting.

Shahadah: Declaration of Faith: to believe in One God and Muhammad as the Prophet of Allah.

Shi'a: a Muslim who adheres to the Shi'a branch of Islam followed by about a tenth of all Muslims.

Sunni: Muslims who follow the Sunnah, the Way of the Prophet.

Tawhid: the belief in the Oneness of Allah and the unity of His being.

Torah: the revelations given to Musa.

Transcendence: God is outside the world, beyond everything and outside time.

Usul ad-Din: the foundations of faith in Shi'a Islam; the Five Roots.

Wudu: the symbolic washing and purification of the mind and body before salah.

Zakah: almsgiving to the poor which benefits the Muslim community.

Judaism

REVISED

Amidah: prayer in synagogue; standing; eighteen blessings.

Aron ha-Kodesh: Ark of the Covenant which houses the Sefer Torah scrolls.

Bar mitzvah: the service for a Jewish boy to become a full member of the Jewish community.

Bat mitzvah: the service for a Jewish girl to become a daughter of the commandment.

Bimah: reading platform in the centre of a synagogue.

Brit milah: birth ceremony for boys in which the boy is circumcised.

Covenant: agreement made between man and G-d.

Creator: characteristic of G-d; that G-d created the world from nothing.

Key moral principles: justice (tzedek), healing the world (Tikkun Olam) and kindness (chesed).

Kosher: food that is allowed under the Jewish dietary system.

Messiah: 'anointed one', whom Jews believe will come to liberate them.

Mitzvot: 613 commandments in the Hebrew scriptures covering religious and moral conduct.

Ner tamid: perpetual light/lamp, found in synagogues and representing G-d.

Oral laws: Talmud; the laws that are not recorded in the five books of Moses; includes commentaries by rabbis from history.

Pesach: festival of the Passover celebrating the Jews' escape from Egyptian slavery.

Pikuach Nefesh: the principle of saving a life which overrides all other religious laws.

Promised Land: believed to be Israel (plus a broader area) given to the Jew by G-d as part of the covenants.

Rosh Hashanah: the Jewish new year.

Shabbat: the Jewish holy day, beginning Friday evening and ending Saturday evening.

Shechinah: the divine presence.

Synagogue: Jewish place of worship; means 'coming together'.

Ten Commandments: the laws given to Moses on Mount Sinai.

Tenakh: the Jewish scriptures combining Torah, Nevi'im and Ketuvim.

Treyfah: food that Jews are not permitted to eat.

Yom Kippur: the Day of Atonement and the holiest day for Jewish people.

General teachings of the six major religions

Use of teachings is very important in this GCSE (in the Religion section as well as the Theme section). It will always be easier to score marks and to make points more clearly if you use teachings that are specific to the topics. The examiner will be able to clearly see the point you are making and the relevance of the teachings; you will be able to make your points in fewer words, more correctly and concisely. You will find many such teachings in this guide. However, in the exam it might be difficult to remember those specific teachings, so this section gives you some general teachings which can be applied to many topics. They form the key beliefs/teachings of the religions – so learn them.

Buddhism

- Karma – our words/actions shape our future.
- Each of the actions of the Eightfold Path, especially Right Action, Livelihood, Speech.
- Compassion, the Five Precepts, including not hurting others (ahimsa), not clouding the mind, kind language, not taking what is not freely given, no sexual misconduct.

Christianity

- Jesus said, Love God, love your neighbour.
- God created us all equal as He made us all.
- Justice – everyone is equal so we all deserve fairness.
- Forgiveness, love, compassion.

Hinduism

- Hindu virtues state compassion, ahimsa, respect for life.
- Tolerance, support for others, service.
- Self-discipline, wisdom, honesty.

Islam

- Ummah – brotherhood of all Muslims, so equality and respect.
- Equality of the Five Pillars.
- Shari'ah law applied to life's issues.

Judaism

- Ten Commandments.
- Love G_d, no idols, no misuse of G_d's name, keeping the Sabbath.
- Respect parents, don't kill, steal, commit adultery, tell lies, want what others have.
- Equality, love, respect.

Sikhism

- Sikh values of sharing, sewa, duty, tolerance, chastity, humility.
- The Khalsa vows – meditation and service to God, no use of intoxicants, do not eat meat that has been ritually killed, equality of all, fight injustice, do not hurt others.

Many of these can be applied to a variety of topics, so you can learn one teaching and use it again and again – less learning! And across religions – less learning!

Relationships and families

Sex

REVISED ☐

People choose to have sex for many reasons, for example love, fun, lust, to create life, money …

Society's attitudes to sex and relationships have evolved over the last 50 years. **Homosexuality**, for example, is far more acceptable today whereas it used to be illegal to be gay. Now many people do not get married and divorce rates are much higher.

As relationships change, attitudes to sex change, but the religious view remains traditional – you need to know both secular and religious views for this theme.

Contraception

REVISED ☐

Contraception is a precaution taken to prevent pregnancy so that a couple can 'family plan'. Using contraception is seen as a responsible way to bring children into the world – when a couple have decided the time is right for them, they are in a position to look after and provide for the child.

Contraception allows a couple to enjoy a sexual relationship without getting pregnant, and reduces the need for abortion of unwanted pregnancies and the spread of sexually transmitted diseases.

Methods include:
● artificial devices – these are 'made', such as condoms
● natural methods – these are behaviours to limit the chance of pregnancy, such as withdrawal or rhythm methods
● permanent methods – these are operations to prevent the production of eggs or sperm. Commonly known types include the Pill, the coil and the cap.

Only the permanent methods are 100 per cent guaranteed.

Relationships

REVISED ☐

People marry for many reasons – for love, sex, to make a marriage legitimate, for children, money, companionship and because it is an accepted way in society and within religions. Others choose not to marry but are still in a solid relationship.

Some people have a free choice about who to marry, some have marriage partners chosen by parents, and some religions advocate marriage to someone in that religion.

Adultery: married person having sex with someone other than the person they are married to – an affair.

Age of consent: the legal age a person is considered old enough to have sex – 16 in Britain (though many young people have sex under this age, which is in fact against the law).

Celibacy: abstaining from sexual relations.

Chastity: being sexually pure; in a relationship, waiting to have sex until married.

Commitment: a relationship based on a promise to be faithful and supportive.

Contract: binding agreements, such as a marriage contract.

Heterosexuality: a sexual relationship between a man and woman (i.e. opposite sexes).

Homosexuality: a sexual relationship between a same-sex couple (i.e. man/man or woman/woman).

Responsibility: what must be done as part of the commitment agreement; what a person has a duty to do.

Sex before marriage: a sexual act between two people before a marriage has taken place.

Types of marriage and cohabitation

Cohabitation is living together as if married. The couple have no marriage licence, however, so do not have the same legal rights as a married couple.

Many people in the modern world accept cohabitation and same-sex relationships, believing people should live in a way that makes them happy. Nevertheless, some people still see cohabitation as 'living in sin' and the relationship as 'unofficial'.

As a cohabiting couple have a sexual relationship, this is seen as sex outside marriage and not in line with what many religions teach.

Same-sex relationships are legally protected through **civil partnership** or a marriage in a registry office. But many religions do not accept same-sex relationships. Under Islamic Shari'ah law, it carries the death penalty. Many religious people, while accepting people are gay, believe they should refrain from sexual relationships.

Sex is for the pro-creation of children and as a same-sex couple cannot naturally have a child then some people would question the need for a sexual relationship. Many same-sex couples now do have children through the aid of medical science as they want a family just as much as other couples do. Some religions accept this and some don't.

Civil marriage: a marriage for a couple (or same-sex couple since 2014) carried out at a registry office – (they may be divorced or are not religious).

Civil partnership: the legal registration of a same-sex couple, giving them some legal and financial protection.

Religious marriage: a marriage service for a heterosexual couple carried out in a religious place of worship.

Roles in marriage

Marriage vows or promises can help us understand the different roles within marriage. People promise to be good to each other, to be faithful, to love and cherish, to support each other through good and bad times until death – so the intention in marrying is to make a life-long commitment to someone.

Roles have a practical angle focused on looking after the household and finances. Roles have changed in this respect; now it is often about what works best for each couple – who works, who looks after the children, who cooks and cleans is their choice rather than conforming to the expectations of society. Money is also a big factor in decisions.

The nature and purpose of polygamy

Polygamy is the practice of a man being married to more than one woman at the same time, and often having children with each wife. It is illegal in the UK.

Under Shari'ah law polygamy is allowed under certain circumstances. Some British Muslims marry 'Islamically' – no British marriage licence is signed, allowing several marriages. None would be recognised under British law and the couple(s) have no protection under the law.

Muhammad allowed this system because *at the time* many women were war widows so unable to support themselves. Rather than leave them unprotected, polygamy was condoned.

Today the rules are difficult to implement – the man must seek consent from the first wife, treat the women all the same, spend time and nights with each one, help with bringing up children with each one, and financially support all of them.

Now test yourself

1 What is the difference between 'religious' and 'civil' marriage?
2 Why do people marry?
3 What are the roles in marriage?
4 Explain 'polygamy'.

TESTED

Theme A

Religious attitudes to sexual matters

Buddhism

- Sex is about desire and craving (tanha) – both prevent enlightenment.
- Buddhism has a strong tradition of celibacy. Sex is natural but rewarding as part of a loving relationship, so chastity is encouraged. Contraception is allowed to limit family size.
- The Five Precepts say to avoid sexual immorality, including adultery.
- Sex before marriage or homosexuality is fine as part of a loving relationship.

Christianity

- Generally only married couples should have sex, and only with each other. Many Christians tolerate sex before marriage in a relationship which is leading to marriage. Catholics believe every sexual act must be within the framework of marriage. Chastity is a virtue. Celibacy is practised in monastic life and the priesthood.
- For many Christians, homosexual sex is considered unnatural (it is against scripture, with no chance of pregnancy). People can be gay but not have sex.
- Responsible parenthood is encouraged, so the use of contraception is accepted. Contraception is against Catholic teaching because it cancels out the chance of pregnancy. Most Catholics follow natural methods of contraception as pregnancy should be possible within every act of sex.
- The Bible says 'Do not commit adultery'; Jesus says that even a lustful look is wrong, so affairs are wrong and a sin.

Hinduism

- Sex can happen only in the married householder stage. For the other three stages, the man should remain celibate. Sex before marriage and homosexuality are both wrong. Sex is a gift from the Ultimate Reality (God), for enjoyment and to have children, and must be treated with respect.
- Chastity is important, with a person's only sexual partner being the person to whom they are married. Hindu virtues are self-discipline and respect – adultery goes against both of these.
- Hindus encourage contraception. Family planning is stressed, though Hindus need to have a son to carry out certain religious rituals and this often leads to less use of contraception. There are 208 days – festivals, holy days and a full/new moon – on which sex should be avoided, which acts as birth control.

Islam

- Marriage and having children is a religious duty. Every person should be a virgin before marriage. They should observe chastity before and during marriage. Celibacy is wrong within marriage.
- Muhammad said sex was special within marriage – pleasurable, and providing the blessing of children, if the couple so wish. Muslims can and should use contraception as part of responsible parenthood.
- Sex before marriage, adultery and homosexual relationships carry severe punishments under Shari'ah law.

Judaism

- The Torah says a woman is made to be man's companion, so there should be marriage.
- Sex within marriage is for pleasure and having children. Humans are to be fruitful and multiply. Celibacy within marriage is not recommended.
- Orthodox Jews accept contraception – they often use the Pill because it does not cause the wasting of seed, which is forbidden in the Torah.
- The Torah says sex before marriage, adultery and homosexuality are wrong and chastity should be observed. Adultery breaks one of the Ten Commandments, and the Torah prescribed the death penalty for this. Homosexuality is accepted by some Jews only.

Sikhism

- Sex is a gift from God but only within marriage. Sex before marriage is wrong. Married life is seen as the norm. Chastity is highly valued before and within marriage as it shows self-control.
- Although most Sikhs see homosexuality as wrong – a form of haumai (selfishness) – some accept it as part of what God has created in a person.
- Adultery is wrong – haumai.
- Sikhs follow responsible parenthood so allow contraception.

Symbolism within religious marriage ceremonies

Buddhism

- Marriage is a cultural not religious act, but is seen as a social good. There are some common rituals. The vows – to love each other, be kind and considerate, be faithful – set the tone for the relationship. The wife must perform household duties, be hospitable, protect and invest earnings and the husband must delegate domestic duties and provide gifts to please his wife.

Christianity

- Marriage is a gift from God and a symbol of Christ's relationship with the Church.
- The vows symbolise the nature of the marriage – full of love and respect, good times and bad times, faithful to each other and life-long.
- The rings symbolise the everlasting nature of the marriage – that love, like God, is eternal and only death can end this contract.

Hinduism

- The marriage is a life-long commitment to each other and the ceremony actually ends with prayers to show the marriage cannot be broken.
- The bride's father pours out sacred water to show he gives his daughter away and the groom accepts the duties and responsibilities of being her husband.
- The bride's scarf is tied to the groom's shirt to symbolise their external union, for which rings are exchanged. They are expected to be faithful to each other.

Islam

- Marriage is the joining not just of two individuals but of two families. A successful marriage is the basis of a successful society as the couple treat each other with respect, kindness and love and children will learn this behaviour as normal.
- The mahr is symbolic of the need for the groom to provide financially for his bride and family. Men are seen as the protectors and maintainers of the family.
- The signing of the contract shows the couple are now together freely and they must be faithful to each other. Marriage is the acceptable place for sex and, in time, children.
- Wives must obey their husbands under the laws of Allah, look after them and their children, and bring them up in the Muslim faith. Often rules are agreed and signed so that both husband and wife are happy in the marriage.

Judaism

- Placing the veil over the bride's face shows that the husband will protect and look after his wife.
- Wine is drunk, the first of seven glasses, to show the couple are at the start of building their marriage. Creating something successful is never easy and needs to be worked at.
- Rings are exchanged – they are plain and undecorated to symbolise the hope of a harmonious marriage. Troubles will occur and so the groom crushes a glass under his foot to reflect the destruction of the temple in Jerusalem.
- The couple should be faithful and should have children.

Sikhism

- The Palla ceremony is where the bride's father takes the end of the groom's scarf and gives it to the bride, symbolising the 'giving away' of his daughter into the care of the groom. This is the external symbol of the two now being together.
- The lavan means 'joining together'. There are four marriage hymns which are read by the granthi. The bride and groom circle the Guru Granth Sahib for each lavan and bow to show they have accepted the advice. This is the internal symbol of the two now being together.

Exam tip

While it is unlikely that you will be asked to describe an actual marriage ceremony, knowing the symbolism might help with questions on the roles within a marriage and how to make a marriage successful.

Families and parenting

A nuclear family is a family unit consisting of mother, father and children. It is considered the normal family unit in the Western world.

An extended family is the nuclear family plus other relatives, usually including grandparents, who may all live together. This is a common structure in many areas of the world, such as Africa, the Far East, the Middle East and South America. It is also common in many poorer parts of the world and in the Muslim and Hindu traditions.

A single-parent family is a family of one parent and child(ren).

One of the main reasons for marriage is to have children, and a key role is good parenting. Having children shows commitment and love, fulfils a relationship and is a religious duty. It may well be unplanned or a way to keep the marriage together.

Marriage is seen as the correct environment to have children for all couples. The children bring a new purpose and new responsibilities to the relationship. Parents need to provide stability, a consistency in behaviour and life, so that the children feel safe and protected. Part of caring is to educate, enabling children to become successful individuals.

Children should show respect to their parents for their love and commitment.

Educating children in a faith

Religious parents often believe that introducing their children to the faith gives them the best start in life. They believe a religious upbringing will help their children be happy and ready to do well in life. Many have initiation ceremonies to 'officially welcome' the children into that religious group. Growing up, children are taught the beliefs and how to worship.

Religion provides a structure and behaviour code, helping children's development. It provides them with access to supportive people and to involve themselves in activities.

Some say it is wrong to 'force' religion on people, but religious people do not see it that way. Having an identity, being part of something – the benefits far outweigh the negatives. They do accept that some children may reject the faith when they grow up, but many return later in life, too.

Many same-sex couples have the same ideas about bringing up their children in the faith. They also believe it provides the best environment for their child to develop.

Exam tip

This is a good area for discussion. Hence the topic lends itself to not only evaluation (12 marks) questions but also similarities (4 marks) questions. You could be given a statement such as *When couples have children they should always bring them up in their faith* (12 marks) or *Explain two similar religious beliefs about parenting* (4 marks). Could you answer these now from the information above?

Divorce

Why is there a need for divorce?

Marriage is 'til death us do part' so there will inevitably be difficulties because there are many pressures in life. Some serious issues might be illness, jobs, addictions, affairs and abuse, which are very difficult to overcome, so **divorce** is seen as the only solution.

The debate is whether divorce should be allowed or not and if allowed, how easy it should be to get one. Many religious people believe vows are absolute, so divorce is always wrong. Others would agree that it is wrong, though at times necessary, but it should not be an easy option. All marriages should be worked at – marriage is a serious commitment and difficulties should be worked through.

In 1969 the Church of England in the UK was key in getting the divorce laws relaxed because the Church believed that a couple living in a loveless marriage or separated were not being given the chance to move on with their lives. Also, Jesus taught compassion, forgiveness, understanding and second chances – divorce is compatible with that.

> **Annulment**: the Roman Catholic way of ending a marriage – the marriage is set aside as if it were never real. However, a legal divorce must still happen to officially end it.
>
> **Divorce**: the legal ending of a marriage.
>
> **Remarriage**: a person's second (or more) marriage, after a divorce.
>
> **Second marriage**: this can happen after the death of a partner so the one left marries again.

What support is available?

Couples will find support from their families, religion, friends, charities, support groups and marriage counselling services. Differences can be overcome if people are prepared to listen, change or alter ways of doing things. Divorce should be the last resort.

Religion would also encourage prayer – asking for God's help.

That divorce rates are high in the UK suggests that people are rushing into marriage or not taking their vows seriously, or that the couple give up too easily – and divorces are too easily obtained.

It must be remembered that some people have no choice – for their own and their children's safety, welfare and life chances. Very few people would disagree with divorce in such cases.

Remarriage

Remarriage can be to a different or the same partner after divorce. Failure of one marriage does not mean another cannot be successful.

What does religion think of remarriage? This really depends upon what the religion's view of divorce is. If the religion disagrees with divorce, then it will disagree with remarriage because it believes the first marriage still exists. Some religions say divorce is not recognised by God so neither is remarriage.

Some might say they see that new happiness has been found but although it is good that people want to remarry, they cannot accept that vows made before God can simply be set aside.

Others would allow a remarriage, just not a religious one. They would support a civil marriage while perhaps offering a blessing to that couple.

> ### Now test yourself
>
> 1 What is divorce?
> 2 Give two reasons a couple might divorce.
> 3 What do religions think about divorce?
> 4 What do religions think about remarriage?
>
> TESTED

Religious attitudes to divorce

Buddhism

Vows are a serious commitment which should not be broken easily. Since marriage is seen as keeping society stable, divorce is discouraged. Sometimes divorce has to be seen as the right option as two people causing themselves and others great suffering by staying together breaks the Precepts, creates bad karma and goes against Buddhist principles of compassion and ahimsa.

- Keep the Five Precepts.
- Be compassionate.
- Thoughts, deeds and actions should always be positive because they have a karmic value which shapes our next lifetime(s).

Christianity

For Roman Catholics, divorce is always wrong. Marriage is a sacrament, which cannot be broken. Promises are made to God and each other to stay together 'until death do us part', and these promises are binding.

For most other Christians, divorce is discouraged but accepted as a last resort. It is sometimes the lesser of two evils and also a necessary evil.

- God hates divorce (Old Testament).
- Whoever divorces ... then marries another; it is as if he committed adultery (Jesus).
- Forgiveness and love (Jesus).

Hinduism

Hindu law forbids divorce to the Brahmin caste, but it is available to all others. It happens throughout Hindu society, though it is frowned upon. The law allows for divorce in the case of cruelty, non-production of children and for other reasons. Clearly, divorce is both available and within the religious teachings; however, it is not a common event. There is great stigma over divorce, and it is especially difficult for women who have been divorced. Couples tend to stay together because of these pressures.

- 'I promise never to abandon her, whatever happens' (wedding vow).
- Marriage is one of the spiritual stages in life.
- Divorce is granted for specific reasons (Hindu Marriage Act (1955) and Manusmriti scriptures).

Islam

Divorce is a last resort – families are expected to mediate, there is a three-month waiting period, and the second part of the dowry must be paid.

- Of all legal things, the one Allah most hates is divorce (Qur'an).
- Marry and do not divorce (Hadith).
- The throne of Allah shakes due to divorce (Hadith).
- If you fear a breach between a man and his wife, appoint two arbiters (Qur'an).

Judaism

Marriage is a sacred commitment and union. Although divorce is allowed, it is as a last resort. Time should be allowed for reconciliation to take place.

- G-d hates divorce (Nevi'im).
- When a man puts aside the wife of his youth, even the very altar weeps (Talmud).
- A court can grant a woman divorce, if she can show that she can no longer live with him (Maimonides).

Sikhism

Divorce is not the Sikh way, but it is accepted by the faith. Marriage should be a lifetime commitment and a couple should work at it, especially when times are difficult. Families help to mediate for reconciliation.

- Marriage is a sacrament.
- Marriage is the union of two souls and a life-long commitment.
- If the husband and wife are in dispute, their concern for their children should reunite them (Adi Granth).

Exam tip

Remember not only to use (state) the teachings but also to apply (explain and relate) them to the question.

Exam tip

Try this formula/sentence structure to help:

In the .... (holy book) it says .... (give the teaching) which means .... (explain the teaching). Therefore .... (name of the believers, e.g. Christians) would believe .... (topic of the question) is .... (acceptable/wrong).

Gender equality and prejudice

Prejudice is the pre-judgement of others based on a characteristic they have, rather than on what they are really like.

In some societies women are not the decision-makers, making them less powerful and seen as less important. This is gender prejudice. It can lead to different treatment (discrimination), so that women are given fewer opportunities – for example, not getting the same chances or promotions at work.

It may be that a culture sets stricter rules for women than for men – for example, where women are not allowed to leave the house, or must be chaperoned, or where girls are not allowed education beyond a certain age. It may be that women do not contribute to decision-making, so a female perspective is never considered. Prejudice within power structures can mean that when women are treated negatively, there is no consequence for the perpetrator, and this further encourages that negative behaviour. Gender discrimination spans from unkind comments to murder – it definitely has an impact.

Ultimately gender prejudice makes women (feel) powerless, affecting their confidence and self-esteem. It keeps women less powerful, making society work for men rather than for everyone. The UK has laws to prevent gender discrimination, and employment law looks at equal pay issues between the sexes.

Given that most religions are very old, it is ingrained for leadership to be assumed by men. In many cases, leadership has been seen as scripturally correct. Some say this has led to inequality between the genders within religion, with men having bigger, more important and decisive roles, and women reduced to supporting roles. In most religions, more progressive forms of the religion reflect more the changes society has accepted in status, but an Orthodox form of a faith, for example, will not have women as religious leaders.

Activity

Support or challenge?

'Men and women are equals in all religions.' Evaluate this statement. Refer to religious and non-religious arguments. You should agree and disagree with the statement, and come to a justified conclusion.

Use the list of arguments below to help you write a strong answer to this question. They are mixed up though, so first you need to work out which ones agree (support) and which ones disagree (challenge) with the statement. Remember that a conclusion should not just be repeating what you have already written, so it is worth keeping back a good argument to use there. You may have to read the next page to find some religious arguments to help with this.

Argument	Supports statement in question	Challenges statement in question
They don't let women lead religious services in lots of religions.		
Women are equal but with different roles.		
God created everyone, so all must be equal.		
Women stay at home and have children and look after them (go forth and multiply) – as men interact with the world, they have more power.		
Both men and women are needed to keep the religion going.		
Women are considered unclean during menstruation, men are never in that situation so are never unclean.		

Religious attitudes to gender equality

Buddhism

- If a man denies the possibility of enlightenment of women, then his own enlightenment is impossible (Lotus Sutra).
- The practice of Buddhism is the same for men and women, showing no inequality of demands on either.

Christianity

- There is neither Jew nor Gentile, neither slave nor free, nor is there male and female, for you are all one in Christ Jesus (Galatians).
- So God created mankind in his own image, in the image of God he created them; male and female he created them (Genesis 1:27).

Activity

Read the teachings for your religion. Write a short paragraph to state the attitude of your religion(s) to gender equality.

Hinduism

- Good treatment of women is seen as a blessing (Laws of Manu).
- Where women are honoured, there the gods are pleased (Manusmriti).

Islam

- Men and women have the same spiritual nature, according to the Qur'an.
- Prophet Muhammad said, 'I command you to be kind to women.'

Judaism

- In Progressive Judaism, women can be rabbis.
- The equality of men and women begins at the highest possible level, as G-d has no gender. Both men and women were created equally and in G-d's image (Genesis).

Sikhism

- Man is born from a woman ... woman is born from woman; without woman, there would be no one at all (Guru Granth Sahib).
- Waheguru (God) is neither male or female (Guru Granth Sahib).

Now test yourself

1 What is gender prejudice?
2 How do religions treat men and women differently?
3 What is meant by 'different but equal'?

Attitudes to the role of men and women

There is a religious debate about the role of women. They are treated differently, yet all religions condemn any kind of discrimination.

- In Christianity, women cannot be priests in the Catholic Church.
- In Islam, all Imams are men.
- In Orthodox Judaism, women sit separately and do not take part in synagogue services.
- With the exception of ISKCON in Hinduism, Brahmin priests are male.
- Theravada Buddhist women pray that their reincarnation will be as a man.
- In Sikhism, while either gender may read the Guru Granth Sahib at services, it is unusual to see women fulfilling this role.

Denying access to certain roles could be said to be discriminatory. However, religion would say that roles are different but equal. If women are happy with their roles then it is not discrimination. The issue arises when women want to do something as part of their religion but are not allowed to because they are women.

Activity

Fix it!

Read this answer and suggest ways to improve it.

Explain two contrasting ways in which religions view gender equality. (4 marks)

Religions believe in gender equality because they say men and women are different but equal. Also they don't because Christians don't let women be priests so they can't lead church services.

Exam question practice

What questions on this section look like:

Theme A – Relationships and families

This page contains a range of questions that could be on an exam paper. Practise them all to strengthen your knowledge and technique while revising. Check back to pages 13–14 to see the marking grids that examiners use: this will help you to mark your answers.

1 Which of the following means to be 'sexually pure'?

   (a) Celibacy   (b) Chastity   (c) Adultery   (d) Contraception   [1]

2 Which of the following terms means to live together as if married?

   (a) Polygamy   (b) Civil partnership   (c) Civil marriage   (d) Cohabitation   [1]

3 Give two reasons people divorce.   [2]

4 Give two religious reasons for having children.   [2]

5 Name two types of family.   [2]

6 Explain two contrasting religious beliefs about contraception in contemporary British society. In your answer you must refer to the main religious tradition of Great Britain and one or more other religious traditions.   [4]

7 Explain two similar religious beliefs about sex before marriage. In your answer you must refer to one or more religious traditions.   [4]

8 Explain two contrasting religious beliefs about divorce. In your answer you must refer to one or more religious traditions.   [4]

9 Explain two religious beliefs about divorce. Refer to sacred writings or another source of religious belief and teachings in your answer.   [5]

10 Explain two religious beliefs about remarriage. Refer to sacred writings or another source of religious belief and teachings in your answer.   [5]

11 Explain two religious beliefs about homosexual relationships. Refer to sacred writings or another source of religious belief and teachings in your answer.   [5]

12 'A vow should never be broken so divorces should not be allowed.' Evaluate this statement. In your answer you should:
   ● give reasoned arguments in support of this statement
   ● give reasoned arguments to support a different point of view
   ● refer to religious arguments
   ● refer to non-religious arguments
   ● refer to a justified conclusion.   [12]

13 'To have a sexual relationship before marriage is the sensible thing to do.' Evaluate this statement. In your answer you should:
   ● give reasoned arguments in support of this statement
   ● give reasoned arguments to support a different point of view
   ● refer to religious arguments
   ● refer to non-religious arguments
   ● refer to a justified conclusion.   [12]

14 'Women as well as men should be able to be leaders in their religion.' Evaluate this statement. In your answer you should:
   ● give reasoned arguments in support of this statement
   ● give reasoned arguments to support a different point of view
   ● refer to religious arguments
   ● refer to non-religious arguments
   ● refer to a justified conclusion.   [12]

ONLINE

Commentary

Level 2 students use simple language and simple sentence structures. They generally make mistakes in spellings. If this is you, try using more connectives, and take more care with spellings.

Level 5 students use a mix of simple and complex sentencing. Their use of connectives can be limited (and repetitive). If this is you, become more consistent in writing better sentences and find a range of connectives so that you aren't always using the same (boring!) three.

Level 8 students use complex language and sentencing – they sound very impressive!

Religion and life

Scientific truth	Religious truth
Comes from a hypothesis and then repeated testing to confirm an idea	Comes from religions and holy books – from God and personal experiences
It describes the world and how it works	Religion explains why we are here, who is God, what happens at death
It answers the what and how questions – function and process	It answers the why, purpose and meaning questions
It is always developing its truths – as it finds more evidence – not absolute but conditional on the testing conditions	It is open to interpretation, but the words stay the same and remain relevant at all times

Origins of the universe

REVISED

Science and religion disagree about how the universe began, but are they actually compatible or conflicting kinds of truth?

The Big Bang Theory says that the universe began 20 billion years ago. There was nothing and then a huge explosion made clouds of dust and gas and over time the universe formed. The earliest signs of life appeared millions of years before the land and sea settled. The earth was hot, covered in primordial soup – a mix of liquids, chemicals, minerals, proteins and amino acids. These fused to give the first life forms and from these all life developed, including humans.

Scientific evidence supports this theory. Scientists know the universe is expanding, and they can track the expansion back to a singular point – explosions cause everything to be flung outwards. Background microwave radiation from the explosion can still be detected in space.

However, questions are still asked about how nothing can actually explode. How can a totally ordered and structured world come from an explosion? Don't explosions cause chaos?

Evolution

REVISED

The work of Charles Darwin

Charles Darwin was a natural scientist who through years of research wrote *The Origin of Species*. He suggested the world was a place of change and that the huge variety of creatures is the result of years of adaptation (evolution).

There is a struggle for survival between creatures through climates, resources and habitat and where species failed to adapt they became extinct. Only the fittest (best suited) survived, which Darwin called natural selection.

Places change creatures because of the environment they are forced to live in, so over millions of years species have evolved.

Environments are different across the world, and creatures live in appropriate places – polar bears reside in the Arctic, not in Africa! As environments change, if creatures don't adapt they die, leading to extinction of species. Adaptation is the key. This theory suggests that it is wrong to think that creatures were designed to look as they do today. A God of creation does not fit with this theory.

However, even Darwin asks: where does all the intelligence in life come from, its complexity or its interdependence? We see design via intelligence and adaptability. Without the guidance of a designer, surely the world would be chaos? Darwin's theory actually makes God an even greater figure of awe and wonder. Perhaps science is just part of God's creation.

Now test yourself

TESTED

1 What is science? What is religion?
2 Briefly explain the Big Bang Theory.
3 Briefly explain evolution as a theory.

Activity

Support or challenge?

'It is impossible to believe in both science and religion regarding the origins of the universe.' Evaluate this statement. Refer to religious and non-religious arguments. You should agree and disagree with the statement, and come to a justified conclusion.

Use the list of arguments below to help you write a strong answer to this question. They are mixed up though, so first you need to work out which ones agree (support) and which ones disagree (challenge) with the statement. Remember that a conclusion should not just be repeating what you have already written, so it is worth keeping back a good argument to use there. You may have to read the next page to find some religious arguments to help with this.

Argument	Supports statement in question	Challenges statement in question
No proof of religious stories.		
Religious stories don't make sense to a reasonable person.		
Science can't tell us why it all began.		
Science deals in theories not facts when it comes to the origins of the universe.		
Scientific ideas like the Big Bang seem illogical – how can something come from 'nothing'?		
Religious ideas are what people said before science.		

Genesis

Genesis is the first Book of the Hebrew Bible. The Genesis creation story believed by Jews, Muslims and Christians.

In the beginning there was nothing. Then over seven days God created light and dark, the heavens, land, sea and vegetation, sun, moon and stars, birds and fish, land animals and humans. On the seventh day God rested – it was a 'good' creation.

How is this story understood?

Some people believe it is literally true. God is all-powerful so it is easy to believe that God did all this in literally seven days.

Others believe that it is true but not literally. It is a simplified version of what happened, for example a 'day' is a 'God-day' – so a long period of time. It uses the knowledge and language of the time.

Yet others would say it's about the message – God as the creator deliberately made the world; it was not an accident or chaos. Humans, made in God's image, are given a purpose to live by God.

Can we believe in science or religion or both?

Some believers would say we only need religion. Genesis is accurate, God created the world in seven days as He can do anything. Humans don't need to understand, they just need to believe. Accepting the scientific view is impossible with this interpretation of Genesis.

Some accept totally the scientific view of the origins of the universe and so see the religious view as nonsense.

Some people believe that God's involvement is what started the Big Bang. So here science and religion go together to explain how it all began.

Some believe that Genesis is simply there to give us a message – that humans have a purpose. So the story is telling us why humans are here whereas science is telling us how we came to be here. Thus together science and religion give humans a more complete answer.

Is science more important than religion then?

Here we must go back to look at the nature of the truths. Depending on the situation, sometimes one is more important than the other. Sometimes we need hypotheses and testing, they help us make sense of how things work and repeated testing shows us things work. It is not enough to simply believe that medicines work, they need to be tested. At the same time religious truths give life meaning and purpose, a sense of well-being, as well as hope of something else after life here. Science and religion simply answer different questions.

There is no absolute proof as to the origins of the universe. Science does challenge religion here, but they both contribute something to our understanding.

> ## Now test yourself
>
> 1 Outline a religious creation story.
> 2 What are the three religious interpretations of this?
> 3 Are science and religion compatible on the origins of the universe?
>
> TESTED

The value of the world

The world is important, for humans both now and in the future.

Religious people believe they have a duty to look after it (stewardship) and treat it with respect. Life is sacred to all religious believers.

Humans have dominion (power) over nature by permission of God. The world's beauty fills people with awe, making many think of God and so worship Him.

Environmental damage

REVISED

Pollution: damage and solutions

Pollution causes damage to the air, sea (water) and land. In fact, anything can be polluted – there is both light pollution and noise pollution, for example.

Factories and transport cause the most air pollution – toxic CO_2 in the air damages the ozone layer, thus reducing its ability to keep the earth cooler. Rain picks up the chemicals and drops them as acid rain, polluting land, water, crops and buildings. Factories empty waste into rivers and farming chemicals drain from the land into the water sources, killing fish and wildlife.

Pollution is the main reason for **global warming** – it causes the greenhouse effect as greenhouse gases heat the earth.

Poor air quality causes health problems. Contaminated food and water sources mean animals/fish die. Ecosystems change, becoming unbalanced.

Solutions? We can cut CO_2 levels with government control over factories, reduce the use of fossil fuels and replace with cleaner energy, alter travel habits and be aware of our 'carbon footprints'.

> **Global warming**: the heating up of the world's atmosphere, causing climate change.
>
> **Pollution**: the presence/ introduction of something that is toxic to the environment.

Global warming

REVISED

Global warming causes climate change as the earth become hotter. Extreme weather patterns – too hot, too wet, too dry – all lead to floods, droughts, damage to animals' habitats, ice caps melting, more deserts and a reduction in rainforests.

The earth heats up and cools off naturally, but scientists tell us that human activities over the last 100 years have speeded up temperature change. The change alters ecosystems so plants and animals have to adapt or die out.

Solutions? Scientists tell us we need to change our energy use. Alternative, cleaner energies have to be found. Coal, oil and gas need to be used less and energies such as wind, solar, water and nuclear need to be used more. These are sustainable (they do not run out) and cleaner (so cause less harm) but are expensive. Humans have to be able to meet their needs – heating, lighting, industry and transport – while not damaging the environment (as is currently the case).

World leaders are attempting to address these problems via (inter)national agreements (e.g. Earth Summits) to reduce CO_2 levels. As more individuals become aware of the damage their actions cause, more of them try to help fix it.

> **Exam tip**
>
> Make sure you know:
> - definitions of all the topics in this chapter – they make good 1-mark questions
> - for 2-mark questions, two causes (reasons) and two effects (consequences) for all the environmental topics
> - for 2-mark questions, two solutions for each problem.

> **Now test yourself**
>
> 1 Why should religious believers treat the world with respect?
> 2 What is pollution?
> 3 What is global warming?
>
> TESTED

Destruction of natural habitats

REVISED

This refers to activities that damage forest and areas of nature beyond repair so that creatures' living space is lost. Pollution is a key cause of this, with acid rain destroying the canopy in rainforest areas, oil spills contaminating the seas and coastline areas, and deforestation (cutting down of huge areas of forest) taking land for grazing, house building, mining and roads, and planting of cash crops like palm oil plantations.

Rainforests are millions of years old and cannot just be regrown; as trees take in CO_2 and produce O_2 we lose the help they give to fighting global warming. Many rainforest plants have medicinal qualities, which we might lose for ever.

Man's needs here are being seen as more important than nature's, hence cutting the forests. Many countries regard building houses and farming land as development to provide for their people.

Solutions? We must protect these areas and provide those countries, which are often poor, with other alternatives to cutting down these areas. Timber is a major money earner, but alternative ways of earning money need to be found.

Use and abuse of natural resources

REVISED

Natural resources include vegetation, minerals and fossil fuels, which have taken millions of years to form. However, humans are overusing them and they are running out because they are limited in quality and non-renewable. When a coal or oil field is empty, for example, that's it … gone!

Solution? Humans need to find renewable energies to fuel the world and our lifestyles.

Caring for the world

REVISED

Sustainable development is the idea that technological advances should be long-lasting and within reach of all nations.

Conservation, meanwhile, is the act of protecting an area or species. Areas of nature need to be returned to their original state of natural beauty, before they suffered the damage inflicted by humans. This could be done by repairing an area through planting trees, creating nature reserves, etc.

Conservation includes breeding of animals, establishing protected areas, even people using their holidays to work for environmental projects.

What can you do to help reduce these environmental problems?

There are many things people can do to help reduce these problems:
- Make small changes to life patterns.
- Adopt animals in reserves where their habitats are protected.
- Recycle.
- Join an environmental organisation – Greenpeace, for example.
- Pray for people to work together.

Many religious people believe this is God's world and as its stewards are motivated to care for the earth.

Activity

Fix it!

Read the answer to this question. Work out how it can be improved. Then rewrite it to achieve better marks.

Religious people have a greater responsibility to look after the world than non-religious people. (12 marks)

I don't agree with that. Everybody lives in the world, so everybody has a duty to look after it. We all mess it up as well, so we all have a reason to fix it and be stewards.

Answers at www.hoddereducation.co.uk/myrevisionnotesdownloads

Animal rights

Animal rights are the rights animals have to live without cruelty and to have good treatment. This means we cannot just do what we want with/to them. They have the right to be treated properly, fairly and with kindness, even when we intend to kill them.

Laws in the UK protect domestic animals (pets) and endangered species by enforcing their care – food, water, shelter and no cruelty.

Animals have many uses:
- as pets – cats, dogs, birds, mice, hamsters, rats, guinea pigs
- as helpers – beasts of burden to move heavy loads or do heavy work, for example cattle, horses
- as work animals – guide, police, customs and hunting dogs, hunting birds
- as providers – sheep (wool), cows (milk), hens (eggs), bees (honey)
- as food – lamb, cows, hens, deer, pigs, fish
- as experimental test subjects – mice, rats, monkeys, dogs
- as sport – bull-fighting, shooting and hunting.

Hence there are plenty of opportunities to both look after animals and, unfortunately, abuse them.

Animal experimentation

Some animals are bred deliberately for life as an experiment subject. Most experiments test for toxicity, of medicines and medical techniques. Animals are also tested on to improve surgical skills for operations.

There is a big debate over the use of animals for experiments, focusing mainly on the two issues of experimenting for medical products like vaccines and testing for cosmetic products.

Religious people would support medical experiments as they are done for the benefit of human beings, which indicates that there is the belief that humans are more important than animals.

The key issues about these experiments are:
- Animals can and often do suffer greatly in experiments and any animal used in an experiment is then humanely destroyed, even if the experiment was successful.
- Many experiments seem unnecessary, for example to test yet another version of a product which has already been tested in the USA.
- These animals cannot live natural lives in any way.

Scientists have developed other means of testing, without using animals, but they are very expensive.

Use of animals for food

Some religions have rules about the food they can or cannot eat; some simply have guidelines. Most food rules are about the eating of meat.

Many people are vegetarians because they have medical problems, or they do not like the taste, or they disagree with farming or slaughter methods, or they think it is morally wrong to eat meat.

Buddhism

- Many Western Buddhists are vegetarian out of respect for all life – animals are also part of the cycle of rebirth. The skilful means of keeping the First Precept of non-harming would encourage vegetarianism.

Christianity

- Many Christians eat no red meat on Fridays; many eat no meat at all during the period of Lent – in both cases out of respect for the sacrifice of Jesus on Good Friday.

Hinduism

- Most Hindus are vegetarian out of respect for life and ahimsa (non-violence). The Yajur Veda forbids the killing of animals.

Islam

- No pork is to be eaten (the pig is an unclean animal), only meat from an animal which has been ritually slaughtered (halal) so Allah has been thanked and the meat is blessed.

Judaism

- The mitzvot give strict rules around food: no meat and milk together, no pork, only meat from certain animals and which have been ritually slaughtered, no blood, only fish with fins, backbone and scales.

Sikhism

- No meat from an animal which has been ritually slaughtered (this is considered cruel treatment); many are vegetarian (it is a vow for Khalsa Sikhs) out of respect for God's creation.

Activity

Good technique makes your answers sound really good – and makes them easy for the examiner to mark. Have a look at this question and the answer, which is annotated to show you the good technique.

Explain two religious beliefs about the status of animals. Refer to scripture or sacred writings. (5 marks)

The Bhagavad Gita says, 'On a Brahmin, cow, elephant, dog – wise men look with an equal eye.'[1] This means that for Hindus all living beings are equal and should be treated with respect.[2] The Brahmin is the most respected in a community, so maybe most important; the dogs are often strays and not looked after, so maybe the least important.[3] However, this teaching says animals and humans are equal.[4]

In the Guru Granth Sahib, it says 'God's light is in every creature'.[5] Sikhs believe all life is sacred because of this. Many Sikhs do not eat any meat at all, and being vegetarian is a rule for Khalsa Sikhs.[6] From this we know the status of animals is high in Sikhism.[7]

[1]Straight away a quote is written to meet the demand in the question. This is a good quote because it is directly relevant to the answer – no need for extended explanations to make it fit, or for the examiner to have to work it out. The mark scheme automatically awards a mark for this.

[2]The quote is clearly explained, but in a concise way.

[3]The explanation is developed to show how the quote differs from what you would expect.

[4]The last sentence gives the overall point about status (as per the question).

[5]There is a new paragraph to signpost for the examiner you are making a new point. Straight into the next quote.

[6]The quote is explained in a way to answer the question.

→

[7]The explanation develops the idea, but to make sure the examiner can see it is relevant to the question, a final statement about status is given.

Now read the answer to this question. What has the student done well in their answer? Use those clues on good technique to help you annotate/highlight it for technique.

Explain two religious beliefs about the use of animals for food.
Refer to scripture or sacred writings.   (5 marks)

In the Yajur Veda, it is forbidden for Hindus to kill animals. This is because all animals have a soul (atman) just as all life forms have. They are on the start of their journey to enlightenment and should not be killed. By eating meat, they might not be killing the animal themselves, but they are encouraging an industry where animals are killed. They believe this would bring bad karma to them.

A second belief is that violence of any kind is wrong. Hindus are taught to believe in and practise ahimsa (non-violence). It is obvious that violence has to be used to kill an animal for its meat – even when done humanely, it is still a form of violence. Hence, Hindus do not eat meat out of respect for the principle of ahimsa, which in turn brings them good karma.

Now it is your turn to use the same techniques and write your own high-level answer to this question:

Explain two religious beliefs about pollution. Refer to scripture or sacred writings.   (5 marks)

Exam tip

Two clear paragraphs make it easy for the examiner to spot that you have done exactly what the mark scheme asks for. Reference to scripture in the first sentence is good. There is good explanation of the point – it is clearly understandable.

Activity

Match the below concepts to the correct definitions.

Concept	Definition
Pollution	Eating meat and meat products.
Global warming	Human use of what nature produces.
Destruction of natural habitats	To put too much of something into the environment, which spoils it.
Use and abuse of natural resources	When humans destroy natural areas, so destroying habitats.
Animal experimentation	The heating up of the environment, causing climate change.
Use of animals for food	Experiments carried out for the purpose of toxicity and medicines.

Theme B

AQA GCSE (9–1) Religious Studies Specification A   131

Religious attitudes to the environment and animals

Buddhism

- All life should be respected. As we will use the earth during many lifetimes, we protect it for ourselves as well as for our children. Ignorance and greed (two of the Three Poisons) lead to most of the pollution being caused – e.g. companies building factories in the third world so they can pay the workers less, have fewer pollution levels to keep to, all leading to bigger profits.
- The First Precept tells us to not harm other sentient beings.
- Right Livelihood implies that Buddhists should not work in a job that exploits animals.
- All living things fear being put to death – let no one kill or cause others to kill (Dhammapada).

Christianity

- God gave us the world, entrusting us with this great gift. Humans have the responsibility to look after it as stewards. We also have a responsibility to each other, the poor of the world and our future children to make sure the world is still intact for many generations to come.
- Animals are part of creation and deserve respect and protection (Assisi).
- Scientists must abandon laboratories and factories of death (Pope).

Hinduism

- Brahman is in all life. The ideas of sanctity of life and non-violence are built into the religion. All life is interdependent – plants and animals depend on the environment so everyone needs to protect it. Souls will be reborn so we need to live on earth again and if God is in all nature then we show an act of worship by looking after it.
- Avoid harming all forms of life (ahimsa).
- Hindu worship includes respect for all and many deities are linked to specific animals.
- Avoiding harm to animals will make humans ready for eternal life (Laws of Manu).

Islam

- The world is the work of Allah – humans are khalifahs, trustees of His world. Allah knows who damages His creation and punishment will follow on Judgement Day. The idea of the ummah means we have a duty to pass on the world undamaged to the next generations.
- Nature is inferior to humans and can be used to improve people's well-being.
- Showing kindness to an animal is an act rewarded by Allah (Sunnah).
- Muhammad (pbuh) insisted animals were well treated.

Judaism

- G-d gave us the duty of stewardship. We should respect it. Tikkun olam (repairing the world) is interpreted as tackling environmental issues; tzedek (justice) means justice for the world itself. To 'love your neighbour' you have to not wreck the world.
- G-d made the world and all in it (Genesis).
- A righteous man looks after his animals (Torah).
- Do not be cruel to animals (Noachide Laws).

Sikhism

- The world is a gift from God, existing because God wants it to. Sikhs perform sewa for others so safeguarding the world is essential. The Gurus said God is within everything so damage the world, damage God.
- God's light is in every creature (Guru Granth Sahib).
- Many Sikhs are vegetarian out of respect for God's creation – the langar, for example.
- Guru Gobind Singh stated that he enjoyed hunting, so it is not forbidden.

Revision tip

Remember you need to learn only two of each from the religion/s you have studied. Easy! Just don't forget to be able to mention scripture.

The value of human life

Religions would say that human life is the most valuable and special of all life forms.

Religious believers think humans are the highest form of creation and within the highest levels of spiritual development. This means that the value of human life is beyond measure, so it needs protection and care. Most religious believers are 'pro-life' in issues relating to life and death.

The sanctity of life

This is the belief that all life is special as it was created by God, so it needs to be protected.

Everyone believes life is special in one way or another. Christians, Hindus, Jews, Muslims and Sikhs all believe life is special because it was created by God. Buddhists and Hindus believe it is special because it strives for enlightenment.

Religions also consider animal and plant life as special, as a creation of God.

Quality of life

This phrase describes how good a person's life is – how they feel, how comfortable they are, how easy it is for them to live. It is also about whether life is worth living if they have a medical condition.

Sometimes decisions are made about whether someone lives or dies and quality of life is a key factor in this. Abortion and euthanasia are such issues.

Activity

Support or challenge?

'Quality of life is more important than the sanctity of life in decisions about the end of life.' Evaluate this statement. Refer to religious and non-religious arguments. You should agree and disagree with the statement, and come to a justified conclusion.

Use the list of arguments below to help you write a strong answer to this question. They are mixed up though, so first you need to work out which ones agree (support) and which ones disagree (challenge) with the statement. Remember that a conclusion should not just be repeating what you have already written, so it is worth keeping back a good argument to use there. You may have to read the next page to find some religious arguments to help with this.

Argument	Supports statement in question	Challenges statement in question
No point living a life of pain with no respite.		
My life, my body, my decision.		
God created all life, so it must be protected.		
Life is so special, it can only be protected.		
The intrinsic value of every individual – regardless of their situation – outweighs the concern for quality.		
How valuable is life if is not enjoyable anyway?		

Religious attitudes to life

Buddhism

- Life is special and must be protected.
- The First Precept is to help others, not harm them.
- The heart of Buddhist practice is to overcome suffering (dukkha).
- The Dalai Lama has said, 'Where a person is definitely going to die, and keeping them alive leads to more suffering, then termination of life is permitted under Mahayana Buddhism.'

Christianity

- God created life in his own image (Genesis).
- Do not kill (Ten Commandments).
- I, your God, give life, and I take it away (Job).
- The Catholic Church teaches that life must be respected from conception until natural death.
- Doctors do not have an overriding obligation to prolong life by all means possible (Church of England).

Hinduism

- Those who carry out abortions are among the worst of sinners (Atharva Veda).
- Compassion, ahimsa, and respect for life are key Hindu virtues.
- The result of a virtuous action is pure joy; actions done from emotion bring pain and suffering.
- The one who tries to escape from the trials of this life by taking their own life will suffer even more in the next life (Yajur Veda).

Islam

- Neither kill nor destroy yourself (Qur'an).
- No one can die except by Allah's leave, that is a decree with a fixed term (Qur'an).
- Each person is created individually by Allah from a single clot of blood.
- Do not take life – which Allah has made sacred – except for a just cause (Qur'an).
- Euthanasia is zulm – wrong-doing against Allah.

Judaism

- Do not kill (Ten Commandments).
- G-d gives life and G-d takes away life (Job).
- The foetus is 'mere water' until the 40th day of pregnancy.
- If there is anything which causes a hindrance to the departure of the soul then it is permissible to remove it (Talmud).

Sikhism

- God sends us and we take birth, God calls us back and we die (Guru Granth Sahib).
- Life begins at conception.
- God fills us with light so we can be born (Guru Granth Sahib).
- All life is sacred and should be respected.

Now test yourself

1 What is meant by quality of life?
2 What is meant by sanctity of life?

TESTED

Answers at **www.hoddereducation.co.uk/myrevisionnotesdownloads**

Abortion

The central question here is: when does life begin? The law states it is at birth but the Abortion Act 1967 bans **abortion** after 24 weeks.

If abortion is after 'when life begins', it can be seen as murder. At any stage from conception the foetus is a potential life.

> **Abortion**: the deliberate expulsion of a foetus from the womb, with the intention of destroying it.

The law in the UK

The law in the UK (excluding Northern Ireland) begins by stating that abortion is illegal, then gives exceptions. Abortion can be carried out only in a registered place before 24 weeks if two registered doctors agree that at least one of the following is true:

- There is a danger to the woman's mental and/or physical health.
- The foetus will be born with physical and/or mental disabilities.
- The mental and/or physical health of existing children will be put at risk.

Breaking the law carries great penalties for all those involved.

The debate

Pro-life: disagree with abortion	Pro-choice: accept abortion
Pro-lifers support the foetus' right to life.	This view defends a woman's right to choose what happens to her body. The arguments are about the woman rather than the foetus.
All life is sacred and must be protected.	A woman should have the right to decide what happens to her body.
God has created life and as stewards, humans have to protect life.	Where the pregnancy is a result of rape or incest, it would be wrong to not allow an abortion.
Abortion is murder.	If having a child is going to put a woman's life at risk, then she should have the right to an abortion.
The foetus can't defend itself, so someone else has to do it for it.	The foetus should not be classed as a life in its own right until it could survive outside the womb.
When a foetus will be born with disabilities, we cannot say what the quality of its life would be, so should not decide to forbid it that life.	It is cruel to allow badly damaged foetuses to be born.
	Banning abortion does not stop it, rather it makes it unsafe. We need to protect women.

What does religion say if the woman's life is at risk?

- Buddhism: the primary intention is the key – helping to save the woman's life is compassionate even if the foetus dies.
- Christianity: if the pregnancy threatens the woman's life it is justified (Church of England). Where abortion is a side effect of a medical procedure to save a woman's life it can be accepted (Roman Catholic Church) – this is known as the Principle of Double Effect.
- Hinduism: the woman's life takes priority, when at risk.
- Judaism: before birth the foetus has no rights over the mother – actual life has priority.
- Islam: the life of the mother takes priority as she is a fully developed human being.
- Sikhism: abortion would be a 'necessary evil'.

Euthanasia

Euthanasia is mercy killing – helping someone to die if they have a terminal illness. It is done out of compassion and love.

Voluntary euthanasia is a person asking to end their own suffering. It could be active – with the person being given something to end their life so the illness does not kill them – or passive – where medication is refused/stopped so the illness kills them.

Non-voluntary euthanasia is when the patient is incapacitated so their family members decide, maybe to turn off a life support machine or to withdraw medication/food. This is passive as it is allowing the person to die.

A doctor's oath says, 'I will give no deadly medicine to anyone if asked or suggest such actions.'

The law in the UK

Euthanasia is illegal in Britain. It is forbidden to help someone to die. Active euthanasia carries a 14-year jail sentence. If viewed as murder, it carries a life sentence.

Doctors do switch off life-support machines (passive) when patients have no sign of brain activity, they do allow patients to refuse treatment or food/water (passive) and they administer drugs to ease pain, which also shortens life. None of these actions is regarded as euthanasia in the UK.

The debate

Arguments for the right to die	Arguments against the right to die
It is the person's body, so they should have the right to decide.	Life does not belong to us, it belongs to God – euthanasia is playing God.
Surely it should be a human right?	To allow euthanasia would be to encourage it – people may force it on others for their own advantage, e.g. making an elderly relative feel a burden.
Only the person can really say when their life is not worth living.	
It is compassionate to put animals in pain to sleep, so we should allow the same compassion to humans to avoid agony and suffering.	People in their last days need care and love rather than being helped to die.
	Doctors and nurses take oaths to protect life, not to end it.

Remember these terms? People say that euthanasia is all about the quality of life – that for those who want euthanasia, they are suffering too much, having no quality of life. Others say that, regardless of quality, life must be maintained because the sanctity of life means it is too special to end.

Caring for the dying

Hospices are homes for both children and adults dying of an incurable disease. They provide palliative care until death, or respite care.

A basic ethos is that when someone is dying, they cannot be cured, only cared for. If that care covers all aspects of their being, they will not wish for euthanasia.

Hospices aim to:
- relieve physical symptoms of illness
- relieve mental and emotional symptoms of dying
- support the families of patients after the death – they suffer too
- educate others about caring for the dying.

Now test yourself

1 What is euthanasia?
2 Why do some people disagree with euthanasia?
3 Why do others agree with it?

TESTED

Answers at www.hoddereducation.co.uk/myrevisionnotesdownloads

Religious attitudes to abortion and euthanasia

Buddhism

- The First Precept is not to take life, therefore generally speaking, abortion and euthanasia are wrong. However, intention is key, so at times it may be the case that an abortion or euthanasia is actually the right action.
- Existence is suffering; karma and craving result in suffering. Compassion is a positive response. If we face death with anxiety, anger and upset, our next rebirth is negatively set, so a comfortable death, where the dying accept death, is facilitated. Buddhism supports hospices, which help people to face their death with calmness.

Christianity

- Abortion is morally wrong, although some people accept it as a necessary evil. While death might mean going to heaven to be with God, it should not be hastened.
- Life should always be protected. Where the mother's life is at risk, most would accept procedures which save her life, which is sacred, even if they lead to the ending of the pregnancy.
- Few Christians support active euthanasia, regardless of what a person might themselves wish for. This is seen as killing, so it is wrong. However, in countries where euthanasia is legal some Christians see it as an act of love and compassion and a good use of the medical knowledge God has granted us.

Hinduism

- Life is sacred and must be protected, therefore abortion is wrong. In each lifetime, a soul creates new karma for the next and 'pays off' the consequence of bad karma. By terminating a pregnancy, we deny the soul that chance to create/repay karmic consequences in a lifetime. So we block the soul's progress towards union with the Ultimate Reality. Where a woman's life is at risk, however, abortion is acceptable, as her life takes priority.
- Passive euthanasia is acceptable. Families respectfully care for their elderly, suggesting euthanasia should not be necessary. Active euthanasia is considered murder. Hindu principles support care for the dying, not ending life.

Islam

- Life is created by Allah, hence abortion is wrong. The issue is when ensoulment takes place: at conception, at 40 or 120 days? Before that time, technically an abortion is acceptable. Where a mother's life is at risk, Islam defends the woman's right to life.
- No one knows Allah's plans. Allah has planned for this experience, so it must have some value. Life will end when Allah wills it, so euthanasia is against that. Passive euthanasia would be accepted where there was no hope.

Judaism

- Life is sacred. Foetal life has no rights until birth and abortion would be allowed, if for example the woman's life was in danger, or for medical reasons. Some rabbis have extended this idea of endangerment to include a woman's mental health being in danger, such as after rape.
- Death should be calm. It is important to protect life and to care for the dying, so active euthanasia is wrong. Does euthanasia shorten life or shorten the act of dying? The latter allows a person a 'good death' and so is acceptable. Euthanasia can be seen as throwing life away, which is always wrong.

Sikhism

- Life is sacred – every soul is on a journey to achieve liberation. Life begins at conception so abortion is murder; it is destruction of God's creation. Sikhs may contemplate abortion – as a necessary evil.
- Sikhs should not harm or end life. Suffering may be seen as working through the negative karma of previous lifetime(s), so must be lived through, not avoided. A Sikh's duty to the dying is to care for them until God decides they die, not to hasten their death.

Exam tip

Many attitudes to abortion or euthanasia in religion are dictated by belief in the sanctity of life. If you can articulate that, you can work out the likely attitude to abortion/euthanasia.

Life after death

Death is when the brain and body stop functioning permanently. Religious people believe that at death the soul/spirit/self leaves the physical body. Though religious beliefs vary, all religions believe there is a continuation and some other kind of life.

Buddhism

(See also p.28) Buddhists believe in rebirth. There is no permanent soul, rather a mix of ever changing skandhas – emotions, feelings, intelligence and so on.

After the death of the body, this mix fuses with a new egg and sperm at conception. The actions and intentions of each life shape the quality of the next. The goal is to achieve enlightenment, and stop being reborn.

Christianity

(See also p.43) Christians believe in the physical resurrection of the body. At death, the body waits until Judgement Day. Catholics call this purgatory.

At judgement, the person faces God and Jesus to evaluate their deeds. If they were good in life, they go to heaven (paradise and wonderful forever). If they were bad, they go to hell (eternal punishment).

Hinduism

Hindus believe in reincarnation. Their atman (soul) lives through many lifetimes, each one shaped by the thoughts, words and actions of their past lifetime(s). Its goal is to achieve enlightenment and become one with the Ultimate Reality, so no longer being reincarnated.

Islam

(See also p.70–71) Muslims believe in resurrection. At death, the body waits in the grave (barzakh) and sees the events of its life.

On Judgement Day, people are sorted according to their beliefs and actions. The wicked are cast into hell; the truly good go straight to paradise. All others cross As-Sirat bridge, carrying the book of their deeds (sins make it heavier). The bridge is sharp and so they are purified from sin before going to paradise.

Judaism

(See also p.93) Judaism focuses on this life rather than the next. Some teachings mention a heavenly place. Jews talk of the 'world to come', which is when the Messiah will come to rule the earth in peace and the dead will be woken to live through that time. However, the crucial point is to focus on getting it right this time, not worrying about what comes next.

Sikhism

Sikhs believe in reincarnation. The soul is born into many lifetimes, whose quality is decided by the words, thoughts and deeds of the previous lifetime(s).

The point of each life is to serve and worship God, so that eventually the soul can be reunited with God (waheguru) and stop being reincarnated.

Activity

Below are two answers to the same exam question. Neither is perfect, so what is wrong each time? Remember the key rules of needing two teachings and having to explain points clearly. Then write your own perfect answer.

Explain two religious beliefs about life after death. Refer to scripture or sacred writings in your answer. (5 marks)

Student A:

Buddhists believe after we die, we are born again many times until we get enlightened. Christians believe we get judged by Jesus and if we were good, we go to heaven.

Student B:

The New Testament says that we can have life after death because Jesus was resurrected. He died as a sacrifice for humans' sins, opening heaven to humans. So, after death, our soul is awakened for Judgement Day, then judged by Jesus. If we had been good in our lives, we can go to heaven; if bad, we go to hell.

Now test yourself

1 What is meant by death?
2 Give two ideas used by religions about what happens at death.

Answers at **www.hoddereducation.co.uk/myrevisionnotesdownloads**

Exam question practice

What questions on this section look like:

Theme B – Religion and life

This page contains a range of questions that could be on an exam paper. Practise them all to strengthen your knowledge and technique while revising. Check back to pages 13–14 to see the marking grids that examiners use: this will help you to mark your answers.

1 Which of the following is not an effect of global warming?
   (a) Conservation   (b) Deforestation   (c) Pollution   (d) Climate change   [1]
2 Which of the following terms means to protect an environmental area?
   (a) Conservation   (b) Sustainable development   (c) Stewardship   (d) Recycling   [1]
3 Give two effects of pollution.   [2]
4 Give two reasons a person may be vegetarian.   [2]
5 Give two reasons for animal experimentation.   [2]
6 Explain two contrasting religious beliefs about abortion in contemporary British society. In your answer you should refer to the main religious tradition of Great Britain and one or more other religious traditions.   [4]
7 Explain two similar religious beliefs about animal experimentation. In your answer you must refer to one or more religious traditions.   [4]
8 Explain two contrasting religious beliefs about euthanasia. In your answer you must refer to one or more religious traditions.   [4]
9 Explain two religious beliefs about the sanctity of life. Refer to sacred writings or another source of religious belief and teachings in your answer.   [5]
10 Explain two religious beliefs about caring for the world. Refer to sacred writings or another source of religious belief and teachings in your answer.   [5]
11 Explain two religious beliefs about the Genesis creation story. Refer to sacred writings or another source of religious belief and teachings in your answer.   [5]
12 'Pollution can never be stopped.' Evaluate this statement. In your answer you should:
   ● give reasoned arguments in support of this statement
   ● give reasoned arguments to support a different point of view
   ● refer to religious arguments
   ● refer to non-religious arguments
   ● refer to a justified conclusion.   [12]
13 'Everyone should be vegetarian.' Evaluate this statement. In your answer you should:
   ● give reasoned arguments in support of this statement
   ● give reasoned arguments to support a different point of view
   ● refer to religious arguments
   ● refer to non-religious arguments
   ● refer to a justified conclusion.   [12]
14 'Religion proves that God created the world.' Evaluate this statement. In your answer you should:
   ● give reasoned arguments in support of this statement
   ● give reasoned arguments to support a different point of view
   ● refer to religious arguments
   ● refer to non-religious arguments
   ● refer to a justified conclusion.   [12]

ONLINE

Commentary

Level 2 students give unsupported opinions in answers to evaluation questions. This means they often give only their own ideas on something and rarely give two sides. If this is you, try to think of and present an alternate view to your own.

Level 5 students give more than one side in evaluation answers; however, they often do not focus closely enough on the statement. So reasoning is loose and limited. If this is you, underline key words/phrases in the statement and always check back to it with each argument you write.

Level 8 students give more than one side, focus clearly on the statement and develop their reasoning with good detail.

The existence of God and revelation

Christian One God; three aspects/persons	Islamic One God; no partners	Hindu One Ultimate Reality; many forms
One almighty, absolute God. Trinity – three-in-one: Father; Son; Spirit. The Father is the creator of the world; the Son was God incarnate (made flesh) as Jesus; the Holy Ghost is God with us now. All-powerful, all-knowing, all-loving.	One God: Allah – Allah has no partner and cannot be split (like the Christian God). Creator of all. Judge. Most compassionate. Most merciful. All-powerful, all-knowing, all-loving.	Ultimate reality – Brahman; pervades the universe in all its aspects. Trimurti of three major forms: Vishnu, Shiva and Brahma. Many other forms of gods to explain aspects of the Ultimate Reality, such as Ganesha, Lakshmi, Durga – each has specific qualities, e.g. Lakshmi is the goddess of wealth and fortune.

Why the different ideas about God?

REVISED ☐

There are various reasons why people have different ideas about God:
- Upbringing: their parents describe God in a certain way and that is what they come to believe.
- What holy books say: they are about God, after all.
- What religions/religious leaders say: they interpret the holy books, and many people believe they are closer to God or in contact with God, so what they say carries a lot of weight.
- They inherit a description of God from their cultural viewpoint or from their community.
- Experiences of God: if you experience God as a loving, kind being when you are in an emotionally difficult period in your life, you will think God is loving and kind. If something bad happens when you are feeling guilty about something, you might think God is vengeful because he has done this to you.

Some differences
- While Muslims believe there is only One God, who is indivisible, Christians believe that God has three persons (Father, Son and Holy Spirit) in the Trinity.
- Muslims give 99 names for God, each of which is a quality, but they believe it is impossible to properly know God. Christians believe they can have a personal relationship with God through the power of the Holy Spirit.
- Hindus believe there is something of God in everything. The Buddha told his followers not to look to a God at all.

> **Activity**
>
> *Explain two similar religious beliefs about God. In your answer you must refer to one or more religious traditions.* (4 marks)
>
> These answers to the question make common mistakes – can you spot them?
>
> A – Christians and Muslims believe God is very powerful, the most powerful possible. They believe God created the universe, which shows His power, as it says in Genesis and the Qur'an.
>
> B – Christians believe that God is omniscient; that God knows each of us so well he understands us perfectly. Muslims believe this as well.
>
> Christians believe God is omnipotent; that God is powerful beyond anything else, so He could create the world. Muslims believe this as well.

A – gives one belief only.
B – gives two beliefs, but does not explain either well.

In the beginning was the Word, and the Word was with God, and the Word was God. (John 1:1)

I am that I am. (G-d's response to Moses request for His name – Exodus 3:14)

He is Allah, One, Allah, the Eternal Refuge. (Qur'an 112)

There, where there is no darkness, or night, or day, or being, nor nonbeing, there is the Auspicious One, alone, absolute and eternal. (Shvetashvatara Upanishad 4:18)

> **Exam tip**
>
> There are many characteristics of God, but only six are stipulated by the Specification. It is helpful to be able to refer to others in your answers, so when you meet others in this Theme, learn them.

Omnipotent	Means 'all-powerful'; as powerful as it is possible to be.	**Like!** Makes God very different to humans. Explains how God could have created the world (the Genesis creation story). **But!** If God is so powerful, why not fix the obvious problems in the world?
Omniscient	Means 'all-knowing'; God's intelligence knows no limits.	**Like!** Makes God very different to humans. Explains how God can know what humans will do (Islamic al-Qadr). **But!** If God knows humans so well, why does he not stop 'evil' people?
Personal	Means humans can have a close relationship with God, shown in the prayer 'Our Father …'.	**Like!** Allows humans to feel watched over and protected by God, who must love them because of His personal nature. Means that we can come to some understanding of God as this personifies God, hence 99 names for God in Islam. **But!** Isn't God supposed to be completely different to us in every way? So how can we relate to God?
Impersonal	Means that God is not something that humans can have a close relationship to or can understand – there is a distance between the two.	**Like!** Emphasises the difference in status between God and humans, which is sensible if we also want to believe in God as creator, absolute, etc. Explains why humans cannot understand God, e.g. as the Ultimate Reality, the divine can only be known through enlightenment. **But!** How can humans have a relationship with this kind of God – something many religions are built on?

→

| Immanent | Means that God is active in the world, for example through the life of Jesus, or the Holy Spirit with Christians. | **Like!** Allows a personal relationship. Shows that God will act in the world, e.g. performing miracles. **But!** Does this make God too much like humans? |
| Transcendent | Means God is beyond space and time, controlled by neither. | **Like!** Explains how God could create the world – outside it and not affected by time or space, e.g. all religions say God is eternal and absolute. Explains the gap between God and humans. **But!** How can humans build a relationship with this God, as Christianity encourages? |

Now test yourself

TESTED ☐

1 What does omnipotent mean?
2 What does omniscient mean?
3 What does personal mean in relation to God?
4 What does impersonal mean in relation to God?
5 What does immanent mean?
6 What does transcendent mean?
7 Why might people prefer one idea of God over another?

Revision tip

For these characteristics, make sure you learn:
● what each word means
● a quotation or teaching to go with each
● why that characteristic is helpful to believers
● why there might be difficulty with each characteristic for believers.

Activity

Support or challenge?

'The most important quality of God is His transcendence.' Evaluate this statement. Refer to religious and non-religious arguments. You should agree and disagree with the statement, and come to a justified conclusion.

Use the list of arguments below to help you write a strong answer to this question. They are mixed up though, so first you need to work out which ones agree (support) and which ones disagree (challenge) with the statement. Remember that a conclusion should not just be repeating what you have already written, so it is worth keeping back a good argument to use there. You may have to read the next page to find some religious arguments to help with this.

Argument	Supports statement in question	Challenges statement in question
This allows God to have created the world.		
Means God is completely beyond humans – exactly what a God should be.		
Better for God to be immanent, as He is with and helps us.		
A personal God who loves us and cares for us is better.		
How can we have a relationship with God if we cannot understand anything of Him?		
God must be eternal and absolute to be God.		

Arguments for the existence of God

There are many arguments for the existence of God as well as the ones on this course. It can be helpful to know of some others, to use particularly in evaluation questions. Check out the ontological argument or the argument from religious experience or the argument from morality, for example.

For the course, you need to know the gist of three arguments for the existence of God, something of their strengths and some of their weaknesses. For the exam, you will need to know only a small number of strengths/weaknesses, so that is all you are getting here. However, you could try to work out some of the problems for yourself (which would help you to understand the actual arguments).

> **A posteriori reasoning**: arguing from experience; arguments generated from facts, not from suppositions.
>
> **First Cause argument**: postulates that God is the Uncaused Cause of the universe.
>
> **St Aquinas**: writer of the First Cause argument, which is one of a set of proofs of God's existence.

The argument	Its strengths	Its weaknesses
First Cause argument (cosmological argument) Put forward by Thomas **Aquinas** (13th-century monk), who claimed: • everything natural is caused by something else (e.g. flowers grow because of sun and rain) • nothing natural causes itself (everything relies on something else) • yet, for anything to exist now, there must have been first uncaused cause (something which did not rely on anything else for its existence) • this Uncaused Cause was God.	This is a logical argument – for example, it makes more sense that something started the chain of existence than that it randomly simply began itself, given nothing else in the world just spontaneously starts. It is an argument we can see evidence for (**a posteriori reasoning**) – we can see the links and chains in nature and in events (think of the cycles you learned about in science); to a human that is our normal experience. So the argument works from something we already know to be true, giving it weight.	Aquinas said that 'all people' recognise the Uncaused Cause to be God – he could not have asked everyone, so this is a sweeping statement and unfounded assertion. Similarly, Aquinas said that 'nothing is self-caused'. While it might be difficult to think of something, that does not mean he is right; again he is making an unprovable statement. He also then uses God as a solution ('there is no uncaused cause ... oh, yes there is – God'!).

Activity

Fix it!

Read the answer to this question, then write an improved version of your own.

Explain two religious beliefs about the existence of God. Refer to scripture or sacred writings in your answer.   (5 marks)

One religious belief about God is that there is a God. Christians say the Bible proves it. Another religious belief about God is that God is the Uncaused Cause which started the whole universe off.

The argument	Its strengths	Its weaknesses
Design argument Many versions, this one was put forward by **William Paley**, a 19th-century Christian theologian. He claimed: ● objects on earth look like they were designed – he uses the example of finding a watch, never having seen one before ● it seems to have a purpose, which means it was thought about and deliberately made ● just so, the world looks like it was designed, e.g. ecosystem, seasons, human eye ● these all seem to have specific purposes, as if deliberately thought about and designed to be this way ● the world must have been designed ● it must have been designed by God (no one/nothing else is capable of this).	This is a compelling argument, also a posteriori. We can see amazing things in nature which just seem so perfect for the job they do, so we like to think there is some reasoning behind these things, i.e. that they were deliberate – which means there has to be a mind at work. We can also see the regularity of the cycles and systems within nature – you do not suddenly have day following night, for example. This a posteriori reasoning allows us to think there is a co-ordinator behind it all, keeping systems in check (Newton's great watchmaker), which can only be God (a human couldn't do it!).	Evolutionary theory removes the need for something designing and keeping the world in check. We could also say that if there was something, it isn't doing a great job when you consider all the suffering we see ('blind watchmaker' idea). Paley's argument only makes a compelling argument for a designer – is that all God is?

Now test yourself

TESTED ☐

1 Name two arguments for the existence of God.
2 Briefly, what does the First Cause argument say?
3 Briefly, what does the Design argument say?
4 Why are these arguments compelling?
5 Why are these arguments flawed?

Activity

Support or challenge?

'There is no such thing as God.' Evaluate this statement. Refer to religious and non-religious arguments in your answer. You should agree and disagree, and come to a justified conclusion.

Use the list of arguments below to help you write a strong answer to the question. They are mixed up though, so first work out which ones agree (support) and which ones disagree (challenge) with the statement. Remember, a conclusion should not just repeat arguments, so it is worth keeping back one to use to strengthen your conclusion.

Argument	Supports statement in question	Challenges statement in question
There is no proof of God.		
The teleological argument is compelling because we see evidence all around us.		
The First Cause argument is logical.		
There is too much suffering in the world.		
Many people think they are personally responsible and should not look to a supernatural being.		
There are more religious people than non-religious people in the world.		

Design argument: aka teleological argument; argument which postulates that since the world looks designed, it must have had a designer – God.

William Paley: writer of this particular teleological argument.

Revision tip

Paley's teleological argument is not the only version – you could check out other versions such as Newton's thumb (for design) or the Kalam cosmological argument.

Argument for the existence of God from miracles

A **miracle** is an event contrary to the proper workings of nature, in other words, what is classed a miracle is something which should not happen in our universe, given the mechanics of it. Some people see as a miracle something which inspires awe and wonder within them, for example the miracle of birth/life. Sometimes people claim a miracle when they 'see' God, such as the seeds in an aubergine looking like the word 'Allah' (God).

The argument	Its strengths	Its weaknesses
Argument from miracles Within an essay debunking any notion of miracles occurring, David Hume, an 18th-century philosopher, actually gave good criteria for being able to label something a miracle. Hume claimed that any 'miracle' should be disregarded if: ● there was another (natural) solution ● the people claiming it had any links to religion (they would be biased/lying/misinterpreting events) ● they are claimed by people with little scientific knowledge. We can use this to reduce the number of events claimed as miracles. However, events claimed as miracles still seem to happen – a person being declared dead, then coming back to life (with no scientific explanation), a plane crash with no fatalities, someone being declared terminally ill with no hope of recovery suddenly being free of a disease (spontaneous regression). God must perform miracles (no one/nothing else explains these occurrences). The **Christological Argument** claims that Jesus rose from the dead (miracle) only because God exists (hence is proof).	There are certainly events which cannot be explained by science. When these events are positive/good, it is compelling to believe that a good force is behind them. If you believe in God, this argument makes sense; we should accept God helps us, and not question it. This fits with the idea of Jesus performing miracles, and his resurrection being one.	The random nature of miracles is a big problem – why do seemingly bad, even wicked people have them, and really good people don't? That suggests no thought behind the awarding of a miracle. Jesus said miracles were to showcase God's power – it seems unfair that someone should suffer just to give people a glimpse of a so-called loving God.

Examples of miracles

For the course, you have to know an example of a miracle. There are many in history, and in religious scripture.

John 11 tells the story of Jesus raising Lazarus from the dead. Lazarus had been ill and Jesus did not visit, in spite of requests, until four days after Lazarus had died. Jesus then told the mourners to move the stone from the tomb and called Lazarus out. Lazarus walked from the tomb (alive and well).

A modern-day example is that of Nev, who was dragged into a machine at work. His upper arm was snapped in several places and the nerve was completely severed, rendering him paralysed in that arm. Medical science says a severed nerve cannot be fixed. Following a year of paralysis, sensations and then movement returned. The arm is now almost fully functioning. Doctors cannot explain this, other than 'it is impossible' (so a miracle).

> **Christological argument**: argument stating that Jesus' miraculous resurrection is proof of God's existence.
>
> **Miracle**: an impossible event, contrary to the laws of nature, always good, attributed to a deity.

Arguments against the existence of God

Many people just do not see a reason to believe in a supernatural being. They think that we should just live in a morally good way and live the life we have (not seeking intervention or motivation from a being that cannot be proven to exist). However, many people feel that there is good proof that God does not exist. There are many such arguments, but for the course you could be asked questions directly only about two of them.

Moral evil: human words/actions which cause suffering to self/others.

Natural evil: events in nature which cause suffering to sentient beings.

Science: systematic study of the natural world through observation and experimentation.

The problem of evil and suffering as proof God does not exist

Suffering is mental/emotional/physical pain caused by events in nature (**natural evil**) or the behaviour of other humans (**moral evil**). It can be caused directly (e.g. someone thumps me) or indirectly (my parent dies, so I grieve).

Our experience of the world proves to us that there is suffering. We see/experience evidence of it every day. If God exists and is all-loving, all-knowing, all-powerful, why does He allow this evil/suffering to continue?

No argument to defend God has ever been satisfactory and there is no argument to prove God has enough strength to overcome the doubts caused by our own experience of evil/suffering. That God 'allows' evil/suffering proves there is no God.

Science as proof God does not exist

Science involves making hypotheses which are subject to tests to support their veracity, and the observation of regularity. Science is knowledge based on these.

Science is evolving and so our scientific knowledge increases minute by minute. What was considered to be true hundreds of years ago according to science may have been debunked by modern science (e.g. illness was thought to be caused by bad 'humours' in the body, it is now known to be through viruses, etc.).

Science says there is a logical explanation for every event – even if we do not yet know it, at some point we will. Hence, science does not need to use God to explain things – if anything, God is the 'joker in the pack', a 'god of the gaps' – that is, what we say when we do not know the real answer. God does not actually exist.

Activity

Develop the notes

A student ran out of time in the exam to write a full answer to the question. Use their notes to write a well-argued, detailed answer. Remember it needs a conclusion.

Science proves God does not exist.

(12 marks)

Agree
- Science is logical ideas based on observed evidence.
- Science grows all the time to explain new things.
- Science tells us not to opt for a being we can't even prove exists over explanations we can work out.
- We get more science lessons than RS ones!

Disagree
- Science can't explain everything.
- Even scientists agree some things are miracles.
- Science could just be us finding out how God runs the world.
- If science is so good, why is it always changing (when religion doesn't)?

Answers at **www.hoddereducation.co.uk/myrevisionnotesdownloads**

Revelation

What is revelation?

The term **revelation** refers to experiencing the presence of God, or the divine. If the revelation is direct, that is, seeing God or hearing God, it is a special revelation. If it is about sensing God's presence rather than directly seeing/hearing God, we call it general revelation.

> **Revelation**: when God reveals Himself; when God makes Himself known to a person either directly or indirectly.

Special revelation

Many holy books describe examples of this, such as the Qur'an describing Muhammad's prophethood. Many of these books also claim to be the word of God, for example Orthodox Jews believe the Torah was dictated by God to Moses. Many religious leaders claim to have met/spoken with God, which gave them the conviction to spread the word of their religion, for instance Guru Nanak.

One example from the New Testament is basically about how one of the key figures in Christianity, St Paul, became a Christian. Saul was his Jewish name. He spent his time seeking out Christians to be tried by the Jewish courts for blasphemy. Then, on his way to Damascus (modern-day Syria), he was blinded by a light that only he could see. He then heard the voice of Jesus asking why Saul persecuted him. Blind, he was taken to a nearby village. A Christian came to help him, sent by God, and cured his blindness. Saul asked to be baptised, changed his name to Paul and spent the rest of his life converting people to Christianity.

> **Revision tip**
>
> For the course, you should have studied one 'vision' or special revelation. There are many, and you know some from your study of a religion. Get those notes out, and recycle them for this Theme!

A special revelation provides personal proof of God to the recipient, affirming their religion or life choices. It can be a life-changing experience, so they do new things or behave very differently thereafter. It also gives insight into the character of God, so provides religious truths, and leads to new (interpretations of) religions.

General revelation

This revelation is available to everyone. It is indirect. It is knowledge of God/the divine, gleaned from experience of the natural world. There are many types, but you need to know about two:

- Knowing God through nature: God created the world, so we can appreciate God through it – we get a sense of amazement, awe and wonder. Maybe the world and the patterns within it make us think there must have been a designer, who was God. Maybe the beauty of the world – flowers, sunsets, etc. – make us think of God, or of some supernatural, divine power working behind the scenes. The hymn 'All Things Bright and Beautiful' is a perfect example of this mindset.
- Knowing God through scripture: 'scripture' is 'holy books' or 'sacred texts'. Many are said to be divinely inspired, or dictated by God. A central theme will be to describe God or aspects of God either directly, such as Psalm 103, or indirectly, for example by describing historical events which God has 'manipulated' (so suggesting justice, or goodness, or wrath, etc.). The reader is reading revealed truths.

A general revelation brings more knowledge of God, a sense of having 'special' knowledge. The person might feel reassured in their religion or life choices. They may feel they have a closer relationship with God.

Enlightenment as a source of knowledge of the divine

Enlightenment means 'awakening'. You could say it is when someone suddenly realises the truth of something. In this case it could be the grasping of a truth about God. Many religious people throughout history have claimed to have gained an understanding of God/the divine through revelation. It seems that the enlightenment allows a person to see things in a new way.

Many religious people study their sacred scriptures to gain better insight and so become enlightened (if only partially). For Orthodox Jews, study of the Torah is very important. Studying and learning about God through reading, debate, meditation/reflection and worship may give insight.

However, if God is absolute, omniscient, transcendent and so on, as described by religions such as Christianity, Islam and Judaism, you could ask whether it is actually possible for our puny human brains to comprehend God at all (even on the lowest level). Does your pet goldfish really understand you?!

In the case of Eastern religions such as Buddhism and Hinduism, enlightenment means full realisation of the truth of life, which leads to escape from rebirth/reincarnation (nibbana).

Hinduism splits life into four ashramas, the final two being devoted to religious study in pursuit of enlightenment. Through this study, and because Hinduism believes in the existence of the Ultimate Reality (divine/God), Hindus believe they can come to understand the nature of God, becoming finally reunited with God via enlightenment. So they can gain knowledge and finally fully comprehend the divine.

Buddhism seeks to realise the true nature of everything – impermanence, no self, and suffering (not just understanding the Buddha's teachings about it). Once this realisation takes place, so does enlightenment. This takes many lifetimes of study. Some Zen Buddhists use koans to gain partial enlightenment – a glimpse of that true nature.

Reality or illusion?

There are other explanations for revelation and enlightenment:
- Why real?
  - Personal evidence.
  - Life-changing experience.
  - Trust self.
- Why illusion?
  - It could be a figment of imagination, due to drugs/being drunk/dreaming/being delirious.
  - There is no empirical evidence to prove the event or the realisation to anyone else.
  - Religious people want to see God, so make themselves believe they have done so.
  - There is no such thing as God, so there can be no revelation of God.

> **Enlightenment**: realising a religious truth; attaining nibbana (release from the cycle of samsara).

Activity

Below are two answers to the same exam question. Neither is perfect, so what is wrong each time? Remember the key rules of needing two teachings and having to explain points clearly. Then write your own perfect answer.

Explain two religious teachings about enlightenment as a source of knowledge about the divine. (5 marks)

Student A:

Christians have the Psalms in the Bible. Psalm 103 describes God. If a Christian reads this, they learn about God and so can better understand God. Also people like Teresa of Avila used to meditate and communicate with God through this. So she had a better understanding of God and was able to write books about it, like 'Interior Castle'.

Student B:

Christians read about God in the Bible, like in the Psalms where God is shown to be merciful, loving, strong and so on. By reading it, they can gain insight into the nature of God, so they understand him better. Muslims can't know God, because God is too 'God'.

Tip: The marks awarded by examiners are: a mark per valid teaching (× 2) and a mark per clear explanation (× 2), plus a final mark for another religious teaching. 'Teaching' is any reference to scripture, to what religious leaders have taught.

Answers at **www.hoddereducation.co.uk/myrevisionnotesdownloads**

Exam question practice

What questions on this section look like:

Theme C – The existence of God and revelation

This page contains a range of questions that could be on an exam paper. Practise them all to strengthen your knowledge and technique while revising. Check back to pages 13–14 to see the marking grids that examiners use: this will help you to mark your answers.

1 What is meant by 'personal' in relation to the divine?
   (a) Beyond understanding   (b) Able to have a close relationship with God   (c) Absolute   (d) All-knowing   [1]

2 What is meant by immanent?
   (a) Absolute   (b) All-powerful   (c) Beyond time and space   (d) Active in the world   [1]

3 Give two alternative explanations to the claim that a person has met God.   [2]

4 Give two reasons why scripture helps people to understand God.   [2]

5 Give two reasons why some people believe the design argument is weak.   [2]

6 Explain two contrasting religious beliefs about visions in contemporary British society. In your answer you should refer to the main religious tradition of Great Britain and non-religious beliefs.   [4]

7 Explain two similar religious beliefs about ideas about the divine. In your answer you must refer to at least one religious tradition.   [4]

8 Explain two contrasting religious beliefs about proving the existence of God. In your answer you must refer to at least one religious tradition.   [4]

9 Explain two religious beliefs about enlightenment as a source of knowledge about the divine. Refer to sacred writings or another source of religious belief and teachings in your answer.   [5]

10 Explain two religious beliefs about general revelation. Refer to sacred writings or another source of religious belief and teachings in your answer.   [5]

11 Explain two religious beliefs about God being immanent. Refer to sacred writings or another source of religious belief and teachings in your answer.   [5]

12 'It is impossible to know what God is like.' Evaluate this statement. In your answer you should:
   ● give reasoned arguments in support of this statement
   ● give reasoned arguments to support a different point of view
   ● refer to religious arguments
   ● refer to non-religious arguments
   ● refer to a justified conclusion.   [12]

13 'The existence of evil proves that God does not exist.' Evaluate this statement. In your answer you should:
   ● give reasoned arguments in support of this statement
   ● give reasoned arguments to support a different point of view
   ● refer to religious arguments
   ● refer to non-religious arguments
   ● refer to a justified conclusion.   [12]

14 'Miracles prove God exists.' Evaluate this statement. In your answer you should:
   ● give reasoned arguments in support of this statement
   ● give reasoned arguments to support a different point of view
   ● refer to religious arguments
   ● refer to non-religious arguments
   ● refer to a justified conclusion.   [12]

ONLINE

Commentary

Level 2 students often struggle with key terms, which means they miss out questions, simply not knowing what they are being asked. If this is you, start by learning the key terms.

Level 5 students usually know the key terms, but their understanding can be limited. This means answers are often limited. If this is you, you need to work on knowing more detail (e.g. relevant teachings).

Level 8 students know the key terms and use them fluently and well, illustrating to the examiner their clear understanding.

Religion, peace and conflict

Buddhism
- Speaking out about injustice shows compassion (karuna) and could be seen as Right Speech.
- **Justice** is to understand the issues, respond with compassion and avoid violence as it only breeds more violence.

Christianity
- God requires humans to live in justice and freedom and wars should be fought justly.
- Wars can lead to conditions no better before the war, but can be fought for the greater good.

Conflict: disagreement which can lead to fighting.

Justice: in regards to war has two parts – to put right injustice and to carry this out in a just/right way.

Peace: To live in harmony and without fear with all people.

Reconciliation: making things right between parties after conflict.

Hinduism
- Wars must be morally justifiable – for a just cause Hindus will take up arms.
- Self-defence is justifiable but all actions should be done with a moral approach.

Islam
- Muslims strive for 'justice', which can mean armed conflict to strive for the common good.
- Islam condemns violence so wars should be carried out in the right way to achieve freedom.

Judaism
- Justice is key for Jews – war is justifiable in self-defence but must be justly carried out.
- Any weapon for self-protection is justifiable, even nuclear weapons, as it is not an aggressive act.

Sikhism
- Sikhs will fight for justice in a righteous war. Weapons which kill indiscriminately are wrong.
- Only minimum force should be used to achieve a goal.

Justice and reconciliation

Reconciliation is the idea of bringing sides together to help resolve issues so people can live in peace; otherwise any peace cannot last.

Justice as a reason for war means that wars are fought to put right injustices – this could be to help people who are oppressed by the regime that rules their country. Religious people cannot stand by whilst people suffer – they feel duty bound by the teachings of their holy books to act.

Any such action must be carried out in a fair way so that this sets the example and sees people being able to live in peace.

Reconciliation is the act of bringing sides together to help put issues right so that there can be lasting peace. This can in the first place prevent war and in the second bring the victor and the defeated together. War on its own does not bring peace, as issues need resolving through discussion and diplomacy so that all sides can contribute to a peace that they are part of making.

Forgiveness

Forgiveness is a theme that runs through all religions and is taught by religious texts and leaders past and present. It is the idea that after wrongs have been committed, there has to be a way forward for that relationship. Often we accept an apology as the person has seen the error of their actions and put the wrongs behind us. After war-time atrocities, some forgive unconditionally (without an apology) as it is the only way they can get on with their lives. Their example has led to enemies actually coming together – an example would be concentration camp guards meeting camp survivors. Forgiveness can lead to understanding both of what happened for both the perpetrators and the victims. Often people can never forget, and nor should they, but people of strong religious faith can forgive. Often the benefit of forgiveness is of more value to the person doing the forgiving then to the person forgiven.

Religious attitudes to forgiveness

1. The Buddha suggests that anger is 'like holding a hot coal – intending to throw it at someone –but you are the one who gets burned' (anger eats away at people so forgiveness prevents more hurt).

2. Jesus said, 'Love your enemies' (a person must forgive to love, leaving no one to be the enemy).

3. Gandhi said, 'Forgiveness is the attribute of the strong' (the stronger person is the one who is able to forgive despite what may have happened to them).

4. The Qur'an says, 'Those who pardon and maintain righteousness are rewarded by God' (forgiveness is a higher quality that Allah will reward after being faced with injustice).

5. Joshua Liebman said, 'We only achieve inner health from forgiveness' (not forgiving can eat people away inside and make them 'ill').

6. Guru Amar Das said, 'Dispelled is anger as forgiveness is grasped' (here forgiveness is the healer for the victim – allow people to move on with a peaceful mind).

Now test yourself

TESTED

1. What is justice when speaking about war?
2. Why might justice be needed after war?
3. What does 'reconciliation' mean?
4. Why might reconciliation be difficult after war?

Exam tip

Remember these key words – justice and reconciliation – are religious principles that can be applied to many topics. So learn them and use them widely.

Violence and violent protest

Religious people have a duty to fight/protest against injustice to create freedoms and peace. Wars can result from injustices. Religious believers have to try to stay true to and indeed balance the beliefs that they hold with the conflicts they face. Most religious teachings focus on peace, yet sometimes peaceful means do not work. When violent protest and violence seem to be the only way to achieve a common good, they become a 'necessary evil'.

What do religions say?

Buddhism

- Generally not accepting of violent (not ahimsa, causes dukkha, unskillful action).
- Speaking out about injustice is compassionate, is Right Action and Right Speech.
- Peace can happen only with mutual respect.
- Violence, although against Buddhist teachings, has been used when peaceful protest has not worked. Violence can gain attention, though there is still no guarantee of a positive outcome.

Christianity

- Teaches against violence as Jesus said 'Blessed are the peacemakers'.
- Christians are told to love their enemies.
- Humans have free will and where non-violent protest is ignored, violent protests are used for the common good.
- Often situations are so bad, religious principles get overridden because of the needs of justice.

Hinduism

- Non-violence is the only way to achieve anything long term.
- Ahimsa is key, but injustice should not be tolerated – protest can be a religious act if done in the right way. Again in practice, violence can erupt.

Violence or not?

Islam

- Action should be peaceful but violence can be used in self-defence.
- Unfairness must be protested against and violence avoided, but it is still often used.

Judaism

- Jews should protest against injustice as they are stewards, but their protest should be non-violent.
- Jews have suffered wicked evils in their history so want to help others – the focus of that help should be peaceful protest.
- Despite teachings, violence has often erupted as civil disobedience has failed to bring change.

Sikhism

- Teaches not to harm others but Sikhism is a warrior religion.
- There is a willingness to use violence to protest/fight against injustice.
- Sewa means Sikhs will defend the persecuted, always with peaceful intention but in practice violence happens.

Now test yourself

TESTED

1 What is violent protest?
2 Why might religions be reluctant to use violent protest?
3 Why might religious people choose to protest violently?

Answers at **www.hoddereducation.co.uk/myrevisionnotesdownloads**

Activity

Support or challenge?

'Religious people should never protest violently.' Evaluate this statement. Refer to religious and non-religious arguments in your answer. You should agree and disagree, and come to a justified conclusion.

Use the list of arguments below to help you write a strong answer to that question. They are mixed up though, so first work out which ones agree (support) and which disagree (challenge) with the statement. Remember, a conclusion should not just repeat arguments, so it is worth keeping one back to use to strengthen your conclusion.

Argument	Supports statement in question	Challenges statement in question
Most religions believe in non-violence, e.g. Hindus and ahimsa.		
Jesus was a man of peace – he stopped his disciples from fighting when he was arrested.		
If all else fails and there is still injustice, protest violently.		
Non-violent protest does not carry any weight with bad people, e.g. Hitler did not stop the Holocaust when faced with protests.		
Violent protest makes you as bad as what you are protesting against, so is self-defeating.		
Religious people should respect life always, so violence shows disrespect and is wrong.		

Terrorism

The UN Security Statement

Terrorist acts are 'acts intended to cause death or serious bodily harm to civilians with the purpose of intimidating a population or compelling a government or an international organisation to do or abstain from doing any act'. In other words, terrorists do terrible things to some people in order to intimidate other people, making them scared in their ordinary lives. The intention is to get their own way with one or more governments. These acts are considered criminal. This separates acts of war (which if done properly are not criminal) from acts of **terrorism**.

Terrorism in the world today

Today terrorism is a word used widely. The early 21st century has seen acts of terror come to the fore, either because of attacks carried out or attacks being threatened, and of course counter-terrorist measures and all the money and people these involve.

Terrorism is not new, but media coverage has brought it more to people's attention. Suicide attacks have taken terrorist acts to a new, perhaps more frightening, level.

The terrorism of today targets anyone: ordinary people, buildings, businesses, the internet, historical sites, sports events and market places – anywhere people gather.

Reasons for terrorist attacks

Terrorists often claim they are:

- fighting for God or to defend the faith
- fighting for social justice and against political injustice
- fighting poverty
- asserting their religious beliefs
- fighting because their wishes will not be heard any other way.

Why others disagree

All acts of terror because of their nature are wrong:

- Those targeted are innocent, with no direct link to the actual issue.
- Religion is wrongly associated with such acts – murder is wrong under all religious law.
- Terrorists are power driven rather than religious activists.
- Their causes are illegitimate.
- Murder, beheadings, kidnaps, rapes – all used in 21st-century terrorism – are never justified.
- Places that are terrorist strongholds are places of fear for ordinary people.

> **Terrorism**: an act of violence intended to create fear.
>
> **Terrorist**: a person who plans or carries out acts of terror.

Some religious teachings

Buddhism: no one should kill, nor incite others to do so.

Christianity: those who live by the sword die by the sword.

Hinduism: the pursuit of truth does not permit violence being inflicted on one's opponent.

Islam: the greatest sin is to take another man's life.

Judaism: when siege is laid – surround only three sides so that those who want to escape to save their lives can.

Sikhism: peace through justice is the ideal.

> **Exam tip**
>
> Terrorism is a difficult topic to ask questions about. This is because it is a very emotive topic. If asked about it, treat it sensibly and objectively.

Religious responses to the reasons for war

War is a major issue in the world today – wars between nations, civil wars, the war on terror, futuristic wars such as nuclear and cyber wars. The world has enough weapons to destroy the planet many times.

Many reasons have been used to justify wars, but not all people agree or disagree with these.

So why do wars start?

Wars are fought over land, in self-defence, for power, to keep agreements (treaties) and in support of other nations. These factors can also be interpreted as greed, self-defence and retaliation. These are the reasons you could be asked about in this course.

Greed

- This is war to gain more land, more power and more resources.
- In general, most religious teaching would not support this as a reason.
- Greed comes from selfishness – both not approved of by religions. Considering the numbers of people who die in war, greed is not justifiable as a reason for war.
- Greed is one of the Three Poisons in Buddhism, keeping us bound to the wheel of samsara; it is haumai in Sikhism.

Self-defence

- Religious holy books/texts describe wars, the Old Testament, the Qur'an, the Bhagavad Gita, the Guru Granth Sahib all suggest that war may be necessary in self-defence.
- If a country or religion is under attack then conflicts can happen. It would be seen as entirely right and proper to defend your country against attack.
- The problem comes when the response is disproportionately large and self-defence turns into aggression for its own gain.

Retaliation

- At times, a country will be attacked in a way that provokes retaliation. For example, the First World War began as retaliation against a political assassination.
- The problem with retaliation is that it is often a knee-jerk reaction which leads to the escalation of a situation with war. Religions would all say that peaceful negotiation and discussions to resolve issues are better than simple retaliation – they defuse rather than explode issues.

Religion and belief as a cause of war

Religion or religious teachings do not cause war. Many teachings are ambiguous, so interpretations cause the problems. However, some teachings are unclear, leaving the door open to use violence/war in the name of religion.

If religion is declared as a reason for war, it gains support from members of that religion. But people need to be guarded about this as many people directing war misuse religion to increase their own power – which actually is the whole point of the war.

Points to note are:
1 It is true that religion is involved in war if two different countries with different religions are in conflict. Religion is not the actual cause here, for example in the Israel/Palestine conflict.
2 It is true that religious beliefs divide people and when splits in religions have occurred, violence has often erupted.
3 Religions often try to show the differences between themselves whereas actually there are more similarities than differences. Religious beliefs can bring people together, solve crises and bring peace.

True religious beliefs do not cause war – they bring people together when viewed in the right way.

Now test yourself

1 Give two reasons for war.
2 What is self-defence?
3 Why do most people agree with war in self-defence?
4 Why do some people claim religion causes war?
5 Why should religion prevent/end war?

TESTED

Religious attitudes to war

Buddhism

- The First Precept, to refrain from harming others, is ahimsa and is a core principle of Buddhism.
- Hatred does not cease by hatred, hatred ceases by love (Dhammapada).
- He should not kill a living being, nor cause it to be killed, nor should he incite another to kill (Dhammapada).
- Buddhism does not believe in war – it leads to greater problems than it solves. It is often the result of the Three Poisons, while also encouraging these in us.

Christianity

- Put away your sword. Those who live by the sword die by the sword (Jesus).
- Blessed are the peacemakers (Jesus).
- Love your enemies, and pray for them (Jesus).
- Christianity teaches peace and love, though many fight in wars to defend against invading forces. There has to be a just cause, a last resort and peace restored after.

Hinduism

- Kshatriyas are expected to be the first to battle, and the bravest in battle.
- Even an enemy must be offered appropriate hospitality if he comes to your home (Mahabharata).
- War is not in keeping with Hindu virtues of ahimsa, tolerance, peace, compassion and respect.
- Hinduism sees that if war is a just one, it is a duty to fight and not doing so brings bad karma. In protecting others, fighting may be the only way.

Islam

- Greater jihad is every Muslim's personal struggle to follow Allah, the lesser jihad is holy war in defence of Islam.
- To those against whom war is made, permission is given to fight (Qur'an).
- Those who die in the name of Allah will be rewarded with paradise (Qur'an).
- Hate your enemy mildly; for he may become your friend one day (Hadith).
- Islam has a duty to fight in defence of Allah, the weak and oppressed as a last resort. Muhammad had to defend himself and holy war is a duty. It might be required to bring change.

Judaism

- Get ready for war. Call out your best warriors. Let your fighting men advance for the attack (Ketuvim).
- The sword comes to the world because of the delay of justice and through injustice (Talmud).
- When siege is laid to a city, surround only three sides to give an opportunity for escape to those who would flee to save their lives (Maimonides).
- Judaism previously had war as a religious duty. The Tenakh describes battles fought with G-d on the side of the righteous. War today is still acceptable but only as a last resort in self-defence and against injustice.

Sikhism

- The Sikh khanda includes two swords and Sikhs wear the kirpan, showing a willingness to fight when necessary.
- When all other methods have failed it is permissible to draw the sword (Guru Gobind Singh).
- A true warrior is one who fights for the downtrodden, the weak and the meek (Guru Granth Sahib).
- Sikhism allows war in self-defence and for justice. The Gurus suggested military training for all, went into battle against oppression and an army was set up after the Khalsa. Many Sikh men today join the army.

Activity

Use the teachings on this page to answer these questions.

Explain two religious beliefs about fighting in a war. (5 marks)

Explain two religious beliefs about peace. (5 marks)

Revision tip

Remember, don't just learn the teachings, know how to use them. That means being able to interpret them in the light of the issues today.

Clue: start with your teaching, then say what it means in terms of the question. Finally, develop your point by explaining clearly.

Just war

Within some religions' tradition there are guidelines on the rules for a legitimate war. Those guidelines attempt to control the decision to go to war and then how it is fought, making it somehow just or fair. These sets of rules have allowed religious people to fight, even when their religion purports to be one of peace.

Christian just war

Proposed by St Augustine, written in detail by St Thomas Aquinas in the 13th century, these rules have still been referred to and used as a guiding principle in modern warfare:

- Controlled by just authority – elected government.
- Just cause – must not be for revenge.
- Clear aim – promote good over evil.
- Last resort – all diplomatic methods have been tried first.
- Winnable – it is wrong to risk life if the war cannot be won.
- Fair conduct – reasonable force must be used and civilians protected.
- Good outcome – the benefits of war outweigh the evil of war.

The just war suggests that if you do not fight, you allow a greater evil to happen than the war would have caused. In other words, the war is the lesser of two evils, or a necessary evil.

Sikh just war

Outlined by Guru Gobind Singh when he set up the Khalsa:

- Sikh refer to just war as dharam yudh: 'in defence of justice'.
- War is the last resort.
- The cause must be just – a Sikh defends himself, his nation and the weak.
- War should be fought without hatred or the wish for revenge.
- Territory must not be taken.
- All soldiers must behave justly and civilians must not be harmed.
- Only the minimum necessary force should be used.
- When aims are met, the war should end and peace be established.

Holy war: war fought in the name of God; believing God has sanctioned the war; in Islam, there are criteria for this kind of war.

Just war: war fought under the auspices of the just war criteria, relates to Christianity and Sikhism; believing it is right to fight a legitimate war in the interests of justice and peace.

Pacifism: belief that all war and killing is wrong, that peace is the only way.

Activity

Fix it!

Read the answer to this question, then try to improve it.

Explain two contrasting beliefs about war in contemporary British society. In your answer you should refer to the main religious tradition of Great Britain and one or more other religious traditions. (4 marks)

Some people think that any war is acceptable if the government can give a good reason for it, like fighting the Iraq war when they thought Saddam Hussein had weapons of mass destruction.

Religious people, on the other hand, believe a war is only acceptable if it meets the just war criteria, because then it is allowed by God.

Holy war

Christian holy war

- Fought for God or faith.
- Last resort – enemy must have the opportunity to make peace.
- Believers are obligated to fight.
- Conducted fairly – there should be just treatment of the enemy.
- Protection of civilians and the landscape.
- Justice and peace restored.

Islam holy war

- A holy war is a just war with rules laid down in the Qur'an.
- Jihad can be fought only as a last resort and not against another Muslim nation.
- Muslims have a duty to join the army and fight if a just leader begins a war.
- Not all Muslims have to fight. Muhammad said one man from each two should fight, so that there are still men to defend and look after the towns and villages.
- Sane Muslim men, not boys, whose families will cope without them fight.
- Soldiers on the battlefield must fight – running away is wrong because that makes it more difficult for other soldiers.
- If a town is attacked, everyone – men, women and children – have to fight back.
- It may begin only when the enemy attacks and it ends when the enemy shows they want peace.
- Civilians must not be harmed, attacked or mistreated. Crops should be left alone. Holy buildings especially should not be damaged.
- Prisoners of war should be treated well. Money collected for zakat can be used to pay for food for them.
- When people regain their rights, the war ends.

Now test yourself

1 What are the conditions for just war?
2 What is the difference between just war and holy war?
3 What are the conditions for holy war?

Activity

Spot the problem!

Read the answer to this question. Work out how it can be improved, then rewrite the answer to achieve the marks.

Explain two contrasting beliefs about just war. Refer to scripture or sacred writings in your answer. (4 marks)

Muslims say Allah allows these wars – sanctioned by Allah. The Qur'an gives the rules for fighting these wars, so if Muslims keep to the rules, they are right with Allah.

Secondly, they believe that not everyone has to fight in a holy war. It is important that some people stay behind to protect civilians and keep things going. If the battle comes to their town, then everyone has to fight the aggressor.

Exam tip

Think about whether these ideas can be applied in the modern world today.

Remember, not all religions make reference to just wars or holy wars. If the exam question is about either of these, you may need to refer to other world religions you are not using as your main focus – it's the only way!

Explain two similar religious beliefs about just war. (4 marks)

Explain two different religious beliefs about holy war. (4 marks)

Victims of war

War results in many victims through injuries and death, destruction of buildings and land, contamination of land and water, refugees, famine and disease, captivity and the defeated. There are organisations that try to help the victims of war, both when war is happening and after it.

It is part of all religions to help those in trouble and defend those who cannot defend themselves. To help the victims of war fits with the basic teaching of the Golden Rule: treat others as you would be treated, which every religion subscribes to.

Christian Peacemaker Teams (founded in 1984) covers a wide range of Christian denominations. The organisation sends small teams to work on peacemaking in conflict zones – this is an example of third-party non-violent intervention.

The Buddhist Peace Fellowship (founded in 1978) works by applying Buddhist principles to resolve issues in the world. It raises awareness of issues, tries to strengthen leadership in the troubled areas, and acts with other groups to make change happen. It supports victims of war by helping bring peace back to an area and doing relief work for victims of war.

Khalsa Aid (set up in 1999) bases its work on the Sikh principles of selfless service (sewa) and universal love. It provides relief assistance to victims of war, funded through donations from Sikhs all over the world, as well as other disaster and relief work.

Individual religious believers can help by joining an organisation to strengthen its work through contributions, taking a job which directly works with victims of war, campaigning politically and encouraging others to do so, and praying for peace.

Peacekeeping: how is religion involved in wars today?

There are three key areas for answers:
- Is religion the defining factor in wars?
  - Yes – as communities are divided by war, religion often comes to the fore.
  - No – religion is often misused just to try to explain who is fighting who. Religion is drawn in but war is more about land and power.
- Does religion play a part in ending war?
  - Yes – many religious leaders call for peace, including employing peace negotiators. The majority of believers want peace and should be able to bring into line those who don't.
  - No – religious people call for peace but they are ignored. Religious extremists will always find excuses for war.
- Does religion keep the peace?
  - Yes – all religions have a central message of peace, expressed through key principle sayings: ahimsa, do not kill, love enemies, etc.
  - No – teachings talk about peace but religious believers may not want it; indeed, some want war. Even with their best peace efforts there are greater overriding factors, such as the craving for power, etc.

Now test yourself

1 Who are victims of war?
2 How do religious organisations help victims of war?
3 How might individuals help them?

TESTED

Exam tip

The above are the types of questions that could be the basis of questions in any exam, so learn the for and against points. It would also be useful to have a couple of teachings from your chosen religions to show that peace and not war is what religions strive for.

Weapons of mass destruction (WMDs)

Most religious people disagree with weapons of mass destruction (WMDs) and many have joined protests against them.

WMDs are capable of killing and maiming large numbers of people.

It is almost impossible to only target military operations.

WMDs are controlled from far away, so whoever releases the weapon does not experience or see the effect directly.

So they are indiscriminate in who they kill and the area they destroy. This is why most people disagree with them and why most forms are forbidden under international law.

Types of WMDs

WMDs use conventional (i.e. ordinary) weapons with a warhead with the WMD-type load. The explosion of the weapon causes widespread scattering of the contents/effect of the warhead. Other than nuclear ones, all are banned under international law.

Nuclear weapons – atomic bombs – cause immediate destruction of all life and structures within their range. The radioactive fallout will have long-term effects, contaminating land for long periods.

Biological warfare – germ warfare – uses live disease-causing bacterium or viruses such as anthrax to bring death or serious illness.

Chemical warfare uses non-living toxins such as nerve agents and mustard gas to cause death, incapacity or illness.

Radiological weapons – dirty bombs – are weapons using conventional explosives to disperse radioactive material. As well as killing people, they contaminate the impact areas for long periods (potentially years).

Religious attitudes

- Use of WMDs is wrong because of uncontrollable/extreme effects.
- It is against just war and holy war theories.
- It is against the principles of peace, justice and sanctity of life.
- WMDs are used as a means of oppression.
- Some believers accept that a nuclear deterrent needs to be maintained.

Should countries have nuclear weapons?

Nuclear weapons are often seen as the acceptable side of WMDs. They are held by a finite number of governments and are subject to international regulation. They are seen as 'defensive weapons', being held to keep the peace (working on the principle 'if I have this weapon, you will not attack me').

Reasons for proliferation (increase in nuclear countries) are:
- they discourage attack – have a deterrent value
- they maintain peace
- use of other WMDs is made less likely.

Reasons for disarmament (removal of nuclear weapons) are:
- nuclear proliferation makes use more likely
- there is no moral justification for their use
- WMDs are a waste of valuable resources (nuclear is extremely costly) which could be used more effectively
- it encourages other countries to develop them.

Now test yourself

1 What are WMDs?
2 Why do some people support the holding of WMDs?
3 Why do many religious believers reject WMDs?

TESTED

Religious attitudes to peace and pacifism

REVISED

Theme D

Buddhism

- Peace can exist if everyone respects all others (Dalai Lama).
- The Buddhist message is one of peace, not war. It is wrong to harm others (First Precept).
- Golden Rule: 'I will act towards others exactly as I would act towards myself.'

Christianity

- Everyone must commit themselves to peace (Pope John Paul II).
- The Christian message is one of peace. Jesus taught a message of love and Christians have a strong pacifist tradition.
- Golden Rule: 'Treat others as you wish to be treated.'

Hinduism

- Key Hindu virtues include ahimsa (non-violence), tolerance, compassion and respect, as well as protection of others.
- The Hindu message stresses that justice can be achieved only through non-violence. Since all life is sacred because Brahman is within all, the atman, war destroys this ideal.
- Golden Rule: 'This is the sum of duty: do nothing to others which if done to you could cause the pain.'

Islam

- The Muslim greeting is salaam alaikum ('peace be upon you').
- One meaning of the word Islam is peace. One of Allah's names is As-salaam, which means 'the source of peace'. It is said that if all people followed the Muslim way of life, there should only be peace.
- Golden Rule: 'None of you truly believe until he wishes for his brothers what he wished for himself.'

Judaism

- It shall come to pass ... nation shall not lift up sword against nation, neither shall they learn war any more (description of G-d's Kingdom).
- The Jewish message is tikkun olam – to heal the world. For this to happen, peace must be at the centre of all that people do.
- Golden Rule: 'What is harmful to yourself do not do to your fellow man.'

Sikhism

- The Lord is the haven of peace (Adi Granth). Peace is believed to come from God.
- The Sikh message of peace obtained through justice is the ideal for all.
- Golden Rule: 'As you value yourself, so value others – cause suffering to no one.'

Pacifists will never participate in war, regardless of the reasons for the war. Conscientious objectors refuse to fight directly but will assist in relief work, be medics or mediators – all seen as peacemaking roles.

The Quakers are a Christian group with a peace testimony never to use violence. They believe they follow the true teachings of Jesus, opposing all wars, and love should be the key between nations.

Gandhi, the Hindu leader, used non-violence for all his political actions – speeches, sit-ins, marches – showing it could be used effectively and be just as powerful as any physical force.

Bonhoeffer, a German pastor, used pacifism to oppose the Nazis. He believed helping the oppressed was a test of faith. In the end he did sacrifice his principles for the greater good – he planned to assassinate Hitler but was arrested and executed for treason.

Now test yourself

TESTED

1 What is peace?
2 What is the Golden Rule and how does it influence people towards peace?
3 Explain a religious attitude to peace.

Exam question practice

What questions on this section look like:

Theme D – Religion, peace and conflict

This page contains a range of questions that could be on an exam paper. Practise them all to strengthen your knowledge and technique while revising. Check back to pages 13–14 to see the marking grids that examiners use: this will help you to mark your answers.

1 Which of the following is not a reason for war?

   (a) Greed   (b) Terrorism   (c) Self-defence   (d) Greed   [1]

2 What does WMD mean?

   (a) Weapons of mass devastation   (b) Weapons of major destruction

   (c) Weapons of death   (d) Weapon of mass destruction   [1]

3 Give two reasons for forgiveness.   [2]

4 Give two effects of conflict.   [2]

5 Name two reasons for a country to keep nuclear weapons.   [2]

6 Explain two contrasting religious beliefs about violence in contemporary British society. In your answer you should refer to the main religious tradition of Great Britain and one or more other religious traditions.   [4]

7 Explain two similar religious beliefs about peace. In your answer you must refer to one or more religious traditions.   [4]

8 Explain two contrasting religious beliefs about pacifism. In your answer you must refer to one or more religious traditions.   [4]

9 Explain two religious beliefs about terrorism. Refer to sacred writings or another source of religious belief and teachings in your answer.   [5]

10 Explain two religious beliefs about helping victims of war. Refer to sacred writings or another source of religious belief and teachings in your answer.   [5]

11 Explain two religious beliefs about reconciliation. Refer to sacred writings or another source of religious belief and teachings in your answer.   [5]

12 'All religious believers should be pacifists.' Evaluate this statement. In your answer you should:
   - give reasoned arguments in support of this statement
   - give reasoned arguments to support a different point of view
   - refer to religious arguments
   - refer to non-religious arguments
   - refer to a justified conclusion.   [12]

13 'War can never bring peace.' Evaluate this statement. In your answer you should:
   - give reasoned arguments in support of this statement
   - give reasoned arguments to support a different point of view
   - refer to religious arguments
   - refer to non-religious arguments
   - refer to a justified conclusion.   [12]

14 'Greed is the greatest cause of war.' Evaluate this statement. In your answer you should:
   - give reasoned arguments in support of this statement
   - give reasoned arguments to support a different point of view
   - refer to religious arguments
   - refer to non-religious arguments
   - refer to a justified conclusion.   [12]

ONLINE ☐

Commentary

Level 2 students do not make it easy for the examiner to give marks. Their writing can be confused, too brief and too vague. If this is you, you just need to learn the content better – start by making notes that work for you.

Level 5 students use a mix of clear and vague ideas. Often the examiner has to look for where new ideas start. If this is you, try giving more clues – a new idea means a new paragraph, and you say 'Firstly' and 'Secondly' before your points.

Level 8 students write clearly and use – as the norm – clear signals for the examiner to work with.

Answers at **www.hoddereducation.co.uk/myrevisionnotesdownloads**

Religion, crime and punishment

Laws

Most religions also instruct their followers to keep the laws of the country in which they live. They should break a law only in certain circumstances – to protect life, for example, or if they are being challenged to break a key principle of their own religion.

Religions recognise that laws are for our own and society's good and safety, so must be right. Most laws are not unlike religious ones anyway.

Religion and rules

Religions have their own rules and laws that believers must follow, giving people a framework and guidance to help them live their lives correctly to achieve their spiritual aims. For example, the Ten Commandments apply to Jews and Christians, and Sikhs follow a code of conduct called the Rehit Maryada.

When a believer breaks one of their religious laws they commit a religious offence (sometimes called a **sin**). Just as in society when someone breaks a law, they are punished; there is also the belief that believers who sin will be punished in some way. Ultimately their afterlife could be affected, meaning they are going to hell or being reborn in a lower life form.

To decide what is right and wrong, religious people have several sources of authority to guide them. Nevertheless, they should always be guided by their **conscience**, sometimes described as the voice of God inside your head telling you what is right or wrong.

Religious traditions accept that everyone makes mistakes, but they also teach the ideas of punishment for the wrong-doing, repentance by the individual and compassion from the victim, which then allows them to forgive. A victim can offer **forgiveness** even if the criminal shows no remorse.

Some people believe that forgiveness is the best way for both criminal and victim to rebuild their lives. Punishment, though, is a clear part of the process. Jesus discusses forgiveness on many occasions but that does not mean to the exclusion of punishment. When Jesus was on the cross his comments about the two criminals being crucified with him can be interpreted as forgiveness; however, there was no reference to their punishment being stopped or cancelled.

Conscience: the voice in our heads that tells us right from wrong.

Evil: an act which is very wicked or immoral.

Forgiveness: letting go of anger towards someone for a wrong they have done to us.

Justice: a belief in what is right and fair.

Law and order: rules of our society, and how they are enforced.

Morality: a person's or religion's beliefs of what is right and wrong in behaviour and action.

Sin: an act which goes against God's will; a religious offence.

Suffering: a feeling of pain, harm, distress or hardship which is caused by the actions of others when they commit crime.

Exam tip

Learn these key terms, they form good 1-mark questions and underpin the whole topic in general. If you know their meaning you will be able to apply them in 4-, 5- and 12-mark questions.

Crime

Think about it … Which crimes do you think are the worst? Always have two or three reasons to be able to explain why, and some examples. Can any crime ever be justified?

Types of crime

When someone breaks the law they commit a crime. Most people experience the effects of crime at some point:

● Crimes against the person: causing direct harm to a person, for example murder, hate crimes.
● Crimes against property: damage or depriving people of their property, for example arson, burglary.
● Crimes against the state: potentially endangering everyone or affecting the smooth running of society, for example terrorism, selling state secrets.

Causes of crime

There are various factors that may lead to crime:

● Upbringing: the morals of family/friends/neighbourhood are a factor, as is whether a person is surrounded by crimes or criminal activity.
● Mental illness: a person's state of mind – they may have no understanding of right or wrong, no feeling of guilt or compassion, or are the victim of an abusive upbringing.
● Poverty: there is no alternative way to survive – a person may have no money, no job, they cannot provide for themselves or their children.
● Addiction: a person may need money to fund an addiction.
● Greed/hate: these emotions are often responsible for crime.
● Opposition to existing laws: crimes may be committed in protest about laws that are considered either unfair or for the benefit of a select few in society. Sometimes laws have to be broken to get them changed.

Evil: what is it and is it linked to crime?

Evil is immoral and wicked; good is virtuous and righteous. There are those who suggest that people who commit the worst crimes are evil. Look at these possible 12-mark questions:

'All humans are born with the ability to be evil.'
● Outside religion, some believe that we each have the capacity to do evil – it is part of our mental make-up. Evil depends on our upbringing, the influences in our lives – when those influences are bad, they can trigger or sow the seeds for evil actions. However, evil is not a force within us but rather a psychological phenomenon, so the person themselves has the potential to be evil. The level of the crime depends on how much evil has been triggered.

'People are not evil, they just do evil things.'
● Others say actions are evil, not the person themselves. However, we cannot punish the action – we have to punish a person for committing the wrong/evil deed. Most religious people believe that as it is the action that is evil, not the person, they are not themselves evil, so can be brought back to good ways. This then affects how people view punishments too.

'All evil has to be punished severely.'
● Evil, because of its wickedness, disturbs people's sense of well-being and safety, thus having a great impact. The direct victims have to be helped, the person punished and everyone else reassured.

Exam tip

These paragraphs can be used in answer to any of the three evaluation statements – providing you with a two-sided argument. Look at the next page for the religious arguments you would also need to include in your answer. Simply put all the ideas together and hit Level 4: 10–12 marks!

Now test yourself

1 What is meant by 'crime'? Give examples.
2 Why do people commit crimes?
3 What is meant by 'evil'?

Answers at **www.hoddereducation.co.uk/myrevisionnotesdownloads**

Good and evil

Theme E

Religious ideas about the origins of evil

Buddhism

- You cannot have good without evil.
- An act is not itself good or evil – the impact it has makes it one or the other.
- Three Poisons – greed, anger and ignorance – motivate humans to be evil.
- Every person is subject to these, it is how they manage their thoughts and intentions that causes the impact. We are each responsible for our own actions and their consequences i. e. behaving skillfully or unskillfully.

Christianity

- Evil is the abuse of the free will God gave humans, allowing them to choose right from wrong.
- In order to be able to see and appreciate good, evil has to exist.
- Most Christians believe in a figure called the devil or Satan, an evil power, though less powerful than God. This devil tries to tempt and encourage humans to behave badly.
- So, evil is a combination of internal and external factors.

Hinduism

- There is a constant struggle in the universe, in the world and in ourselves between light and dark, good and evil.
- Good and evil are natural parts of the creation.
- Human free will allows people to do evil, and as people are ignorant of the reality of the world, selfishness encourages them in the wrong direction.
- By our thoughts/words/actions we create karma – if evil, we will have to make up for that in possibly many future lifetimes.

Evil?

Islam

- The Qur'an says that there is a devil (Iblis) who was an angel. Allah had ordered the angels to bow to Adam, but Iblis refused.
- Iblis was expelled from paradise, but was able to cause Adam and Eve's expulsion from Eden.
- Iblis continually tempts and pushes humans to be wicked. Humans fail to show self-discipline and give in to Iblis' temptations.
- Evil is a mix of a powerful evil being and the weakness of humans.

Judaism

- Adam and Eve were tempted by the serpent to disobey G-d, resulting in the Fall – their expulsion from Eden.
- The serpent represents a malevolent force, which continues to subvert the behaviour of humans.
- Human free will means there has to be evil in the world – if there was no evil then free will would be useless. Observing mitzvot (laws), a Jew avoids evil.

Sikhism

- Selfishness (haumai) is the root of evil.
- It prevents people from following their religion, encourages them to break rules and hurt others. The more selfish a person, the more evil they are capable of.
- Evil lies within the consciousness of any person, and the level of selfishness we have makes it more or less controlling of our actions.

Now test yourself

TESTED

1 For any religion, try to explain their idea of where evil comes from.
2 Use your own intelligence to work out where you think good comes from and how a person might stay good.

The aims of punishment

There are many aims of punishment – this course requires you to study three of them. However, you could refer to any others in answers which are not exclusively about the three specified.

Knowing a fuller range of aims helps you better understand why punishments are given by judges. So here are some other commonly used aims:

- Protection: the key aim is that the law must protect society from the criminal and the criminal from society – to keep everyone safe. When someone is locked up in prison, they cannot cause harm in society so people are safer.
- Vindication: the law has to be tough enough for people to live by the rule of law. People must feel that the punishments given mean the law is upheld. In effect, punishments justify the existence of laws.
- Reparation: the criminal can 'repair the damage done', either with direct contact with the victim of their crime to physically put something right, or by doing something to benefit the local community. They are 'making up for' by 'repairing'.
- Compensation: the criminal pays back something (usually with monetary value) to compensate the victim for the damages done – whether physical, emotional or financial, or damages to items/ property.

Deterrence

This deters (puts off) the criminal from doing the crime again because the punishment is harsh. It also deters other people from committing crimes in the first place because they are put off by the punishment given to others.

Key point: if people were deterred from criminal acts, there would be no crime to punish. Harsh punishments like the death penalty are used as a deterrent in Islam, and available in law in Judaism and Hinduism – there is no chance then of repeated crime. Christianity and Sikhism agree with deterrence but not always through very harsh punishments (which may make criminals worse). Buddhism does not agree with harsh punishments as

they could themselves cause harm, which is against the Precepts. Deterrence can be created in many ways, but there is no guarantee that deterrence will be effective.

Retribution

This is the idea that the punishment 'should fit the crime', almost to the point where it can be seen as taking revenge. The law of course is not actually vengeful – it provides justice by seeing the criminal pay for their crimes and ensuring that they have not got away with them.

The 'death penalty' or a 'life sentence' for a murderer would be retribution – life for life. Islam, Judaism and Hinduism support this idea – for example, the death penalty ensures a 'life for a life'. It ensures justice and no repeated crimes. Christians would say that a whole life sentence is better as it 'takes away the freedom of life' rather than the law carrying out an act as bad as the criminal's murder. Revenge is not an appropriate response, coming as it does from hatred. However, justice is done, and it is costly for a whole life sentence and prison is not always considered harsh enough.

Reformation

Many punishments are given to try to change the behaviour of the criminal – to be able to safely put them back into society, having seen the error of their ways. They realise they were wrong, or see the effect on their victims and reform, so change.

A criminal can be reformed through a harsh punishment or through a positive punishment with education, rehabilitation and counselling programmes. All religions support this aim – but reform is done in different ways. Islam goes with harsh punishment to force reform. This works as no one really wants to suffer, whereas Christianity, Buddhism and Hinduism want to see work done with the criminals so they change their moral outlook and see the inappropriateness of their ways. Reform cannot be guaranteed though and criminals do reoffend.

Activity

Support or challenge?

'Reformation is the most important aim of punishment.' Evaluate this statement. Refer to religious and non-religious arguments in your answer. You should agree and disagree, and come to a justified conclusion.

Use the list of arguments below to help you write a strong answer to that question. They are mixed up though, so first work out which ones agree (support) and which disagree (challenge) with the statement. Remember, a conclusion should not just repeat arguments, so it is worth keeping one back to use to strengthen your conclusion.

Argument	Supports statement in question	Challenges statement in question
It changes people's moral outlook for the better, so changes them for ever.	✓	
Protection is necessary from murderers and those who hurt other people.		✓
Jesus believed in second chances, and reformation helps people appreciate a second chance.	✓	
A victim would prefer to be compensated for what has happened to them – if someone has vandalised my house, I would rather it be fixed.		✓
Not all people can be reformed because their behaviour is too ingrained.		✓
There is something of God in everyone, so everyone can be reformed, and then they would contribute positively to society.	✓	

Reformati I agree with this statement because Reformation changes people's moral outlook for the better so it changes them for ever. However, someone might disagree with this statement because protection is necessary from murderers and those who hurt other people. Another view of this would be that Jesus believed in second chances, and reformation helps people appreciate a second chance.

Religious attitudes to crime and punishment

Buddhism

- The law enforces rules and punishes when rules are broken. Punishment is a deterrent to put off criminals through a need for self-preservation, for example not to murder because 'I don't want life in prison'. Buddhists believe that this is the wrong mindset – criminals need to learn to not do things because they realise they are wrong/hurtful to others, namely Right Intention.
- Some Buddhist values are upheld by the law, for example by prohibiting murder, the value of non-harm is maintained; by punishing thieves, the value of 'not taking what is not freely given' is upheld. The types of punishments given do not always show compassion and understanding. Neither is the treatment of criminals carried out according to Buddhist teachings of compassion and the Noble Eightfold Path. It is not always easy to equate punishment with strict Buddhist principles.

Christianity

- The law has responsibility to punish and care for the criminal while trying to reform them. While prison removes freedoms/rights and separates offenders from their families, it is also concerned that they be reformed and can rejoin society as 'good' citizens. Therefore there can be conflict between severe punishments and the Christian belief in help, love and reform.
- However, some Christians want more of an emphasis on 'justice' based on the 'an eye for an eye' teaching from the Bible. Most believe in people being treated humanely and fairly, giving them the chance to face up to their crime, serve a fair punishment and have a second chance to turn their lives around.

Hinduism

- Scripture says punishment is a ruler's right and through fearing the threat of punishment, all beings should follow their dharma. Punishment maintains social order.
- In the past, punishments allowed for compensation rather than for retribution. This allows for society and criminals to be reconciled and social justice to be restored. In modern law, punishments are given by the state and victims need to be compensated too.

Islam

- The Qur'an emphasises the justice of Allah and the idea, and accountability, of one's actions. Also it talks of mercy and forgiveness. The legal system prescribes punishments for crimes such as murder, rape and theft, including capital punishment, imprisonment and lashings.
- Muslim scholars believe that extreme punishments are not used widely today. Most Muslim countries have modern prisons and principles of fair treatment of criminals. Justice must be done and the victims compensated. Hence victims can accept compensation from the criminal who then is given a lesser sentence, and Allah looks favourably on that.

Judaism

- Jews have to accept punishments dealt out for criminal acts. There is a strong belief in repentance and while a person can repent to G-d, this is pointless if they try to avoid the punishments from society.
- One of the seven laws of Noah states that there is a need for a proper legal system to establish a moral society. Treatment of offenders must be just and fair, with a focus on reform. Revenge as in retribution according to the Talmud is not a Jewish principle.

Sikhism

- There are religious laws and criminal laws. For the former, community service in the gurdwara is used, with an emphasis on penance, humility and renewal of vows broken. Sikhs do not hold power in any state or country and so do not determine punishments.
- Some agree with capital punishment to keep society safe but many believe it is against the nature of God as He decides life and death. Punishments should be just and allow for reform, and forgiveness is consistent with trying to be like God.

Religious beliefs about suffering

Religions condemn suffering caused by human action and all have rules/principles which are there to try to prevent suffering. Teachings tell us it is wrong to cause suffering and that those who do so should be dealt with.

Buddhism believes suffering is everywhere – we all have to look within ourselves to stop this suffering. Other religions want God to help them overcome suffering or be forgiven for causing it.

Religion gives humans the path to righteous actions, but this path is difficult to follow at times. All religions stress how our emotions – love, hate, greed and desires – easily lead to suffering and give us teachings to keep these in check.

Religions support the law to prevent suffering, believing law-breakers should be punished fairly and with justice, and that victims must be helped.

Helping those suffering from crime: the victims

Victims (and witnesses) are supported by the justice system. They are offered emotional and practical support and practical tips to keep safe. There is specific support in certain areas, such as for abuse or rape victims, victims' rights, help for young victims and help for foreign language speakers.

Forgiveness for the criminal

It is very important to forgive and this is a key religious quality. **Forgiveness** is more about the victim than the criminal, and often has more impact on the victim, allowing them to let go of the negative ideas of revenge to move on and let the criminal move on too. It does not mean the victim condones, accepts, excuses or forgets the crime, however.

Some criminals repent, earning forgiveness; some do not but are forgiven anyway. Society deals with criminals with punishment, whereas victims can deal with them with forgiveness.

For Buddhists, forgiving practises compassion and Right Understanding. Without it the world remains vengeful and troubled. For Christians, Jesus said we should forgive 'not seven times but seventy times seven'. Hindus see forgiveness as one of six cardinal virtues. Islam states, 'whosoever forgives and makes amends, his reward is upon Allah'. In Judaism, the Torah explicitly forbids Jews to take revenge or to bear grudges. Sikhs believe 'forgiveness is as necessary to life as the food we eat and the air we breathe'.

Most religions believe that forgiveness is a quality of God, to be copied by the believer.

> **Activity**
>
> Giving yourself timed tests is a great way to boost your exam readiness. So, for a 4-mark question, give yourself 5 minutes. Go!
>
> *Explain contrasting religious beliefs about the punishment of criminals.* (4 marks)

> **Forgiveness**: to stop holding someone's actions against them and move on.
>
> **Repentance**: being truly sorry for what you have done.

> It is not the law's business to forgive. The law deals with the criminal as it has to. It can be described as a process: crimes committed; criminal caught and punished; time served; **repentance** shown (maybe), and new start. The crime is not forgotten, but the criminal has the chance to move on.

> **Activity**
>
> Use the information on this page, and the checklist below, to answer the following:
>
> *'All criminals should be forgiven rather than punished.'* (12 marks)
>
> - The key words are 'all' and 'rather'. Can you think of different crimes which could be forgiven and those which might not be forgivable?
> - Think about two/three reasons criminals should be forgiven, maybe using some examples to demonstrate your points, and then two/three points showing why punishment is necessary too.
> - In these types of questions arguing that both are required often makes a good conclusion.

Punishment

Prison

Prison is the secure confinement of a criminal to deprive them of their liberties. They have a regime to follow day in day out. Most prisoners will be released back into society having completed no more than half their original sentence, as they become eligible for release on parole at that point.

Aims prison fulfils:
- Protection: keeps safe society from the criminal and the criminal from society.
- Deterrence: prison itself should deter the criminal and would-be criminals.
- Retribution: length of sentence fits the crime committed.
- Reformation: work is done in prison to change the criminal for the better.
- Reparation: the criminal might be encouraged to meet their victim and make up for what they have done.
- Vindication: sentences are lengthy for serious criminals so that the law is respected.

Concerns about prison:
- The conditions in which prisoners are kept are not conducive to reform.
- There is debate over which crimes should result in prison.
- How can putting bad people with bad people reform any of them?
- Most prisoners reoffend, so prisons are not effective, but they are costly.
- Crime carries on in prisons – drug use, gangs, assaults, violence, threats.
- Separation from families, detachment from society, readjustment on release are all the source of problems.

> **Revision tip**
>
> The Specification requires you to study two punishments used in the UK: prison and community service. You can refer to others in answering non-specific questions though, to support the points you make.

> **Community service**: doing unpaid work for the community as a legal punishment.
>
> **Corporal punishment**: inflicting physical pain as a legal punishment.
>
> **Prison**: deprivation of liberties as a legal punishment.

Community service

This punishment is given for less serious crimes to repair the damage caused, with a set number of hours spent 'paying back' the community by working on projects. It is more positive than prison so has better outcomes. It can be done around working hours and there is no separation from families. **Community service** offers help to avoid criminal activity.

Aims community service fulfils:
- Reformation: a positive change can come about in the criminal through a positive contribution to society.
- Deterrence: the orange jackets make people highly visible when on community service and they do not want to be seen doing this again.
- Retribution: the project matches the crime – graffiti clean-up. Society is getting them back.

Concerns about community service:
- There are not enough projects available – many not suited to the crimes committed – so it is not helpful.
- It is seen as too soft an option and often does not bring reform.
- Monitoring and management are often poor, so those sentenced to community service do not complete hours or are badly behaved, without any punishment or reprisal.

Corporal punishment

Corporal punishment is physical punishment causing physical pain, such as whipping/branding/amputation. It is not used in the UK, where it is illegal, or most democratic countries. All religions in the modern world (except Islam) would disagree with its use.

Some teachings suggest its use historically, as in Hinduism, Judaism and Christianity. However, modern-day teachings of both Christianity and Judaism are against this form of punishment.

Islamic countries use corporal punishment, with lashes and amputation being the most common forms. The Qur'an sanctions such punishment and as the word of God should be followed.

Corporal punishment is seen as a deterrent and is effective because no one wants pain. It is retribution and quick reformation, but also inhumane and barbaric – revenge is wrong.

Criminals can become hardened, so the lesser forms of corporal punishment have no deterrent value.

Religious teachings about corporal punishment (CP)		
Buddhism	**Christianity**	**Hinduism**
Crimes come from intention – this is what needs to be dealt with, but CP does not target this. CP is not a loving action, breaking the First Precept.	An eye for an eye (Bible). You heard it said, an eye for an eye … I say if someone hits you offer the other cheek (Jesus).	Incapacitation is an aim of danda (punishment), so amputation of the hand for a thief was used historically. CP is not ahimsa though!
Islam	**Judaism**	**Sikhism**
As for a thief, male or female, cut off their hand (Qur'an).	Torah law permits CP. It is forbidden to mutilate a body and CP does that, at least temporarily, so can be seen as wrong.	Fareed, do not turn around and strike those who strike you with their fists. Kiss their feet, and return to your own home (Guru Granth Sahib).

Now test yourself

1 What is prison?
2 What is community service?
3 What is corporal punishment?
4 What is good/bad about each of these types of punishment?

Activity

Support or challenge?

'Punishments in the UK are not harsh enough.' Evaluate this statement. Refer to religious and non-religious arguments in your answer. You should agree and disagree, and come to a justified conclusion.

Use the list of arguments below to help you write a strong answer to that question. They are mixed up though, so first work out which ones agree (support) and which disagree (challenge) with the statement. Remember, a conclusion should not just repeat arguments, so it is worth keeping one back to use to strengthen your conclusion.

Argument	Supports statement in question	Challenges statement in question
Community service is too easy to get out of and no one works hard.		
Corporal punishment would make more people think twice – physical pain has the harshness to deter. The UK doesn't have this.		
Prison is very difficult, depriving of freedoms and keeping a criminal from their family.		
Punishment should be about deterrence and reformation, not harshness – which sounds like revenge and is against religious teachings.		
Many criminals reoffend after they have been punished in the UK.		
Jesus taught forgiveness – even when he was being punished in the harshest way. It is good the UK does not have this kind of punishment.		

Activity

Read the question and both answers. Which answer is better? Use a highlighter and annotations to show why it is better.

Explain two contrasting beliefs from contemporary British society about the death penalty. In your answer, you should refer to the main religious tradition in Great Britain and one or more other religious traditions.

(4 marks)

Student A:

Christians agree with the death penalty because they believe in an eye for an eye. This means murderers should be put to death. Muslims also agree with the death penalty because the Qur'an says it must be carried out for certain crimes.

Student B:

Muslims have the death penalty as Shari'ah Law. The Qur'an surah says which crimes are punishable by death, but also says that life cannot be taken except by way of justice (so the death penalty can only be used for the most serious crimes). Judaism – on the other hand – allows for the death penalty, but never uses it. The Torah gives situations for which the death penalty may be used, and Jewish law defines how capital punishment should be carried out.

The death penalty – capital punishment

In the few countries where the death penalty is legal, it is reserved for the most extreme offences, usually murder. Crimes such as blasphemy, adultery, drug offences, corruption, fraud, treason and war crimes are also capital offences (they carry the death penalty).

- There are 85 countries that retain the death penalty; only 21 use it routinely.
- Since 2000, approximately 1,000 people per year worldwide have been recorded as executed by their governments.

Why the need for such an extreme punishment?

Where the death penalty is used, the crimes are seen as being so bad that no other punishment would be suitable. Society must take revenge on the individuals who commit such heinous acts and deter others from committing such offences.

This meets the ethos of 'an eye for an eye' and also the law of equality of retribution in Islam. A murderer shows no respect for human life, so the state has none for theirs.

Many holy books name certain offences as being punishable by death.

Arguments for CP:
- An 'eye for an eye, life for a life'.
- Deterrence – to put people off committing horrendous crimes.
- Justice for the victims and their families.
- Life sentences do not mean life – murderers walk free after a few years.
- Terrorists murder indiscriminately, they cannot be reformed.
- It is a waste of resources housing criminals for their entire life.
- The death penalty has been used for centuries around the world.
- It demonstrates that society will not tolerate some crimes.

Arguments against CP:
- Retribution is uncivilised – two wrongs don't make a right.
- Most murders are 'spur of the moment', so capital punishment would not deter.
- Killing the murderer does not end the pain of loss for the victim's family.
- It makes executioners seem as bad as criminals.
- Executing terrorists would make them martyrs.
- Innocent people can be executed after an unfair trial.
- All life is sacred, including that of murderers.
- It is inhumane and degrading to put anyone through the mental torture of death row.

Now test yourself

TESTED

1 What is capital punishment?
2 Why do some people support the use of capital punishment?
3 Why do other people disagree with the use of capital punishment?

Activity

In her exam, Jenni wrote this answer. You can see she focused on aims of punishment rather than the pros and cons of the death penalty. Notice how she underlines her key points to make them leap out for the examiner (clever!).

Use the bullet points from arguments for and against the death penalty to write a stronger answer to this.

The death penalty does not solve the problem of crime.   *(12 marks)*

To solve the problem of crime, I think we have to get the punishment right. The death penalty is a good <u>deterrent</u> – who wants to get killed? So it puts people off. It also <u>protects</u> society from that criminal hurting anyone else. So it does solve the problem.

However, it is <u>only useful for some crimes</u>, so it doesn't solve the problem really. Jesus talked about <u>forgiveness</u> – the death penalty is definitely not that!

Religious beliefs about capital punishment

Buddhism

- Buddhists do not agree with punishments that are unduly severe – and the death penalty is.
- The death penalty goes against loving kindness (metta) and compassion (karuna).
- The First Precept is about not taking life.
- The death penalty is a form of revenge, so comes from bad intentions (Three Poisons).

Hinduism

- The laws of man allow for the death penalty for murder, theft and adultery.
- Gandhi said: 'An eye for an eye and we shall all soon be blind.'
- Punishment should allow for the offender to reform.
- In India today only murder and treason carry the death penalty.

Judaism

- 'The Lord does not enjoy seeing sinners die. He would rather they stop sinning and live' (Nevi'im).
- 'If anyone takes the life of a human being they must be put to death' (Torah).
- 'G-d created the world with justice and mercy so that it would last' (Midrash).
- The death penalty exists as a deterrent but is rarely used – atonement is preferable.

Would religion agree with capital punishment or not?

Christianity

- 'An eye for an eye' (Old Testament).
- 'Do not kill' (Old Testament).
- 'God gives life and takes life away' (Job).
- Capital punishment would deny the sanctity of life – 'all life is sacred'.

Islam

- 'The greatest sin is to take another man's life' (Qur'an).
- 'We ordained for them – a life for a life' (Qur'an).
- 'Take not life except by way of justice and law' (Qur'an).
- 'If a man kills unjustly, his family will be entitled to satisfaction' (Shari'ah).

Sikhism

- Many do not support the death penalty because of their belief in the sanctity of life.
- Some would see it as a useful deterrent and just punishment for some crimes.
- If someone hits you, do not hit him back, run after him and kiss his feet (Guru Granth Sahib).

Exam tip

Remember that not all believers will agree with the death penalty, even if teachings suggest it is acceptable. Most holy books have teachings to support and to challenge the use of the death penalty.

This is a popular topic and fits into all the question styles. It could be a definition for 1 mark, reasons for 2 marks, similar or contrasting beliefs about … 4 marks, religious beliefs about … 5 marks, or a 12-mark evaluation. In other words, there is plenty of scope for the examiner to ask it on your exam.

Capital punishment: the death penalty administered officially by the state as a punishment for certain crimes.

Midrash: 'story telling', written by rabbis to interpret the Tenakh, or answer questions arising from it.

Exam question practice

What questions on this section look like:

Theme E – Religion, crime and punishment

This page contains a range of questions that could be on an exam paper. Practise them all to strengthen your knowledge and technique while revising. Check back to pages 13–14 to see the marking grids that examiners use: this will help you to mark your answers.

1 Which of the following is not an aim of punishment?

   (a) Justice   (b) Retribution   (c) Deterrence   (d) Reformation   [1]

2 What is meant by corporal punishment?

   (a) Death penalty   (b) Deprivation of liberties

   (c) Paying compensation   (d) Physically hurting someone   [1]

3 Give two concerns people have with the use of prisons as a punishment.   [2]

4 Give two reasons for the use of community service as a punishment.   [2]

5 Give two reasons to support capital punishment.   [2]

6 Explain two contrasting religious beliefs about the death penalty in contemporary British society. In your answer you should refer to the main religious tradition of Great Britain and one or more other religious traditions.   [4]

7 Explain two similar religious beliefs about justice. In your answer you must refer to one or more religious traditions.   [4]

8 Explain two contrasting religious beliefs about the aims of punishment. In your answer you must refer to one or more religious traditions.   [4]

9 Explain two religious beliefs about forgiveness as an attitude to criminals. Refer to sacred writings or another source of religious belief and teachings in your answer.   [5]

10 Explain two religious beliefs about the need to follow the law. Refer to sacred writings or another source of religious belief and teachings in your answer.   [5]

11 Explain two religious beliefs about people who break the law because of mental illness. Refer to sacred writings or another source of religious belief and teachings in your answer.   [5]

12 'Opposition to an unjust law is the only reason to commit a crime.' Evaluate this statement. In your answer you should:

- give reasoned arguments in support of this statement
- give reasoned arguments to support a different point of view
- refer to religious arguments
- refer to non-religious arguments
- refer to a justified conclusion.   [12]

13 'Murder is not the worst crime a person can commit.' Evaluate this statement. In your answer you should:

- give reasoned arguments in support of this statement
- give reasoned arguments to support a different point of view
- refer to religious arguments
- refer to non-religious arguments
- refer to a justified conclusion.   [12]

14 'Only severe punishment can maintain law and order.' Evaluate this statement. In your answer you should:

- give reasoned arguments in support of this statement
- give reasoned arguments to support a different point of view
- refer to religious arguments
- refer to non-religious arguments
- refer to a justified conclusion.   [12]

ONLINE

Commentary

Grade 2 students show little knowledge of the diversity within or between religions. If this is you, you need to get notes that are better for you to work with.

Grade 5 students show some knowledge of diversity and an understanding of how this influences different people. If this is you, focus your notes and revision on specific groups within religions so that you can write clearly and knowledgably.

Grade 8 students show good knowledge and understanding of the diversity within and between religions. They demonstrate this clearly in detailed answers.

Religion, human rights and social justice

Social justice

This is justice which tries to more fairly distribute wealth, where the law is fair to all, and there are equal rights and opportunities for all. Society must be fair to all, regardless of race, age, gender, sexuality and disability, and it has to be open to all with education, healthcare, housing and social welfare – social justice aims to bring this about.

Social justice is a reason why religions fight for human rights and against prejudice and exploitation, including fighting for the poor and vulnerable. There are always people in society who can look after themselves despite political systems, but there are always those who cannot. The poor may need preferential treatment and a society is judged on how it treats its most vulnerable. Others believe too much help can make people reliant on that help, however, so they do little to help themselves.

Key religious ideals

- Buddhism: selflessness – Right Action, Livelihood, speech, effort and intention should, if carried out properly, lead to social justice.
- Christianity: the teachings of Jesus used in terms of liberation from unjust economic, political or social conditions.
- Hinduism: in India there is a conscious move away from the caste system, which separates people and has created a massive gulf between rich and poor.
- Islam: social justice with zakah and almsgiving are central to the faith.
- Judaism: the concepts of simcha (gladness), tzedakah (charity and justice), chesed (deeds of kindness) and tikkun olam (healing the world) lead to social justice.
- Sikhism: the message of **equality** of all beings shows believers should deal with all mankind with the spirit of universal brotherhood and equality.

Compassion: loving kindness – helping because there is a need to help.

Equality: everyone is equal in value and worth.

Harmony: living together without argument and conflict.

Stewardship: duty to look after – here the poor and less fortunate.

Tolerance: accepting of difference.

Human rights: what are they?

These are the rights humans should be able to expect as a minimum because they are human.

The UN Declaration of Human Rights (1948) and the UK Human Rights Act (1998) include basic rights and freedoms. Some examples are right to life, to not be persecuted by others, to have a fair trial, to free speech, and also the right to have food, shelter, education, healthcare and work.

The UN claims that adopting and following the Human Rights Act is part of the way to build freedom, peace and justice in the world. In other words, where a country commits to human rights, its people enjoy better lives.

Rights bring responsibilities to the self and others through the medium of respect. Being a citizen brings rights within a country, but also confers the responsibility to respect and follow the rules of that country.

Now test yourself

1 What is meant by stewardship?
2 What is meant by responsibility?
3 What is social justice?
4 Give two human rights.

What do religions teach about this?	Is this always the case in practice?
Buddhism believes all religions are just different ways to the same religious truths. People should decide for themselves after hearing/learning the teachings – no persecution and religious freedom is the right path.	However, there have been occasions of Buddhist violence against other religions, for example in Sri Lanka and Thailand.
Many believe the only way to eternal life is through Jesus, so this excludes all other faiths. Hence they try to convert others to the word of Jesus – discrimination should not be shown to peoples of other faiths and neither should persecution be perpetrated.	However, some say as long as the person lives a moral life (through any religious beliefs or none), then eternal life is still available. All religions basically have the same moral code anyway.
Hinduism is open to all other faiths – 'different paths to the top of the same mountain' (Tagore) – discrimination and persecution are wrong.	However, the religion does not believe in trying to convert others to Hinduism, so trouble has broken out with Christians and Muslims in India who try to convert. Also, many do not like non-Hindu practices and Brahmin castes then treat non-Hindus as inferior.
Islam accepts Christians and Jews as 'People of the Book'. Muhammad built relationships with those of other faiths and taught peace and tolerance, inclusiveness and acceptance of other religions. The morally good will be rewarded in paradise, so discrimination and persecution are wrong.	However, some Muslims show intolerance of other faiths, for example Islamic State carrying out mass murders, and Muslim-led violence leading to mass migration in Africa. This is not supported by teachings, but as it is 'Muslims' doing this, it has brought back religious intolerance on other Muslims.
Judaism is seen as the best way to live, but Jews allow others to live as they wish. How people live their lives is the important factor, not who they worship – no intolerances should be shown.	However, there has been much conflict in Israel with Muslims and as well as being political in nature it is religious. This has led to war, death, persecution and discrimination in Israel and elsewhere.
Sikhs must not offend other religions – all are the same flesh and creations of God. Guru Nanak often rejected the exclusiveness of other faiths – no persecution should be shown.	However, some Sikh practices, such as not marrying anyone other than a Sikh, or forbidding the consumption of meat from ritually slaughtered animals, could be taken as disapproval of other faiths.

Freedom from persecution because of religion: the right to be legally protected if someone targets you because of the religion you follow. They would have committed a hate crime, which is a criminal offence.

Freedom of religious expression: the right of any person to follow the religion of their choice and to be open about what they believe. In the UK, you cannot be told (legally) that you are not allowed to follow a particular religion – none is banned.

Should religious people express their beliefs openly?

Some people openly express their faith: by the morally good life they live, through clothing, wearing a specific item like a cross, talking to others about their faith, through the media or through gestures such as sportspeople openly praying before an event.

UK society is enriched by religious beliefs and culture, which promotes diversity with understanding, tolerance and harmony. Laws also allow all this to happen freely. It is a person's right to express their religion and this right must be respected as long as no one is being harmed by it.

For some religions, there is the expectation to 'bear witness', that is to let others know what their faith is, and even to try to convert people to the faith (proselytise/evangelise). Members of these groups will certainly be open about their faith.

However, there are other opinions:

● Some take offence at religion if they are non-religious, seeing any expression as unacceptable, even an attempt to proselytise.
● It could make people targets of hate crimes as they make themselves known, hence some stay quiet out of fear.
● Religion divides people rather than bringing them together, for example where two religions differ in attitude to something.
● Some religions include practices which are not legal in the UK, or which are stricter than UK law, for example the clash between Shariah and UK law on how to deal with adultery, or the acceptance of polygamy. These often lead to negative publicity and discrimination of those perceived to be in that religion.

Activity

Fix it!

Read the answer to this question. Work out how it can be improved, then rewrite the answer to achieve the marks.

Explain two religious beliefs about freedom of religious expression. Refer to scripture or sacred writings in your answer. (5 marks)

One belief is by Christians who say that Jesus told them to go and make everybody into a Christian. So for Christians, they have to convert people. Second belief is by people who aren't religious and they don't want to know about it. They think people should keep their religion to themselves not force it on people.

Exam tip

Watch out for this topic as a 12-mark evaluation, for example *Religious people should be open and proud about their beliefs.* It could focus around whether it is right to express religious beliefs or whether people should just keep their beliefs to themselves. Find examples both of expression and of discrimination to support your arguments.

Prejudice

Introduction

There are many types of prejudice – against colour, religion, age, nationality, sexuality, disability, appearance. The Specification names racism only. It also lists freedom of religious expression and the status and treatment within religion.

Prejudice is about what we think. It is true to say everyone can be prejudiced at times, even by accident – not all people then discriminate.

Prejudice and discrimination can have a great effect on a person's life. In Britain, discrimination is against the law.

Discrimination: to put prejudiced ideas into action.

Positive discrimination: to promote opportunities for minority groups so they are better represented.

Prejudice: to pre-judge something or someone, usually without any real evidence for that judgement.

Causes

These are the reasons/experiences which create the thoughts that may then be manifested in actions:

1 Bad experience
2 Upbringing
3 Media
4 Ignorance
5 Scapegoating.

Types on course

1 Homophobia: prejudice against a person who is (perceived to be) gay (or LGBT).
2 Disability prejudice: this is prejudice against someone because they are disabled. Disability encompasses a variety of conditions – physical, for example having an acute vision problem, being in a wheelchair, not having a limb; mental, for example having a learning problem or a mental illness.
3 Gender prejudice: prejudice against someone's gender, aka sexism.

Role and status of women in religion

(See also pages 121–122.) Most religions allow women supporting but not leadership roles.

In Catholic Christianity women cannot be priests or higher. In the Church of England women can be vicars and in 2016 the Church had its first woman bishop (in Stockport). Orthodox Jewish leaders are all men but the Reform Jewish movement has a woman as its Chief Rabbi.

As religions try to keep pace with modern society, the role of women is undergoing changes.

Role and status of homosexuals in religion

(See also page 116.) Homosexuals are fully accepted within the Christian Quaker tradition and in the Metropolitan Church as leaders and they are allowed marriage services. In other religions gay people are accepted but they should remain celibate, that is not have same-sex physical relationships. Sex is for procreation.

Buddhism accepts homosexuality as part of a loving relationship. In Islam it is not acceptable to even be homosexual and indeed in countries where there is Shari'ah law, homosexuals are in great danger as the status of being homosexual carries the death penalty. Sikhism also disagrees with it as it is seen as an act of selfishness because sex is for procreation.

Now test yourself

1 What is meant by prejudice?
2 Give two types of discrimination.
3 Give two causes of prejudice.
4 Explain religious beliefs about racism.

NB: The core of this answer would be the same if the question were about prejudice or discrimination generally or any specific form of discrimination.

TESTED

Exam tip

Think about qualities that religions preach about: tolerance, harmony, respect and equality. These are handy words to use to support answers as well as specific teachings.

Racism

Racism is the belief that the colour of a person's skin, or their race, affects their ability; that some races are better than others.

'All human beings are born free and equal ... should act in a spirit of brotherhood ... everyone is entitled to all the rights and freedom.'
Universal Declaration of Human Rights

Religious attitudes to racism

Buddhism

- Believes discrimination leads to dukkha (suffering) so it must be wrong and avoided.
- The belief not to harm others or use harmful language and develop metta.
- Everyone is equal because everyone is welcome in the sangha.
- Prejudice creates bad karma and has a negative effect on rebirth.
- The Dalai Lama stated that the best way to live life was to 'always think compassion'.

Christianity

- Believes that all forms of discrimination are wrong.
- 'God created everyone equally.'
- 'There is neither Jew nor Gentile, slave nor free man, male nor female. We are all equal in Christ' (New Testament).
- Jesus told us to 'love our neighbour' and to 'treat others as we wish to be treated'.
- In the Good Samaritan story the man is helped because of his need, not because of who he was or wasn't (in fact, the victim and helper were from enemy nations).

Hinduism

- Hindu Dharma is that Brahma is found in everything, therefore any prejudiced thoughts or discriminative actions are wrong.
- Hindus believe in non-violence (ahimsa), love and respect for all things.
- Compassion is a key belief – needing to improve things for others, not persecute them.
- Hurting others can lead to bad karma, which negatively affects future reincarnations.
- The true self is the atman and as everyone has one, this must mean everyone is equal.

Islam

- Believes that Allah created everyone as equal but different. This was Allah's design, so discrimination is unjustified.
- Allah loves the fair-minded (Qur'an), which makes discrimination wrong.
- Muhammad allowed a black African man to do the call to prayer in Madinah and he welcomed anyone regardless of wealth, status or creed.
- The Muslim Declaration of Human Rights states that everyone is equal.
- On Hajj (the greatest Muslim gathering on earth) everyone is equal in dress and action.

Judaism

- Believes that prejudice and discrimination are incompatible with Jewish law.
- God created everyone equal – prejudice is seen as an insult to God.
- Jews should welcome and not persecute strangers – practise justice, love and kindness (Old Testament).
- Treat others as you wish to be treated (Leviticus).
- Jewish leaders stated that Jews should live in harmony with non-Jews.

Sikhism

- Believes in the principle of justice and to fight for justice where it does not exist. Equality and sewa (service to others) would clearly indicate that discrimination is wrong.
- 'Using the same mud, The Creator has created many shapes in many ways' (Guru Granth Sahib).
- Those who love God love everyone (Guru Granth Sahib).
- God created everyone, therefore all are equal and so deserve the same treatment and respect.
- 'God is without caste' – Guru Nanak.

Exam tip

It is a good idea to know teachings which are specific to racism, not just ones which can be used for both general and specific questions. Having specific teachings makes your answer sound stronger to the examiner – the link to the question is obvious.

Now test yourself

1 What is racism?
2 For one or more religions, explain what their attitude to racism should be.

TESTED

Answers at **www.hoddereducation.co.uk/myrevisionnotesdownloads**

Wealth

How do people become wealthy? They:
- earn it: they are highly educated, get a well-paid job
- win it: perhaps on a talent show, or gambling
- inherit it: from a rich family, as a gift
- achieve it undeservedly: through crime, etc.

Exam tip

Learn a couple from the two religions you have studied plus two from Christianity. Remember it is one of the 'contrasting topics' and it is necessary to be able to write about Christianity.

Religious attitudes to wealth

Buddhism

- Believes that there is essentially nothing wrong with having wealth but rather how it is used.
- Riches ruin the foolish ... through craving for riches, the foolish one ruins himself (Dhammapada).
- Greed for wealth is associated with the Three Poisons and is a form of craving.
- Unskilful thoughts from greed keep us circling in samsara, in an endless round of repetitive, habitual attachment (Kululanda).
- Buddhism teaches Right Action, Right Thought, Right Intention and Livelihood – for the wealthy to see poverty and ignore it would be wrong.

Christianity

- Christians believe that there is nothing wrong with wealth in itself; it is how we use it that matters. Wealth is seen as a gift from God. Our money should come from lawful means. In the Bible there is the warning that the wrong attitude to money could lead people away from God.
- The love of money is the root of all evil (New Testament).
- No one can serve two masters ... You cannot serve both God and money (Matthew).
- Be on your guard against all kinds of greed: a man's life does not consist in the abundance of his possessions (Luke).

Hinduism

- It is important to create wealth (artha) to provide for family and maintain society. The wealthy should not hoard wealth but use it in a stewardship role. Excess wealth can bring problems – overindulgence and materialistic rather than spiritual living.
- Money causes pain when earned, pain to keep and pain to lose as well as to spend (Panchatantra).
- Happiness arises from contentment; uncontrolled pursuit of wealth will result in unhappiness (Laws of Manu).
- Look after everyone and act as if everything belongs to you, but know in your heart that nothing is (Ramakrishnan).
- Life is all about good deeds here and now. This helps the receiver and the giver's own rebirth.

Islam

- All wealth is a gift from Allah – humans are caretakers of Allah's wealth and will be judged by their use of it.
- Riches are sweet, a source of blessing to those who acquire them by the way, but those who seek it out of greed are like people who eat but are never full (Hadith).
- Earning a lawful livelihood is an obligation – no one has eaten better food than what he can earn by the work of his own hands (Hadith).
- It is not poverty which I fear for you, but that you might begin to desire the world as others before you desired it, and it might destroy you as it destroyed them (Hadith).
- Islam teaches that wealth comes from Allah for us to be able to use to benefit humanity.

Judaism

- Wealth earned in the right way is a gift from G-d and can be used for the self and others. If the heart is filled with the desire for money then there is no room for G-d.
- Do not weary yourself trying to become rich (Proverbs).
- He who loves silver cannot be satisfied with silver (Ecclesiastes).
- He who has a hundred, craves for two hundred (Midrash).
- Money should not be craved but it is necessary in life.

Sikhism

- Anyone possessing riches has been blessed by God as they are able to help the poor. Livelihoods should be made by honest means. Anything that is earned dishonestly is seen as the 'blood of the poor'.
- One who lives by earning through hard work, then gives some of it away to charity, knows the way to God (Guru Gobind Singh).
- Be grateful to God for whose bounties you enjoy (Guru Nanak).
- Those who have money have the anxiety of greed (Adi Granth).

Poverty

Causes

The reasons for poverty vary in relation to where in the world people live. In the developing world poverty is a fact of life brought on by things outside people's control – the poverty is not their fault.

In the UK it may be about being born into a poor family situation, but most poverty is about our own inaction or failure to want to take up the opportunities available.

Other reasons for poverty may be family background and upbringing, one's self (addiction, idleness, attitudes to education), or external factors such as high unemployment, unfair trade and lack of opportunities.

> **Excessive loans**: massive interest rates on loaned money that lead to more debt.
>
> **Fair pay**: to be paid a rate appropriate to the work done.
>
> **People trafficking**: the modern-day slave trade.

Issue

- Fair pay is payment for work done at an appropriate level, including issues of fair pay between men and women for the same job.
- Pay is based on different things, such as hours worked, qualifications needed and type of job.
- Some people are low paid (minimum wage); others earn excessive (too high) wages.

Reflecting on the issue

- Do we appropriately value the jobs done – low-paid nurse versus high-paid sports person?
- Low-paid jobs require few qualifications but are still needed by society.
- People have worked hard to get high-paid jobs – for example, lawyer – so deserve more.
- Lowest paid often work the most hours, to earn enough.

Issue

- Excessive loans – the poor borrow money for what they need, in the form of long-term and short-term loans.
- Loans are made available instantly but with very high rates of payback.
- They are often used for emergency money people need but haven't got.

Reflecting on the issue

- People often pay back weekly at the minimum rate so the amount of interest still increases, meaning the debt becomes higher.
- The poor often fall behind on payments, so increasing the debt.
- Companies exploit their needs, their inability to pay and their lack of understanding of how the system works.
- Some people feel forced to take out new loans to resolve the problem of falling behind with an existing one, hence getting further into debt.

Issue

- People trafficking is where people are trafficked by gangs offering a 'better life'.
- The person pays a price for this 'opportunity'.
- Often families pay huge amounts to give one member the hope of a better life
- Major issues of poverty and war in a country lead to greater amounts of people trafficking.

Reflecting on the issue

- People end up 'belonging' to these gangs as slaves, sex workers/prostitutes because when they arrive in the 'better place' the gangs want more money in return for their freedom.
- Many end up as illegal immigrants, living in fear of violence and drugs.
- Some children are sold into slavery with rich families, hoping to earn money to send home.
- This practice preys on the desperation of the poor.

Now test yourself

TESTED

1 What is unfair pay? Why is it unfair?
2 What are excessive loans? Why do people disagree with them?
3 What is people trafficking? Why is it exploitation?

Responsibility to the poor

Who	Why	How
The government – we elect a government to look after the best interests of society, including the poor. They provide for the needs of the country as a whole and as individuals.	They have the means to help: they collect the taxes to finance the running of public services. People will not vote them into power if they don't help.	Provide health/educational/welfare services and links to business – they can bring all these into play to help the poor. They have money, expertise and access to co-ordinate help. Their policy decisions on saving and spending directly affect the wealth of individuals, e.g. cutting benefits or spending more on the homeless.
Charities – a charity by nature is set up to help someone/something. It collects money to help its cause and therefore has the means to help.	To help is the reason they exist. They are set up on religious or humanitarian principles, i.e. compassion and wanting to reduce suffering.	They fundraise through organised events, national charity shops, donation collection. Through experience they then decide how the money raised is best spent.
Religions are about communities and helping each other. The worship of God has to be seen in action as well as words.	The teachings of holy books tell them it is their duty to do God's work. Famous leaders in history and today put the poor at the heart of their work. It shows loving kindness to bring social justice to the world. God rewards such action.	Religions organise community events, donate to religious charities, work with the poor here and abroad, pray for them and simply be there for people in their times of need.
The poor themselves – the poor need to want to help themselves or at least want help from others, otherwise the help is wasted.	The poor should not want to remain poor, they should want to improve their situation rather than staying reliant on society and charity. Some people are poor due to their own action (e.g. drugs) or inaction (e.g. not gaining qualifications) so they do have a responsibility to themselves to change this.	They have to believe things can improve, take the help that is on offer, work hard to become independent again. Many have made efforts to get out of poverty but have been knocked back, e.g. job applications ignored many times, so it is up to society to make it possible for the poor to help themselves.

Charities

Each religion has its own charities working with the poor around the world. Examples include the International Buddhist Relief Organisation, Christian CAFOD, Hindu Sewa International, Muslim Aid, World Jewish Relief and Sikh Khalsa Aid.

In the UK, most are run with volunteers and professionals working in conjunction with the Disaster Emergency Committee to co-ordinate emergency, short- and long-term aid.

Poverty in the UK

Secular charities like Shelter and religious charities like the Salvation Army focus on helping the homeless and poor in the UK today. They provide food and shelter and help people to rebuild lives. Shelter does it out of a sense of compassion, and religions out of compassion and to follow religious teachings.

Issues with giving to charity:

Should we give to charity or directly to the individual? Should we give money or buy them food? Does the money we give actually help the people who need it? How much of each £1 we give to a charity is actually spent on the poor?

> **Exam tip**
>
> Learn two similar religious beliefs behind the work of charities for your 4-mark questions.
>
> The work of charities is always a good topic for an evaluation 12-mark question.

Religious attitudes to helping the poor

Buddhism

- Karuna – compassion – wishing others freedom from suffering.
- 'Today everyone is looking for personal happiness. So, I always say, if you wish to be happy and aim for self-interest, then care for others. This brings lasting happiness' (Dalai Lama).

Christianity

- If anyone has material possessions and sees his brother in need, how can he love God? (New Testament).
- If a brother has no clothes or food, what good is it to wish him well without caring for his physical needs? (James).

Hinduism

- Some believe by helping those in poverty they can improve their own Karma and rebirth.
- It is taught 'it is the same God shining out through so many different eyes. So helping others is no different than helping ourselves'.

Islam

- He who eats and drinks whilst his brother goes hungry is not one of us (Hadith).
- For a debtor, give him time to pay – but if you let it go out of charity this is the best thing to do (Qur'an).

Judaism

- You shall not burden your heart or shut your hand against your poor brother (Old Testament).
- The Torah forbids charging a fellow Jew interest on money.

Sikhism

- A good person always seeks the welfare of others (Bhai Gurdas).
- A place in God's court can only be attained if we do service to others in the world (Adi Granth).

- There is always someone poorer than you, therefore we are all wealthy enough to be able to help others.
- Some people are wealthy enough and have positions where they can deal with some of the greater issues such as loan interest or fair pay.
- We might help for religious reasons or simply out of compassion, but in a modern world with the wealth there is, we could argue that until poverty does not exist we all have work to do.

Exam tip

When learning teachings, keep in mind that you need them for 4/5-mark questions. In each of these you need to give the teaching and be able to explain how it applies to the question. A good way is to start with the teaching, explain what it means and then how it applies in practice to the individual believers today. Then add an appropriate example.

Activity

Explain two religious beliefs about tackling poverty. (5 marks)

Muslims are told 'for a debtor give him chance to pay'.[1] This means that when lending money to the poor, then a fair chance should be given to pay, not to keep putting the person further into debt.[2] So for example they should not be charging excessive loans with massive interest that the poor can never pay back.[3]

[1]Teaching used in first sentence.

[2]Teaching is explained and applied.

[3]Example is used to develop the point.

Read the answer above. It is half of a 4-mark answer. Write the other half, using the same structure. This will help you to get used to how to answer these types of questions for your exam.

Now answer this one in the same way.

Explain two religious beliefs about excessive loans. (5 marks)

Exam question practice

What questions on this section look like:

Theme F – Religion, human rights and social justice

This page contains a range of questions that could be on an exam paper. Practise them all to strengthen your knowledge and technique while revising. Check back to pages 13–14 to see the marking grids that examiners use: this will help you to mark your answers.

1 Which organisation created the Human Rights Act?
   (a) The G7   (b) Amnesty International   (c) United Nations   (d) NATO   [1]
2 What is racism prejudice against?
   (a) Age   (b) Colour   (c) Gender   (d) Religion   [1]
3 Give two reasons why some people are poor.   [2]
4 Give two ways religious believers can fight prejudice.   [2]
5 Give two ways the poor may be exploited.   [2]
6 Explain two contrasting religious beliefs about the status of women in religion in contemporary British society. In your answer you should refer to the main religious tradition of Great Britain and one or more other religious traditions.   [4]
7 Explain two similar religious beliefs about freedom of religious expression. In your answer you must refer to one or more religious traditions.   [4]
8 Explain two contrasting religious beliefs about why people should help the poor. In your answer you must refer to one or more religious traditions.   [4]
9 Explain two religious beliefs about the use of wealth. Refer to sacred writings or another source of religious belief and teachings in your answer.   [5]
10 Explain two religious beliefs about social justice. Refer to sacred writings or another source of religious belief and teachings in your answer.   [5]
11 Explain two religious beliefs about prejudice. Refer to sacred writings or another source of religious belief and teachings in your answer.   [5]
12 'People trafficking is the worst form of exploiting the poor.' Evaluate this statement. In your answer you should:
   • give reasoned arguments in support of this statement
   • give reasoned arguments to support a different point of view
   • refer to religious arguments
   • refer to non-religious arguments
   • refer to a justified conclusion.   [12]
13 'Prejudice can never be stopped.' Evaluate this statement. In your answer you should:
   • give reasoned arguments in support of this statement
   • give reasoned arguments to support a different point of view
   • refer to religious arguments
   • refer to non-religious arguments
   • refer to a justified conclusion.   [12]
14 'There is no good reason to be poor in the UK today.' Evaluate this statement. In your answer you should:
   • give reasoned arguments in support of this statement
   • give reasoned arguments to support a different point of view
   • refer to religious arguments
   • refer to non-religious arguments
   • refer to a justified conclusion.   [12]

ONLINE

Commentary

Level 2 students write very simple, limited answers. If this is you, try to give two answers to every question (bar the first two!), so you pick up a few more marks.

Level 5 students write solid answers, which make sense but lack sparkle. If this is you, try getting a deeper understanding of the subject content to give yourself more personal knowledge to write from.

Level 8 students write answers with a 'wow factor', their answers flow so the reader has no sense of vagueness/confusion after reading.

Key terms from the Specification

As you worked through the guide, you met lots of key terms. A good idea is to go back and create an RS dictionary of your own. If asked to define a word, it must come from the Specification, so these are those words/phrases.

Theme A: Relationships and families

Cohabitation: living together as a couple.

Contraception: precautions taken to prevent pregnancy and to protect against sexually transmitted infections.

Divorce: legal dissolution (ending) of a marriage.

Extended family: the nuclear family plus other relatives, such as grandparents living with the family, but can also include cousins, uncles and aunts.

Family: parents and their children as a group.

Family planning: the planning of when to have family using birth control/contraceptives.

Gender discrimination: acting on prejudices against someone because of their gender.

Gender equality: the idea that men and women are of equal worth.

Gender prejudice: the idea that men and women are not equal.

Heterosexuality: being physically attracted to the opposite sex.

Homosexuality: being physically attracted to the same sex.

Marriage vows: promises made in a wedding ceremony.

Nuclear family: basically mum and dad, plus the child(ren).

Polygamy: the practice of a man having more than one wife at the same time.

Procreation: the biological process of a couple producing children.

Remarriage: marriage a second time after divorce (not usually to the person originally divorced from).

Same-sex marriage: where two people of the same sex get married either through civil partnership or civil marriage.

Sexual relationships outside marriage: having an affair, a sexual relationship with someone you are not married to; often referred to as adultery.

Theme B: Religion and life

Abortion: deliberate termination of a pregnancy, with the intention to prevent life.

Afterlife: beliefs about what happens to our self/soul after we die.

Animal experimentation: use of animals to test for toxicity and validity of medicines.

Awe and wonder: sense of amazement.

Big Bang theory: the scientific view of the beginning of the universe.

Dominion: the idea that humans have the right to control all of creation.

Environment: the world around us.

Euthanasia: mercy killing; ending life for someone who is terminally ill, or who has degenerative disease; this can be voluntary (a person deciding for themselves) or non-voluntary (being decided by others as the individual is incapable).

Evolution: scientific theory which states that life today has evolved from simple forms through a process of natural selection and the survival of the fittest.

Natural resources: the resources the earth provides without the aid of mankind.

Origins of the universe: how the universe began; science = Big Bang, religion, e.g. Genesis.

Pollution: to put too much of something into the environment, causing an overload.

Quality of life: how good/comfortable life is.

Responsibility: duty to do something.

Sanctity of life: life is special; life is created by God.

Scientific views: knowledge coming from observed regularity in nature and experimentation.

Stewardship: duty to look after the world, and life.

Theme C: The existence of God and revelation   `REVISED` ☐

Atheism: the belief that there is no God.

Design argument: the idea that the world is designed so God exists as the designer; teleological argument.

First Cause: the idea that the world was the result of something causing it.

General revelation: indirect revelation, e.g. through seeing God through nature.

Humanism: a belief system which does not include God but sees as central the morally good behaviour of humans.

Immanent: at work in the world, e.g. performing miracles.

Impersonal: beyond human capacity to understand; distant (in intellectual and emotional terms).

Miracles: events which are considered impossible so should not have been able to happen and cannot be explained by science.

Omnipotent: all-powerful.

Omniscient: all-knowing.

Personal: relatable; humans can meet and connect with God.

Reality: what is real or actual.

Revelation: God revealing himself.

Science: the collection of knowledge from observation and testing.

Special revelation: direct revelation, e.g. seeing God in a vision.

Transcendent: beyond space and time, controlled by neither.

Ultimate reality: the idea of a God with total power.

Vision: seeing something which is non-physical, usually of a holy person.

Theme D: Religion, peace and conflict   `REVISED` ☐

Forgiveness: willingness to not blame a person any more for the wrongs they have done.

Greed: unreasonable desire/hunger for something.

Holy war: rules around fighting a war acceptable to Islam.

Just war: rules around fighting a war acceptable to Christianity and Sikhism.

Justice: making things fair again.

Nuclear deterrence: holding of nuclear weapons for the purpose of deterring others from acts of aggression against them.

Nuclear weapons/war: a weapon/war of mass destruction.

Pacifism: the belief that all violence is wrong.

Peace: the opposite of war; harmony.

Peacemaking: activities intended to bring or keep the peace.

Reconciliation: making up between two groups after disagreement.

Retaliation: payback for harmful action.

Self-defence: fighting to protect oneself after the perception of being attacked.

Terrorism: use of violence and threats to intimidate, especially for political purposes to create a state of fear in a population.

Victims of war: those who are negatively affected by war.

Violence: aggression in language or action towards another person.

Violent protest: voicing disagreement in a violent/aggressive way.

War: armed conflict between two or more sides.

Weapons of mass destruction: weapons which cause uncontrollable and untold damage, e.g. nuclear weapons.

Theme E: Religion, crime and punishment   `REVISED` ☐

Aims of punishment: the reasons we punish offenders.

Community service: punishment; the criminal has to do a set number of hours' work in the community as their punishment.

Corporal punishment: physically hurting the criminal as their punishment.

Crime: breaking the law; this can be against a person (e.g. assault), property (e.g. arson) or the state (e.g. terrorism).

Death penalty: capital punishment; execution as a lawful punishment.

Deterrence: aim of punishment; where the punishment puts someone off committing the crime.

Evil intention: morally wrong thinking which can lead to what is considered wicked behaviour; often linked to the idea of a malevolent force, e.g. the devil.

Forgiveness: letting go of anger towards someone for a wrong they have done us.

Hate crime: a crime committed because of prejudice, e.g. beating someone up because you think they are gay. In UK law, it can mean the doubling of a sentence if found guilty.

Law: the rules which govern a country to keep us safe.

Prison: being locked up and deprived of one's liberties as a lawful punishment.

Reformation: aim of punishment; helping the person see how and why they should behave better.

Retribution: aim of punishment; getting back at the person for what they have done.

Theme F: Religion, human rights and social justice REVISED ☐

Charity: giving in order to alleviate problems, in this theme, of poverty.

Discrimination: actions based on prejudice, often negative.

Equality: the idea that everyone is equal, of equal value and worth.

Excessive interest on loans: borrowed money which has to be paid back with unfairly high levels of interest.

Fair pay: payment that is appropriate for the work done.

Gender: the state of being male or female.

Human rights: the rights a person is entitled to simply because they are human.

Justice: getting fairness.

People trafficking: the illegal trade of humans for slavery, e.g. in the sex trade or for work.

Poverty: having less than the basic needs of life, so that life is a struggle.

Prejudice: prejudging someone based on a characteristic they have, e.g. their looks.

Racial prejudice: prejudice based on a person's racial/ethnic origins.

Religious expression: how a person expresses their beliefs.

Responsibility: duty, e.g. the responsibility to work to earn money.

Rights: entitlements, e.g. the right to education.

Social justice: justice in terms of wealth and opportunities in a society.

Stewardship: duty to look after, in this case, other people and those less fortunate.

Wealth: a person's money and possessions.

Revision strategies

Revision is what you should be doing when you read this book. However, just reading isn't enough – you need to find ways to make what you read stick. Then you need to find ways to improve your exam effectiveness – timings and technique. The following are some strategies you may like to try so that you can find out what works for you. Each strategy has been effective for students at GCSE. Try to make your own revision stuff though – don't just beg from your teacher. Making your own stuff is a form of revision, so it is worth the effort.

Strategies for recall
REVISED

Creating revision cards

These are small cards which have the key details on them – key words and definitions, reasons/causes, relevant teachings, examples and so on. The idea is that you would have reduced your own notes to this brief detail – being able to do this demonstrates your understanding of the topics. The words/ideas on the cards are meant to trigger the much more detailed knowledge that you have. So you use them to remind yourself.

You can also put images on the cards – visual images help our brains to recall.

A twist on this is to swap sets with other students. This allows you to check what you know because they may have put in some things which you have missed. Read through the cards and if there is something you feel vague or clueless about, you know you have to go back to a bigger set of notes and start from there.

> Buddhist worship
> Puja – at home or at temple – daily or as wished
>   Offerings – flowers (beauty/impermanence), candles
>   (light of Buddha's teaching), incense (sweetness of teachings
>   goes everywhere); food (dana – giving)
>
>   Meditation; chanting; advice from monk
>
>   Buddha-rupa – centre of shrine; symbolism
>   (meditation; enlightenment; Middle Way; Dhamma)

Creating image cards

These are cards which have as their focus an image – for example, of the Christian belief about life after death. Around the image, you make notes – what it is, key words, symbolism, importance/cause/reason, diversity of practice, teachings. The exact nature of the notes depends on the topic, of course.

So, why an image? Well, your brain likes images and finds them helpful for recall. Most people think visually, so this strategy is effective. Even making the cards is a good form of revision – you have to analyse images, and create an effective set of notes which fits to the card, covering all aspects of the topic.

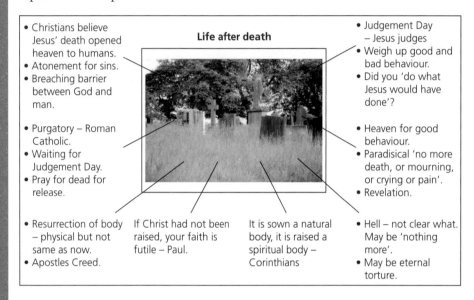

- Christians believe Jesus' death opened heaven to humans.
- Atonement for sins.
- Breaching barrier between God and man.

- Purgatory – Roman Catholic.
- Waiting for Judgement Day.
- Pray for dead for release.

- Resurrection of body – physical but not same as now.
- Apostles Creed.

Life after death

If Christ had not been raised, your faith is futile – Paul.

It is sown a natural body, it is raised a spiritual body – Corinthians

- Judgement Day – Jesus judges
- Weigh up good and bad behaviour.
- Did you 'do what Jesus would have done'?

- Heaven for good behaviour.
- Paradisical 'no more death, or mourning, or crying or pain'.
- Revelation.

- Hell – not clear what. May be 'nothing more'.
- May be eternal torture.

Making mindmaps/thoughtmaps

How do you revise? Do you read page after page and hope it soaks in? If you do, I've got bad news for you. That is one of the most inefficient ways to revise – sorry!

Would you like to be able to put everything about one topic onto one sheet? You can learn here. Some people like to use these at the start of their revision, giving them an overview of what they have to learn. Others use them as a checklist at the end. I'd recommend both ways.

You will need A3 paper, lots of different colour pens and your notes (just in case!).

Look at the chart on page 191 – we'll call it a thoughtmap.

In the centre, in big letters, is the topic name. It needs to stand out, so you know what the page is about. Here it is THE EXISTENCE OF GOD AND REVELATION, but it could be any topic you choose IN ANY SUBJECT (not just RE).

Around it at the first level are the chunks that make up that topic. These are the general issues that the exam questions will be based on, for example questions about how we look after our world. Each chunk has its own colour. When you try to remember the bits of the chart, those colours will help your brain to organise the ideas.

Answers at **www.hoddereducation.co.uk/myrevisionnotesdownloads**

Around each element are the relevant sections. They continue the colour of their element. These make up the foci of the questions, for example saying we look after our world by conservation efforts. You can add the details for each of those sections. They are what your answers will include. For example, where you have key words, you give definitions. You can also add images (if you can draw!).

This chart isn't finished; loads more can be added – try to do that for yourself.

Do this for any topic. Use a sheet of A3 size paper. Stick it on your bedroom wall – you'll read it both deliberately and by accident there. What details you don't remember, check back in your notes. Add any that won't stick.

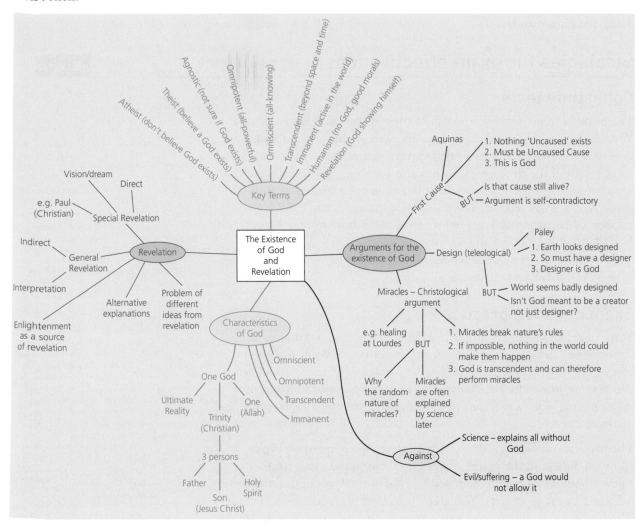

Creating flash cards

Flash cards are simply cards with a statement or question on one side and information on the other. You can take exam-style questions as the questions, or just general ones. We suggest you might use these as questions starters:

- key word definitions ('holy war =')
- what a believer believes about ...
- what is the importance of ...
- how is a believer influenced by ...
- similar beliefs about ...

- different/contrasting beliefs about ...
- reasons to agree with a given statement
- reasons to disagree with a given statement.

You will notice they are close to the questions AQA has said it will use, so the idea is to make you think that way already in your revision, to tailor the way you revise so that it helps you more effectively in the exam.

Of course, they are your flash cards, so put what you want. Get someone to test you with them.

Creating audio files of notes

Any notes you have made or acquired (like the ones in this book) are a prime target for using as audio files. Just record yourself reading them aloud, then play the recording back any time. You can just listen, or listen as you read the notes. You could play low-level music in the background – choose your preferred artist for the topics you find most difficult, so that the positive feel you get from the music helps make the topic more palatable.

You could team up with others and swap files so that you associate a topic with a person, helping your brain to keep the elements of that topic together as one.

These are good to listen to when doing other tasks – walking to school, doing the dishes, and so on.

Strategies for exam effectiveness

REVISED

Doing time tests

The number of people who run out of time in the exam is astonishing. You need to be able to manage your time well so that you get your best chance at the best marks. You need to train yourself to write everything you need to in the time given. So practise a lot – give yourself these approximate timings, get some questions from your teacher or from books or the AQA website, and try to write an answer in the time you set. For a 12-mark question, give yourself 14–15 minutes; for 4- and 5-mark questions, give 5 and 6 minutes respectively; 1- and 2-mark questions need to be done in seconds. You will get better if you practise, so don't just leave it to chance or give up if you find it difficult at first.

Exam question practice

You can get exam papers from the AQA website, from textbooks or your teacher. You can even make them up yourself if you get a good idea of the way the questions have to be worded. The more questions you practise, the more familiar you will be with the wording and the requirements, with a resultant improvement in your technique, speed and marks.

The thing about papers is that you have the range of question types you would meet in the exam, and can do them in the exam time. Authenticity is key here to help you feel comfortable and this familiarity helps reduce exam anxiety. You aren't just checking what you know, or whether you can answer questions – you are also helping yourself develop a positive RS exam mindset.

Learning to be the examiner

If you know how the examiners mark answers, you can shape your answers in a way that makes it easier for the examiner to mark them. So find out about the mark schemes, how marks are awarded, the style which makes your writing clearer. Do this by taking chances to learn and to mark – your teacher probably does this with you in class, so pay close attention.

Answers at **www.hoddereducation.co.uk/myrevisionnotesdownloads**